British History in Pe[rspective]
General Editor: Jere[my Black]

Please note that a sister series, *Social History in Perspective*, is available covering the key topics in social and cultural history.

**British History in Perspective
Series Standing Order:
ISBN 0–333–71356–7 hardcover
ISBN 0–333–69331–0 paperback**

You can receive future titles in this series as they are published by placing a standing order. Please contact your bookseller or, in case of difficulty, write to the address below with your name and address, the title of the series and the ISBN quoted above.

Customer Services Department, Macmillan Distribution Ltd
Houndmills, Basingstoke, Hampshire RG21 6XS, England

The Kingdom of Ireland, 1641–1760

TOBY BARNARD

First published 2004 by
PALGRAVE MACMILLAN
Houndmills, Basingstoke, Hampshire RG21 6XS and
175 Fifth Avenue, New York, N.Y. 10010
Companies and representatives throughout the world

PALGRAVE MACMILLAN is the global academic imprint of the Palgrave
Macmillan division of St. Martin's Press, LLC and of Palgrave Macmillan Ltd.
Macmillan® is a registered trademark in the United States, United Kingdom
and other countries. Palgrave is a registered trademark in the European
Union and other countries.

ISBN 0–333–61076–8 hardback
ISBN 0–333–61077–6 paperback

This book is printed on paper suitable for recycling and made from fully
managed and sustained forest sources.

A catalogue record for this book is available from the British Library.

A catalog record for this book is available from the Library of Congress.

10   9   8   7   6   5   4   3   2   1
13   12   11   10   09   08   07   06   05   04

Printed in China

Contents

Introduction

This account outlines the events between 1641 and 1691, and identifies the processes that substituted a small number of Protestants for the numerous Catholics who had hitherto dominated the government, owned the property, and exercised power in Ireland. It also probes how the new dominance of the Protestants was exercised, what it meant throughout the island, and what were its limitations. Alongside the activities of the governors in Dublin Castle and the nearby parliament, the seemingly humdrum business of ruling the localities is investigated in detail not before attempted. The study necessarily rests heavily on records left by the privileged Protestants. However, these are used to investigate neglected aspects of daily life in the provinces. Much of the text deals with official institutions and those who manned them. Through the officials and their activities, it is possible to recover something of the impact of the British state in Ireland, even on the majority of inhabitants who lacked formal opportunities to participate in public ventures. Accordingly, the strengths and weaknesses of the confessional state erected in Ireland in the late seventeenth century, and maintained for almost a century thereafter, are revealed.

Chapter 1: Land and Peoples

Ireland before 1641

The English intention to rule Ireland had first been acted on when (in 1169) Henry II, king of England and duke of Normandy, was authorized by the pope to invade and annexe the island. Until the sixteenth century, English control waxed and waned. During those centuries, its authority seldom extended beyond the capital, Dublin, a narrow corridor of land around Dublin and the eastern seaboard (known as the Pale from the ditch which demarcated its boundary), and a few ports strung along the coast, such as Waterford, Cork, Drogheda and Limerick. In 1541, worries over security made Henry VIII's advisers assert English authority in Ireland more aggressively. This aggression matched similar initiatives in the north and far west of England and in Wales. The most legible sign was an act, devised in England and passed by the Dublin parliament, which declared Henry VIII king of Ireland. Before this, he and his predecessors were styled simply as the lords of Ireland. The act for the kingly title of 1541 announced an ambition: to bring Ireland completely under English rule and to turn it into a provincial dependency little different from northern and western England or Wales. Distance, an unwillingness of England to spend heavily on the venture, the interference of other European states, and – above all – the distinctive cultures and attitudes of the inhabitants of Ireland conspired to defeat the scheme.

Notwithstanding the setbacks, reputation obliged successive English monarchs to persist with efforts to subject Ireland. Moreover, arguments of security warned that England itself would never be safe so long as Ireland eluded proper control. The Tudors and Stuarts were surrounded

1

by potential and actual enemies: pretenders to their thrones and rivals among continental monarchs. Ireland offered ground from which trouble-makers might assault England. Accordingly, the troublesome and costly English engagement with Ireland continued. Throughout the sixteenth century, and into the seventeenth, efforts were concentrated on trying to extend the systems of English law and administration deeper into the Irish provinces. The creation of shires throughout the kingdom was followed by the introduction of law courts – assizes and quarter sessions – in each. From the 1530s, the danger of Ireland either being wrested from English control or used as a base to destabilize the Tudor or Stuart monarchy became intertwined with the question of religion. Once the Tudors had opted for Protestantism as their state religion, they had to impose it across all their territories. By the end of the sixteenth century, this had been accomplished throughout much of England and portions of Wales, but notoriously not in Ireland. The stubborn devotion of Ireland to Catholicism challenged the contemporary axiom that religious disunity within any state risked serious destabilization.

Before 1641, English progress towards its goals in Ireland was erratic and disappointing. Methods alternated between minimalism, recommended as cheap and less likely to provoke local uproar, and force. The recalcitrance of many local leaders – landowners, priests and lawyers – expressed itself through obstruction in the occasional parliaments, non-cooperation in the localities and (more rarely) in open rebellion. Conspiracies and uprisings strengthened the hands of those impatient with conciliation, and keen on rougher methods. If, as seemed the case, the obstinate Irish would never willingly accept the religion and habits of lowland England, then they should be swept from power and replaced by the tractable.

This political thinking chimed well with the economic pressures which were impelling emigrants westwards from England, Scotland and Wales. Ireland had long beckoned to those seeking seasonal work, permanent betterment, or freedom from the constraints of their own communities. The relative ease of sailing across the narrow, although often stormy, waters between Britain and Ireland meant that many from the western margins already knew Ireland and had kindred and connections there. In the sixteenth century, as more from Britain uprooted themselves to try new lives in America, the popularity of Ireland as a destination for the restless also grew. The government and private investors traded on these impulses, and encouraged immigrants to establish themselves on the properties confiscated from the unruly Irish. First, in the Irish midlands – King's and Queen's Counties, later known as Laois and

Offaly – then more widely in the southern province of Munster during the 1580s and most conspicuously in the northern province of Ulster early in the seventeenth century, settlement by Protestants from Britain (and beyond) was promoted. The official schemes supplemented the spontaneous movement of peoples westward into Ireland in search of subsistence or improvement.

The resulting settlements seldom achieved the size or economic and social impact that had been desired. Yet, in a few districts – the northern counties of Antrim, Armagh, Down and Londonderry and in south Munster around the towns of Youghal, Tallow, Bandon and Kinsale – changes were apparent. By 1641, perhaps 15,000 newcomers from Britain had been attracted into eastern Ulster; and 22,000 into Munster. By 1660 each of the two provinces may have had as many as 30,000 Protestant inhabitants. Thereafter, natural increase among the existing residents added to the stock in Munster. In Ulster, renewed immigration, primarily of Scots, driven out by grim conditions at home, swelled numbers, especially in the 1690s. The landscape took on fresh aspects as English and Scottish styles of building and cultivation were introduced. Houses of stone and lime with chimneys and glazed windows were erected. They were surrounded with orchards, and the holdings fenced, ditched and hedged. Small towns hosted a larger if still restricted range of specialist craftsmen. Forty-six new parliamentary boroughs were incorporated during James's reign, almost doubling the previous total. More settlers were granted the rights to hold markets and fairs in their townships in the hope that they would stimulate trade and industriousness. Over 500 sites were authorized between 1600 and 1641, but many remained on parchment.[1] Not all welcomed the immigrants. Those forced from lands to make way for the newcomers understandably schemed how to regain what had been lost. Even those who had adjusted to – and often profited from – the newcomers watched warily.

The government in Ireland, having invited the newcomers, favoured them, treating them as exemplars of Protestantism, industry and civility. Favours included grants of the most fertile and accessible lands, and appointment to local and national offices. By 1641, it was difficult to thrive in this world of English Ireland unless a member of the established Protestant church, the Church of Ireland. Catholics, having for so long controlled property and power, were understandably discomfited. Some converted to Protestantism, but most protested and considered how best to reverse the trends. Notwithstanding the arrival of Protestant immigrants and the pressures on Catholics to embrace

Protestantism, the percentage of Protestants in the kingdom remained small: hardly 10 per cent before 1641. Without mass defections of the Catholics, natural increase was not likely to transform Ireland into a Protestant kingdom, and so threatened to delay indefinitely that vital precondition for making it peaceful and prosperous.

Natives and New Settlers

Two uprisings by the Catholics – during the 1640s and between 1689 and 1691 – challenged the trends. Their failure precipitated further social and economic engineering. On both occasions, the defeated were stripped of property and offices. The redistribution of land in the 1650s, after the Cromwellian reconquest, aimed to introduce approximately 35,000 new proprietors in place of the old. The Catholics' share of land plummeted. In 1641, they had owned an estimated 59 per cent of the profitable acreage; by 1688, only 22 per cent. Further seizures following a fresh war and further defeats for the Catholics between 1689 and 1691 reduced their total to about 14 per cent. This dramatic change in property-ownership was the basis for the emerging Protestant ascendancy. A few Catholics managed to avoid loss of lands and status. This was easiest west of the River Shannon, in the province of Connacht, but not impossible elsewhere, even in the Pale close to Dublin. The fertile county of Meath was noted at the end of the eighteenth century for a heavy concentration of Catholic notables.[2] The exceptions hardly masked the fact that this was a revolution unlike any seen in either England or Wales, or indeed in Scotland, during the period. The dethroning of a long-established élite paralleled what happened in other European counties: for example, in Bohemia after 1620, where Protestants were supplanted by Catholics.

In Ireland, the redistribution of property was conceived as the prelude to a more thorough imposition of English manners and religion. Successes were at best patchy and frequently superficial. Fewer than hoped of the new owners came to reside on their estates. A landed élite consisting of 3000 to 5000 families emerged. Absentee owners leased their holdings to others, often on generous terms which allowed the principal tenants to flourish. Most landlords expressed a preference for Protestants as tenants. Except in eastern Ulster, there were too few to permit the exclusive ordinance to be enforced. Catholics were able to rent the farms which once they had owned. Even then, by a law of 1704, they were debarred from taking leases longer than 31 years. Legal trusts allowed these prohibitions to be evaded. Ingenuity and subterfuges were required for Catholics to retain even a semblance of the possessions that they enjoyed before 1641, and left them a constant prey to insecurities lest their sleights be discovered and denounced.

Ardent Protestants, having willed this situation and enthusiastically backed the seizures of land, questioned the results. By the eighteenth century, it was alleged – but without compelling evidence – that Catholics had consoled themselves for the loss of lands by moving into urban trade.[3] The stated intention behind English policy was to rid Ireland of those traditionally identified as subversives: the Irish Catholic magnates, priests, lawyers and soldiers. The corpus of Catholics, having been decapitated, would be content to toil as hewers of wood and drawers of water. And indeed the bulk of the labouring population, whether in countryside or town, was composed of Catholics. At the same time, towns, long conceived as agencies of Protestantism and industry, were to be made into Protestant preserves. The government of chartered boroughs was turned into a Protestant monopoly during the 1650s. This control was eroded in the 1670s and briefly overturned in the 1680s, only to be firmly re-established after 1690. Contemporary wisdom made towns, with their councils and trading guilds, 'the best school for the vulgar to learn and to practise virtue and public spirit'. By excluding Catholics and (after 1704) rigid Protestant dissenters from full membership, much of the population was debarred from the associational education which might train them in citizenship.[4]

It was easier to enforce an exclusively Protestant policy on urban office-holding, which was the key to parliamentary representation in the 109 borough and eight county borough constituencies, than in trade and property-owning. Legal barriers had been raised against Catholics owning houses in the strategically important walled towns and ports in the aftermath of the Cromwellian conquest, but these were either lowered or evaded. Nevertheless, Protestants tended to own the most desirable properties in towns, as well as in the countryside. But, just as farms could not be tenanted and worked without Catholics, so few towns outside eastern Ulster would thrive unless they shared trade and work with Catholics. Realists knew that an expulsion of 'Irish papists' would lay waste 'most of our towns and lands which are mostly tenanted by them'.[5] Some Catholics clawed their way upwards into the middling ranks. Obliged to be reticent and frugal so as not to attract the attention of vindictive Protestants, they generally crouched in the shadows. Only as an aggregation can the importance of the Catholic town-dwellers be sensed. In Dublin, probably by the middle of the eighteenth century, the Protestant preponderance in numbers – itself a product of the 1640s and 1650s – ended. Elsewhere in the island, Catholics had remained a majority notwithstanding the penalties. In 1732, Catholics constituted about two-thirds of the population of Cork city, maybe 70 per cent in Limerick, slightly over three-quarters in Drogheda and perhaps four-fifths in Kilkenny. In the western port of Galway, Protestants may have been no more than one-eighth of the total.[6] Catholics tended to be pushed into the poorer districts – often called Irishtowns – beyond the town walls. This tendency can be discerned in Galway in the 1720s. Within the walls, Catholic households constituted 63 per cent of the 343. However, the extramural dwellings divided between 360 Catholics and 75 Protestants. In general, Catholics lived in less commodious houses. In Athlone – within the walls – the average size of the 99 Protestant households was 2.4 hearths; that of the 79 neighbouring Catholic dwellings, 1.7 hearths.[7] Even so, in inner Galway, Catholics had houses with an average of three hearths.[8] This contrasted with the situation at Limerick, with Galway a traditional Catholic stronghold. There Protestants had a bare majority within the walls, owning 50.7 per cent of the houses. Only 5 per cent of the 539 Catholic houses in intramural Limerick had more than three hearths. The average was 1.6.[9]

Catholics come into focus chiefly when the authorities harassed them. They were suspected of attachment to the foreign enemies of England or of involvement in local unrest. Their worship, clandestinely practised early in the eighteenth century, but more openly thereafter, helped to define them, both in their own and in their adversaries' eyes. A fondness for relics, pilgrimages, resort to holy wells and the continuing celebration of festivals were noticed.[10] More reticent communal activities, focused on sodalities and confraternities, are harder to spot.[11] The traditionalism in the beliefs and behaviour of much of the Catholic laity did not invariably delight their spiritual directors. Priests imbued with the ideals of the counter-reformation and lay-people besotted with the new dogmas of politeness and respectability shuddered at habits which smacked too much of carnival, clannishness, vendetta, riot and superstition. Rifts opened – as in Protestant communities – between the avowed reformers and those content with the customary ways. Sometimes they coincided with divergent political stances: whether to accept the new Protestant order or adhere still to the exiled Stuart dynasty.[12] The nuances in Catholic practice interested Protestants less than the resilience of much that was proscribed. By the 1720s, Protestants were aghast that stringent laws passed during the previous 30 years were failing to destroy the ordained priesthood or the cult to which it ministered.

The cultural differences tended to coincide with and be reinforced by social and economic diversification. Protestant Ireland, estimated to number 300,000 to 400,000, had a gilded pinnacle of the prosperous and professionals, but the solid foundations lay among artisans, cottiers and labourers.[13] Neither Catholics nor Protestant dissenters had many high in society, and were disproportionately well represented among the poorer sort. Remote rural areas were, by the late seventeenth century, being drawn more forcefully into a commercial instead of a barter economy. Markets and fairs proliferated. At them, the humble labourer sold what had been garnered – often dairy produce like butter – in the hope of earning enough to pay the rent and buy necessities, such as salt, tobacco, cloth and meal. Beef preserved in barrels and animal skins and fat rendered down into tallow were other staple products in demand among local consumers and as exports. Few required great technological skill or were manufactured. One critic lamented 'that lazy, sleepy, easy way of getting so much money as will just buy them brogues and sneezing and strong beer'.[14] Early in the 1760s, it was reckoned that it took £5 8s 6½d to support a householder in the west for a year. The same household, it was thought, could earn an annual £13. On the Sligo estate of the enquirer who made these calculations, a skilled carpenter was paid 1s 6d daily. Shearers, hired seasonally, received either 10d or 3d each day, depending on age and experience. In contrast, the unskilled hired to cut and save turf and to gravel paths, each received a daily pay of 5d. The least regarded, 'spalpeen labourers', were given anything from 2½d to 5d for a day's toil. In 1772, it was still supposed that peasants earned no more than five to seven old pence for a day's labour.[15] These sums resembled those in rural Wales at much the same date.[16] Further east, especially in the towns, better wages were to be had. In Dublin, journeymen in the textile industries agitated for a rise in weekly wages beyond nine shillings. Craftsmen routinely earned a daily 12d, but it could reach double that figure; general labourers, 10d. Skilled needlewomen and dressmakers could make 4s 6d per week.[17] However, much of this work was intermittent and even seasonal, so the sums guide imperfectly towards annual incomes among the skilled and laborious.

Reformers despaired of the uncertainties when so much employment depended on the vagaries of the weather and the passage of the year. The same uncertainties condemned much of the population to poverty and – notably in the 1720s, 1740s and 1750s – to starvation. Poverty levelled members of the different religious denominations. During the eighteenth century, the numbers and proportion of the population with annual revenues between £5 and £20 slowly increased to 30 per cent. The fortunate minority purchased more commodious housing and more varied food, clothing and furnishings. In these ways, through modes of living and dress, the middle rank differentiated itself more sharply from the drudges and drones. At the same time, even in the 1790s, almost 60 per cent of the population existed on £5 per annum or less.[18]

Ideas of Government

Throughout the sixteenth, seventeenth and eighteenth centuries, rulers and ruled argued about the proper relationship between Ireland and Britain. Theories diverged from practices, and this discrepancy often upset the inhabitants of Ireland. The theory, set out in treatises and official declarations, is recovered more easily than what was happening across the island. The lives of those resident in Ireland is the principal theme of this account. However, a brief review of how Ireland was conceived by those who made policy may be helpful.

Ireland, ruled by the king (or queen) of England and (after 1603) of Scotland, was described succinctly in 1541 'as united and knit to the imperial crown of the realm of England'. Later, in 1689, William and Mary, the new monarchs, were flattered to be told that Ireland was 'one of the most considerable branches of your mighty empire', but still a 'subordinate kingdom to the crown of England'.[19] The latter proposition did not go down well in Ireland, where, it was reported in 1709, 'there is indeed a great reluctancy in all sorts of people here in having it thought that they are a conquered and dependent kingdom'. Despite the Irish misgivings, an act of the Westminster parliament in 1720 announced that the kingdom of Ireland, 'hath been, is and of right ought to be, subordinate unto and dependent upon the imperial crown of Great Britain, as being inseparably united and annexed thereunto'.[20]

These characterisations introduce concepts of conquest, consent and contract, aspirations to the same liberties enjoyed by 'free-born' Englishmen, and relationships of equality or subordination. As a kingdom, Ireland and its peoples notionally possessed rights. In practice they often failed to match those enjoyed by the subjects of England, Wales or even Scotland. The mismatch between theory and practice irritated. By the 1640s, it was noticed that English rule failed to deliver automatic access to English common law, despite the fact that there existed in Dublin and throughout much of the kingdom a replica of the English legal system.[21] Then there were disagreements as to whether Ireland was a conquered territory, whether some of its inhabitants had voluntarily consented to the rule of England, or whether it was a colony peopled from England, Scotland, Wales and Normandy. Whatever the way in which English power over Ireland had come into being, questions arose as to how it was to be wielded. All agreed that sovereignty reposed in the English monarch. How then that figure was to exercise authority was less clear. Did the monarch act alone by virtue of his or her prerogative, in partnership with the English privy council, or through the English parliament? The Westminster parliament, increasing its assertiveness throughout the sixteenth and seventeenth centuries, meddled in Irish matters. The peoples of Ireland felt that English MPs were frequently less friendly than the monarch and his – or her – ministers. Accordingly, some in Ireland were inclined to cry up royal power at the expense of that of the English parliament: an attitude which could only worsen English MPs' suspicions of Ireland. The latter were perturbed by what they took as their kings' wish for freedom from parliamentary surveillance and inclination towards authoritarian styles of rule akin to those favoured in continental Europe. Many in Ireland, especially the Catholics, were suspected of sympathy with these royal ambitions. Suspicions worsened under the Catholic James VII and II (1685–8). A Catholic from Ulster excitedly told the king that, if it lay in his co-religionists' power, 'they would make you as absolute in Ireland as your heart could wish'. Furthermore, Ireland 'by the king's prerogative is at his disposal independently of the parliament of England'.[22]

Such notions made Ireland central not peripheral to the Stuarts' programme. Successive monarchs and their advisers tried to tap its resources. Royal interventions in Ireland were interspersed with parliament's. In 1642, the Westminster parliament decreed that lands belonging to insurgents should be used to repay investors, mainly from England, Scotland and Wales, who were underwriting the reconquest of the kingdom. Next, in the 1660s, Irish trade in live cattle was stopped; in 1699, the export of wool and woollen goods was similarly inhibited. More momentous still was the statute which in giving the English throne to William III and Mary II automatically installed them as rulers of Ireland as well. Shortly afterwards, oaths were imposed by an English statute which ensured that, from 1692, Catholics were debarred from the Irish House of Commons. Then, in 1720, Westminster declared Ireland's constitutional subordination to England. It did so to silence acrimonious and inconclusive assertions in Ireland about the powers of its own institutions, particularly the right of the upper chamber of the Dublin parliament to be the final court of appeal in contested legal cases. Such peremptoriness hardly endeared Westminster, England or their German monarchs to the Irish. A few were provoked to look for an alternative ruler and even to declare Ireland's independence; rather more explored ways in which the practical inconveniences might be lessened and effective control of their own affairs could be regained. This last quest, it will be argued, succeeded triumphantly.

Commentators placed Ireland within the 'empire' of first the Scottish, then the Dutch, and finally the Hanoverian rulers of England. These placements reveal the hybrid nature of the state of which Ireland was a part. It was a motley, collected over the centuries by inheritance, conquest or chance. The Stuarts' and Hanoverians' kingdoms had numerous parallels: the territories ruled by the kings of Denmark, France and Spain, the Habsburg emperor, and the Polish–Lithuanian commonwealth.[23] Each posed, with variants, problems similar to those faced by the Stuarts and Hanoverians in Ireland. So long as English possessions were largely limited to Europe, Ireland was most obviously compared in its rights and treatment with Wales and Scotland, and with the outlying provinces in other composite monarchies.

James VI of Scotland inherited the English throne in 1603. The resulting regal union further complicated dealings with Ireland. The Scots had long concerned themselves with the neighbouring island, the coasts of which were only a short voyage away. Some Scots soldiered there; others colonized accessible lands. Shared culture linked the highlands and islands with Irish Gaeldom. Long-standing ties tightened early in the seventeenth century when the governments in London and Edinburgh, now under a single king, encouraged a joint venture to pacify and exploit Ireland. Scots and English were granted estates in Ulster seized from troublesome locals, notably the earls of Tyrone and Tyrconnell. Official sponsorship merely consolidated already strong connections. The presence of Scots, particularly in the north of Ireland, introduced fresh problems rather than solving existing ones. Distinctive habits and religious practices added to the diversities of Ireland. When the Scottish settlers were attacked during the war of the 1640s, Scotland came to the rescue. In the wake of this warfare, more Scots settled, and a distinctive ecclesiastical system of Presbyterianism was imported and entrenched. Yet, the kingdom of Scotland had no constitutional standing in governing Ireland.

By the end of the century, the way in which their English rulers treated the two separate kingdoms diverged. Presbyterianism was recognized as the state cult in Scotland; in Ireland, despite its strength, it was penalized, along with other forms of Protestant dissent. One Presbyterian in Belfast observed ruefully that, north of the River Tweed 'all trust' was allowed to a Presbyterian regime, yet elsewhere none of that persuasion was favoured with any.[24] In Scotland, a distinctive legal system was also preserved; in Ireland, indigenous codes – the brehon law – were to be eradicated. Scotland, although invaded and subdued by the English in 1650, suffered no expropriation of its occupying owners; in contrast, the defeated Irish lost lands and positions. In 1707, fears that the Scots might prefer their own dynasty, the Stuarts, rather than the Protestant Hanoverians, after Queen Anne died, led to a treaty of union which yoked the Scots to the English. Ireland, although considered as a candidate to be united with Britain, was not incorporated except briefly and awkwardly during the 1650s. Occasionally, a belief that union would improve the condition of Ireland, or specifically the trade of Protestants there, beguiled a few.[25] In practice, the advantages of not being legally united were appreciated. The Scots gained representation at Westminster and lost their own parliament. This loss, it has been suggested, in time diverted vibrant social and intellectual activity into an eighteenth-century Scottish enlightenment. Meanwhile Dublin retained its own parliament, which, as is shown below, became regular and dynamic from 1692. At the same time, something akin to an enlightenment, but more practical than speculative, flourished among the Protestants who crowded into the Irish capital. Scots and Irish were well aware of the parallels and differences in their situations. Both disliked English incursions. But, other than in the 1640s, they hardly coordinated their resistance.

As England's overseas possessions increased, so Ireland was seen, according to taste and need, as a kingdom in a multiple monarchy or as an appurtenance of empire, comparable to the North American colonies or the expanding Asiatic settlements. The uncertainties were further revealed by other portrayals of Ireland. In 1682, an English entrepreneur long settled in Dublin crowed that Ireland, or the parts of it known to him, 'is become West England'.[26] In doing so he expressed an aim which had inspired the lengthy English entanglement with Ireland. Other observers over the next century commended changes in proportion to the degree that they brought Irish economy, society, religion and peoples closer to the English standard. Ireland was conceived as a distant province, in character and potential little different from west Wales, northern and south-western England, all of which had gradually been assimilated to wholesome English ways. Cheeriness was expressed by one Protestant in the Ireland of 1747. He asserted that 'we are now one people; nor is there any material difference between a free Briton born in England and one born in Ireland, more than between a man of Yorkshire and a man of Kent'.[27] These self-assessments overlooked those who prided themselves on their Irishness. Until the mid-eighteenth century, loud declarations of Irishness were seen as a quirk of Catholics rather than of Protestants.[28]

Commentators looked for and found different Irelands: a kingdom, a province, a collection of provinces, congeries of settlements of varying vintages, a near and ancient colony. Depending on the perspective of the viewer, it was portrayed as an unexploited El Dorado, grim Golgotha where the bleached bones of settlers, soldiers and natives attested to the repeated efforts to establish stable English communities, or an Eden forfeited by the transgressions of the occupants. Apprehensions and aspirations were projected into the landscape, so that contradictory descriptions resulted. These Irelands were not all imagined. The island accommodated a rich mixture of peoples, settlements, agrarian societies and towns. Some reminded of the tales of the exotic or barbarous; others matched what travellers saw in Britain and western Europe. Climate and ecology conspired against uniformity. Much of the kingdom seemed underdeveloped and under-peopled, notwithstanding pockets of pleasing industry. In 1719, a sympathizer reported that 'one half of the people of Ireland eat neither bread nor flesh for one half of the year, nor wear shoes or stockings'. He concluded that 'the hogs in England and Essex calves lie and live better than they'.[29] By 1738, it was contended that Irish agriculture lagged one hundred years behind the rest of Europe. Disappointment at the slow pace with which Ireland was being made a second England provoked numerous proposals as to how to quicken the process.[30] However, confidence that Ireland could be transformed was not universal. The glum uncovered structural differences between the two, supposedly sister kingdoms. But, common to virtually all these characterisations was the location of Ireland, physically and typologically, in Europe, albeit on its westerly margin, and alongside Britain, portrayed as an elder sister, even the stern but doting mother.

Such observations lacked statistical precision, but testified to the way in which the perceived deficiencies in the Irish hinterlands offended the lovers of industry and populousness. Conditions in Ireland recalled those of peasants beyond Britain. During the 1720s, an Ulsterman likened the humble houses around Oldenburg without chimneys and with animals sharing the accommodation to those in rural Ireland. The observer linked material backwardness to systems of absolute government.[31] In Ireland, it was easy to blame primitivism on religion. Apologists thought English (after 1707, British) rule a benign system perverted only by the obstinacy of the Catholics. Certain benefits were clear. In the mid-seventeenth century, the population was about 1.3 or 1.5 million. Within a century, it almost doubled. By the mid-eighteenth century, Ireland enjoyed a faster rate of population growth than any other European country.[32] It accelerated as the century progressed. Existing towns expanded and new ones were founded. The growth ensured more labour and greater demand for staples. Few had access to land other than as tenants, cottiers or workers. Wages were small, and diet monotonous, if adequate, thanks particularly to the widespread consumption of dairy produce and the large-scale cultivation of the nutritious potato. Already in the 1650s, an observer stated that the versatile tuber was 'most part of the poor's food … Every one hath his potato garden.'[33]

Delight at this welcome increase in the labouring population turned into consternation when famine recurred, most horrifyingly in 1740–1. The shallow roots of the dramatic growth alarmed the thoughtful.[34] Old projects were revived. Crops and methods which had increased agricultural productivity elsewhere were trumpeted. The manufactures which gave work to town- and country-dwellers in England and Wales were espoused. However, the clover, sainfoin and turnips which flourished in English soils did not always thrive in Ireland. Efforts to weave cloth, forge iron, blow glass or pot utensils seldom answered extravagant expectations. Nor did schemes to grow madder, hops and broccoli invariably succeed.[35] Adventurous entrepreneurs sometimes lost heavily. Making textiles, from the wool and (later) flax which abounded, employed large numbers profitably. Unfortunately, the industry was prone to recession and embargoes. Undismayed, optimists, subscribing to the dogma of improvement, persevered. They sought to refine techniques and introduce novel products. At least with linen, it seemed by the mid-eighteenth century that they had triumphed. By 1751, linen and hemp amounted to half the value of goods exported from Ireland. At the start of the century, the commodities had provided no more than 8.4 per cent by value of Irish exports. In the same period, cattle products had fallen from more than half to 36.5 per cent of the worth of exported goods.[36]

Another fillip to the torpid economy was to people Ireland with immigrants from Britain. This strategy would simultaneously bring the island more firmly into the English ambit, implant scarce skills and diffuse prosperity. From 1172, settlers arrived. Sometimes the newcomers were accused of going native. Inevitably the distinct populations pollinated one another. Arresting sports resulted. By the close of the seventeenth century, pride in ethnic or geographical origins was often reinforced and sometimes complicated by confessional alignments. In general those who cherished an Old Irish ancestry remained Catholic. Among those who insisted on their Englishness, there was greater variety. The seed of planters before 1534 boasted of being 'the English of Ireland'. They were aptly referred to as the 'Old English'. They borrowed from the bible the phrase, 'bone of your bone, and flesh of your flesh', to plead for friendly treatment by England.[37] The Old English, in the main, adhered to Catholicism. Settlers arriving since the mid-sixteenth century – the New English – were usually (but not invariably) Protestant.[38] A visitor to the south of Ireland in 1701 remarked that many inhabitants tried, despite the mixing, to maintain the separate terms of 'Irish' and 'English'. The former 'are the Roman Catholics and ancient natives; the latter, the Protestants, whose predecessors came out of England and Scotland; they are not pleased to be called Irish at home'.[39] Instead, they described themselves proudly as the English of Ireland, or, if of Scottish ancestry and settled in the north of Ireland, as 'British Protestants'. However, from the middle of the seventeenth century, religious confession was becoming the easiest way to sort the population. Confessional affiliation, adopted almost as a shorthand by governments, was widely used by the governed to explain and define differences, some of which were more invented than actual.[40]

Chapter 2: Rebellions and Reconquests, 1641–1691

The Uprising of 1641

Late in October 1641, Catholics in Ulster killed Protestant neighbours, ejected more from their homes and seized the settlers' properties. The insurgents had intended to synchronize their actions with the capture of the English governors in Dublin. Once they controlled the government, it was expected that mastery of all Ireland would soon follow. But the Dublin plot was forestalled. Despite this reverse, others throughout the kingdom soon joined the bands in Ulster. The insurrection was not suppressed until early in 1653. Immediately questions propose themselves. Why did Ireland rebel? Why did the revolt last so long?

The readiest answer is that the insensitive measures imposed by England estranged the indigenous political élite (or substantial sections of it). Provocations worsened in the 1630s, particularly under Charles I's abrasive deputy in Dublin, Sir Thomas Wentworth. Yet, the rebels were not as one either in their timing or intentions. The trouble spread quickly beyond small groups of disgruntled landowners, lawyers and priests, to a wider constituency, sometimes disparaged as 'the rascal multitude'.[41] In time it would be convenient to blame the uprising on those outside conventional politics. Many more Catholics than MPs, landowners, lawyers and office-holders joined the struggle. Desperation, arising from physical privations, helps to explain the widespread activism. Undoubtedly there were tangible resentments: loss of lands, livelihoods and status to the newcomers. Debts bred discontents. Then, too, late in the 1630s, bad weather depressed already modest means, bringing more

15

to – and over – the brink of destitution. The humble, although unlikely to have access to the printing presses or to have their manifestos and utterances preserved, indeed in many cases not functionally literate, were not all innocent of sophisticated political and religious notions.

Scotland rebelled against Charles I in 1637. Inevitably events there touched the Scots in the north of Ireland, who had remained in close contact with their kinsfolk in the northern kingdom. Stirrings of discontent in England as Charles I gravitated towards Rome, suspended representative institutions and collected novel taxes, also affected Ireland, where it was suspected similar policies were in preparation or already being applied. Around Europe, disgruntled subjects schemed to bring rulers to account. Both the theories through which they justified their resistance and the tactics which they then adopted were readily copied. Imitation is clearest and easiest to explain among the traditional leaders of Catholic Ireland. In particular, Catholic priests had studied in continental Europe before they returned to the Irish mission. Traders had set up around the north Atlantic littoral and sustained their co-religionists still in Ireland. Numerous soldiers, enlisted in the armies of Spain, France and the empire, picked up a miscellany of ideas and tactics, which they then spread through Ireland. Political sophisticates took their messages into their communities. The Irish rebels, like their counterparts elsewhere, declared that they fought for law, custom, faith or king. It was not always clear what they meant by these protestations and whether all protestors meant the same.[42]

If events in continental Europe affected the structure and dynamics of insurrection in Ireland, so too did the developing crisis in the Stuarts' triple kingdoms. The upheavals also resulted from factors in train since at least 1541, and arguably from 1169. The results of the Confederate Wars of the 1640s and subsequent Cromwellian reconquest and settlement shaped Ireland for the next 150 years. The revolts, first triggered by localized grievances, protested against the rough methods of the English. During James VI and I's reign (1603–25), even those who had not been stripped of lands were excluded from national office, and from influence over policy. Subtle politicians and lawyers, especially from the region of the Pale around Dublin, did not despair of regaining power. They skilfully exploited the embarrassments of their English rulers, proffering help through taxes and soldiers. Opportunities had opened in the 1620s when James VI and I and Charles I were at war first with Spain and then with France, but closed before the Irish Catholics could negotiate a durable deal, enshrined in a series of demands known as 'The Graces'.

The multiplying difficulties of Charles I after the Scots rose in 1637 once more suggested that he might seek help from Ireland, where his Catholic subjects seemed best positioned to assist.

During the 1630s, Lord Deputy Wentworth (later earl of Strafford) experimented with policies designed to strengthen royal and English authority over Ireland. Wentworth's programme for Ireland had implications – at least potentially – for Scotland and England as well. Strafford was removed from office and eventually beheaded in 1641. He served as a scapegoat for the unpopular policies of the previous decade. His execution guarded against such measures being reintroduced, but created a vacuum in the government of Ireland. The absent king, preoccupied with problems closer to home, left Ireland to drift. On one side, those Irish hopeful of reversing the anti-Catholic programme of recent times saw and seized their chance. They advertised their optimism that soon their plight would be mended. The Catholic cheerfulness alarmed already apprehensive Protestants. The Catholics, while confident about the king's good intentions, doubted his ability to put them into practice. Instead, throughout 1640 and 1641, Charles's opponents, the militant Covenanters in Scotland and their allies in the Westminster parliament, gained ground. The ascendancy of the opposition heralded an intensification not a softening of the offensives against Catholics. A few Irish Catholics, rather than submit to these ominous developments, decided to take advantage of an increasingly confused situation in Britain. Accordingly, they plotted to recover their lost properties and to resume the government of Ireland.

The protestors had their equivalents throughout Europe. Across the continent, many, once powerful, saw their customary rights eroded by administrations bent on centralization and greater uniformity. Most of the discontented professed conservative intentions: merely to restore things as once they had been – or were imagined to have been – and to free their monarchs from evil counsellors. Nostalgia for a distant, and no doubt mythical, golden age in which the now depressed had their due tripped off their tongues. Snobbery gripped others: they derided the newly arrived as uncouth. Conservative aims had often to be forwarded by means which looked (and were) radical, even revolutionary. In particular, as the rising in Ireland spread, it acquired a momentum which swept aside moderates and the undecided. Later, in attempts to extenuate the violence, notables lamented how the insignificant had been emboldened to enter the public scene. Pressures from outside the conventional political élites undoubtedly widened the conflict. Old grudges were also settled.

Opportunists robbed neighbours, carried off clothing and furnishings, felled timber, maimed livestock, snatched horses, and pillaged barns and mills. On occasion, the robbers desecrated objects, notably bibles, sacred to the Protestants, and even dug up their corpses from grave-yards. Whether this was a symbolic act aimed at removing the pollution arising from heretics or a device to make saltpeter needed for gunpowder can be debated. Protestants were killed. Reports soon put the total at 154,000. Panic resulted, and did not make for a cool appraisal of what was afoot. Modern research has reduced the deaths to a more plausible, but still alarming, 3000–4000.

Soon the tides of war surged unpredictably, inundating some zones, especially those on frontiers between different regions, but leaving others unscathed. The writ of the king's government in Dublin, despite the panoply of lord lieutenant, council, parliament and law courts, scarcely ran further than a narrow belt of the Pale. Its proclamations and edicts were increasingly irrelevant to what was happening in the interior of the island. The insurgents set up a rival government at Kilkenny in October 1642. Soon it governed a larger area than Charles's truncated adminis-tration in Dublin. In time it gave a name to the whole movement – the Confederation of Kilkenny. The confederation proclaimed its loyalty 'to God, king and country'. What it meant by the last – 'patria' – remains uncertain: whether an area coterminous with the island of Ireland or a more restricted and even mythic community.[43]

The leaders at Kilkenny had difficulty in imposing orders in remoter districts. As rebellion engulfed the kingdom, neither Catholics nor Protestants were united in their reactions. For many, *sauve qui peut* was the dominant maxim. In this spirit, they turned to whichever side offered the best prospect of material aid. The attitude of magnates could decide allegiances in their territories. Large landowners like the earls of Antrim, Clanricarde, Cork, Inchiquin and Ormond themselves paid troops. The paymasters then dictated where and how they should be used. Longer than in England, where aristocratic leadership of local forces gradually gave way to central payment and control, grandees in Ireland accounted for some of the local variations in alignment and action, giving the wars a baronial aspect. However, the peers' rentals, in the case of the richest – Cork and Ormond – approaching £20,000 annually, could not finance protracted fighting. Ormond, burdened alike as the king's deputy in Ireland and by his own debts accumulated over several generations, saw his disposable income drop to £600 by 1645.[44] Each peer had local rivals keen to clip his power. The burden of paying contingents overstretched the resources of individuals, bequeathing debts which would never be redeemed and which in some instances – Antrim, Inchiquin and Ormond – contributed to the eventual eclipse of the families as major political actors.

At the start of the 1640s, the aristocratic tenor of the revolt was pronounced, as indeed it was in Scotland and England, and Catalonia, Portugal and France. The course of the war not only weakened aristocrats financially, but their poor performance as leaders cast doubt on the notion that they should be, by virtue of their lineage and standing, the natural leaders in times of peace and war. The language, courtesies and gestures of deference continued to be employed long after the 1640s, but the realities of economy, confessional difference and politics attenuated the role of the lay peers. Even in the early episodes of the war, members of modest landed families moved to the fore.[45] On each side, the clergy played disproportionate roles: greater than in the English civil wars. In large measure, it reflected the confessional character of the Irish conflict where the Catholic majority ranged themselves against the Protestants.

War, 1641–1649

Throughout the 1640s, the allies at Kilkenny upheld in theory as well as practice the continuing rule of the Stuarts over Ireland. Only a few dissented. Yet Charles was unable or unlikely to grant all that the Irish Catholics asked. In consequence, the bold pondered alternatives to the Stuart monarchy. Since the 1570s, Irish Catholics, when uprooted from their homeland, put themselves under the protection of the king of Spain. Many exiles settled in one or other of his territories: the Iberian peninsula; the Spanish Netherlands; Milan or the Two Sicilies. Catholics from Ireland travelled to other places, where the sympathetic responses of their princes meant that the pope, the duke of Lorraine, the Austrian Habsburgs and the Bourbons in France were courted as potential protectors of Catholic Ireland. Exploring these options in the 1640s – and later – excited controversy and split Catholic Ireland. Some Catholic theorists, usually priests, had been schooled in doctrines which elevated royal power above the constraints of law and representative institutions. The fieriest contemplated a total repudiation of England's and the English king's authority, and an independent Ireland as 'a free state'. There were precedents for this stance, such as the United Provinces when they threw off Spanish overlordship in the late sixteenth century.[46]

Complete independence for Ireland appealed more as a rhetorical extravagance than as a practicable policy. The fissiparous nature of power in Ireland, still strong despite the unity revered by England, was intrinsic in the system of Gaelic lordships which the English were overthrowing. The idea that a native ruler for the entire kingdom might be found in the person of the successor of the earl of Tyrone, an earlier victim of English pressures, was aired. However, if English rule was to be repudiated, the help of others would be needed. One foreign prince would be substituted for another. Whether Ireland as a distant province of Spain, France or the Habsburg empire would have suffered less intrusive government and colonization and would have reacted positively, even happily, is far from clear. Foreign princes were uninterested in the plight of the Catholics of Ireland except as sources of money and men which might then afforce their campaigns in continental Europe. In short, French and Spanish concern with Ireland differed little from that of the Stuarts.

The pursuit of foreign alliances further complicated the politics of Ireland in the 1640s, supplementing but sometimes cutting across the schemes to strike deals with Charles himself or – in the cases of Ormond in Dublin and erstwhile royalists – with the Westminster parliament. During the 1640s, the Catholic diplomats enjoyed one asset which they soon lost. Governing much of the kingdom and commanding substantial armies, the representatives from Kilkenny negotiated from strength. This position did not bring any helpful alliance. After 1649, negotiators, although toppled from power, could boast of the great potential of Catholic Ireland to supply soldiers and (maybe) money. However, it was hard for foreign powers to take these overtures on trust and in return invade Ireland. In general, Catholic princes bothered with Ireland only when enmity with the rulers of England made campaigns in Irish waters or on Irish soil useful to distract from the main battlegrounds. Later, in 1689, the deposed James persuaded Louis XIV to back his bid to regain Britain from Ireland, and thereby return the Stuarts's territories to the Catholic and pro-French camps. Again, as in the 1640s, the experience, a failure which spelt ultimate disaster for Catholic Ireland, emphasized the interdependence of Ireland, Britain and continental Europe, and the low place customarily taken by Ireland in the ordering of British and European priorities.

In the unfolding crisis in Britain, Charles I was pitted first against rebels in Scotland and then in England and Wales. In Ireland, responses were increasingly governed by the factor which since the mid-sixteenth century divided the inhabitants: religious confession. Catholics, subject to irksome legal discrimination, explored how best to reverse it. If most hoped that their English king would of his own volition relax or cancel the offensive laws, there were doubts as to how best to extract the desired concessions. The cautious advocated diplomacy; the impatient wanted – like the Covenanters who had risen in Scotland or the English parliament which battled against Charles from 1642 – to force him to revoke the obnoxious laws. The leverage of the insurgents was strengthened by their hold on most of the kingdom other than Dublin itself and the eastern fringe of Ulster. At the headquarters in the inland city of Kilkenny, an assembly convened. More important was the executive agency in the shape of a supreme council of 24, recruited from the four provinces of Ireland. Under it, provincial councils for Connacht, Leinster, Munster and Ulster, were designed to meet quarterly and had judicial as well as administrative functions. Across the country, at the several levels of province, county, town and barony, mechanisms were devised to deliver money, men and materials for the government at Kilkenny. The Catholics' regime raised between £60,000 and £70,000 annually and in 1646 had perhaps 20,000 men under arms. These efforts strained weary civilians. New mulcts imposed originally as temporary devices were continued, sometimes under other guises, even after peace returned. The levies further impoverished an already debilitated Ireland.[47]

In the large areas loyal to Kilkenny, Catholic worship was publicly sanctioned. For the first time, the impact on Ireland of the Counter-Reformation was openly displayed. However, the king would not concede one important demand relating to Catholic rites. Pre-Reformation church buildings were not to be restored to the Catholics. The leaders at Kilkenny disagreed about the importance to be attached to this request. Lawyers, such as Nicholas Plunkett, Richard Bellings and Patrick Darcy, and landowners like Lords Mountgarret and Muskerry, pressed secular grievances relating to land and office. Accordingly, they demanded that office be reopened to Catholics on subscription to a simple oath of allegiance to Charles. They also wished that the Irish parliament function as the legislature of a kingdom, by according it greater freedom to initiate bills without prior reference to England, as required by Poynings's Law of 1494. In contrast, clericalists agitated to extend the bare liberty of worship conceded to the Catholics and to put on a surer legal footing what they had achieved in many districts under their control. They reverted to objectives for which the Old English had pressed during the 1620s; similar requests recurred over the next century and a half. In the event, it proved impossible to agree any formula which distinguished between secular and religious allegiances, and allowed the readmission of Catholics to a place in civil government. The arrival of emissaries from the pope – first Scarampi (in 1643) and then (in 1645) Rinuccini – made the clergy more insistent that they repossess the churches built before the Protestant Reformation. Priestly intransigence widened the existing rifts within the supreme council and complicated the task of reaching any durable agreement with the king.

The administration centred on Kilkenny built on structures already in place and added others which copied wartime innovations of the Scottish Covenanters, the English parliamentarians and the English royalists. These expedients have been highly praised. The confederates, it is suggested, governed 'a unitary state'. In addition, this 'highly sophisticated system of government' was the chrysalis from which – in time – 'modern Irish nationalism' sprang.[48] The military machine, once dismissed as disorganized, disorderly and unsuited to Irish conditions, has more recently been reassessed and adjudged successful. The lessons of siege warfare learnt in campaigns in the Low Countries and Central Europe, where numerous Irish Catholics had been fighting since the 1620s, suited the Irish terrain. The armies, at their peak numbering perhaps 20,000, won important engagements. Notable was that at Benburb in 1646. Scottish Covenanters who had come to the aid of the beleaguered Protestants of Ulster were routed by O'Neill's northern force. In relation to the population and wealth of the island, the scale of the mobilization compared favourably with that of the Scots and the English parliamentarians.[49] Yet, the Irish, like the insurgents in Scotland and England, aspired to more than they achieved. The confederates never fielded their full military force: at best, 11,000 of their men combined in any single assault.[50] Central committees at Kilkenny – as in Dublin – struggled to be obeyed in the more distant parts of their jurisdictions. Before 1641 government was underdeveloped throughout much of the island. The confederates inherited and did not overcome localism and noncompliance. How loudly the issues of power and religious freedom resonated among the humbler inhabitants is impossible to detect. In Ireland, no less than in England, Scotland and Wales, locals resented paying ever heavier taxes and seeing those taxes spent on forces which soldiered outside their localities. Civilians, intimidated and coerced by troops supposedly friendly to their interests, fell victim to freebooters and marauders as well as to the enemy.

The authority of the leaders at Kilkenny fluctuated in south Munster, west of the Shannon in Connacht, and in Ulster. In many details, these problems merely reproduced endemic obstacles to uniform administration encountered by all national governments in Ireland. The mechanisms through which to rule remained fragile and incomplete; logistical problems prevented any quick communication of orders from the centre. The personnel manning local institutions had priorities rather different from those of their distant masters, and the latter frequently lacked the means to ensure absolute obedience. In time, as in England, Wales and Scotland, working relationships between centre and localities were hammered out. At least nominally, functionaries in the boroughs and counties complied with the formal requirements, such as swearing confessional oaths and periodically accounting for their stewardship to Dublin. In return, officials in Dublin and London did not enquire too minutely into what their local representatives did so long as they did not trigger more unrest or too flagrantly disobey instructions.

The disunity among the leaders at Kilkenny during the 1640s worsened the centrifugal tendencies in the countryside. The failure of the Confederation to bind all whom it governed into a coordinated campaign helped to explain why it lost the war. Indicative of and an addition to these problems was a divided military command. Thomas Preston and Eoghan Rua [Owen Roe] O'Neill returned to Ireland in 1641 with experience of continental warfare. Preston was associated with the Pale and north Munster; O'Neill, with Ulster. Each represented a different strand of Catholic opinion: Preston, that of the Old English; O'Neill, the arguably more uncompromising attitudes of the uprooted native Irish. Each operated in his own region. The generals cooperated reluctantly and uneasily. Nor were matters helped by the Confederation itself retaining final control over strategy: a situation which paralleled the attempts by the Long Parliament in London to dictate to its commanders and armies. Only belatedly was the administration at Kilkenny streamlined. Local powers were overridden in the hope that all Catholics could be united in a national campaign.

The king's parallel administration, based in Dublin, had even less success in unifying the scattered redoubts of Protestants into a system able to resist and defeat the ascendant Confederates. As the area under Protestant control steadily contracted, so the difficulties of maintaining even a skeletal authority throughout the entire kingdom worsened. A parliament continued to meet in Dublin, but it was reduced to a Protestant rump when the Catholic members streamed away to the rival assembly in Kilkenny. The earl (from 1642 marquess, and later – 1660 – duke) of Ormond governed in the name of Charles I. Something of a protégé of Wentworth, Ormond had his role formally recognized when he was commissioned as the king's lord lieutenant in 1643. He was assisted by a council. It was not as one. A few councillors questioned the wisdom of looking to Charles, while he was so preoccupied with his other kingdoms. A minority in Ormond's council felt it would be wiser to rely on the Westminster parliament to defeat the Confederation. These divisions were as nothing to those which split Protestants elsewhere in Ireland. In Ulster, scene of the first and perhaps most violent stages of the uprising in 1641 and also the area of most intensive settlement by Scots, many pinned their hopes on their kindred among the rebellious Covenanters in Scotland. The Covenanters did indeed send forces to protect the north of Ireland. By 1644, the Scottish contingents under Robert Monro numbered 6500. Thanks to this help, the planters kept a toe-hold in the province. It was threatened by the successes of O'Neill, notably at Benburb. Bit by bit, as the insurgent Catholics were first contained and then repulsed, Scottish influence increased, and with it political and confessional divisions.

In the other main district of recent settlement, south Munster, strategy differed. Settlers split between those who remained steadfast for Charles and those who preferred his enemy, the English parliament. By 1644, the latter looked better placed and keener to assist the embattled Protestants of Munster. Not only did Charles's own sorry condition disable him from sending material assistance, it made him amenable to concessions to the Confederates. Charles, in dire straits, contemplated a deal with his Catholic subjects of Ireland. In return for a guaranteed share in future of the power and property of the kingdom, the Catholics at Kilkenny would divert their resources into the royalist war effort in England. In 1643, a truce was signed on the king's behalf in the hope of freeing part of the royal army in Ireland for service in Britain. Five thousand of the men commanded by Ormond were shipped over to Wales and England, but they soon melted before the heat of parliamentarian fire. Instead of helping the king's cause, they blemished it, since the English did not distinguish between these loyalist troops and the supposedly ferocious Irish who were said to have butchered the Protestants of Ireland in and after 1641.

Charles, now desperate, in 1645 embraced the more ambitious but hazardous scheme of making peace with the alliance at Kilkenny. Through sizeable concessions, he hoped to buy an army of 10,000 from them. The discussions, pursued throughout 1645 and 1646, deepened the existing tensions at Kilkenny, in Dublin, at the king's headquarters in

Oxford, and among the Protestants in the Irish provinces. Surreptitiously (and duplicitously), Charles sent personal envoys – Glamorgan and Digby – rather than relying on the wooden Ormond to strike a deal. The treaty was signed too late to deliver Charles from defeat in England, and was immediately disowned by the clerical party headed by Rinuccini. Protestants in Ireland, knowing that the king and his advisers were scheming to strip them of their privileges, recoiled. In Munster, for example, the provincial leader, Inchiquin, and his deputy, Lord Broghill, a son of the earl of Cork and later earl of Orrery, defected from the king's to the English parliament's side.

The Westminster parliament, close to victory in England and Wales, appointed its own lord lieutenant for Ireland, Viscount Lisle: a rival to the king's man, Ormond. In 1646, Lisle landed with parliamentary forces in the south of Ireland. The expeditionary army did little to contain a resurgent Confederation. By 1647, the latter menaced Dublin itself. The total loss of English control over the island loomed. In this crisis, the king's viceroy, Ormond, more concerned to uphold English than Stuart authority over the kingdom, surrendered Dublin to the English parliament in July 1647. He calculated that the parliament was likelier to keep it from falling to the Catholics loyal to Kilkenny. On 8 August 1647, the confederate army under Preston was defeated. The threat to the capital receded, but most of the island continued in the confederates' hands. Late in 1648, Ormond stitched together an incongruous alliance of confederates and Irish Protestants loyal to Charles. One weathercock, Inchiquin, swung back to the king. Many former combatants abstained from or opposed Ormond's coalition. In particular, Owen Roe O'Neill, powerful in Ulster thanks to the hereditary influence of his dynasty in the province and his victories over the Scots there, held aloof. The nephew of Tyrone, who had fled from Ireland in 1607, he was rumoured to harbour regal ambitions. Were Catholic Ireland to set up in earnest as 'a free state', then O'Neill would be its most plausible head. In the Protestant camp, instincts of self-preservation directed notables in Munster, such as Broghill, and in Connacht, Sir Charles Coote, towards the powerful English parliament.

Cromwellian Reconquest, 1649–1660

The English parliament needed to be secure in England and Wales before it could spare energy and resources for Ireland. In August 1649, it acted. An army of 12,000 commanded by Oliver Cromwell was shipped to Ireland. Cromwell's task was eased greatly by a defeat inflicted on the Confederates outside Dublin at Rathmines shortly before he landed. Thereafter, superior numbers, supplies and finances, together with calculated savagery, concession and luck, enabled the invading force gradually to re-establish English control over the country. In the period between 1647 and 1649, the forces of the Confederation had tended to retreat into their fastnesses. Rinuccini's influence waned, even among some of the bishops. The representatives of Catholic Ireland redoubled the search for allies. Envoys journeyed to Rome, Paris and Madrid. Despite their exertions, no reinforcements arrived in Ireland. This in the end made the difference between victory and defeat. The Protestants of Ireland were saved, first by the tenacious Scots, and then by the enormous English army. This repeated the way in which earlier revolts had been suppressed and prefigured the war won by William of Orange. Other than for modest subsidies and the few ardent cavaliers who repaired from England, Wales and Scotland to Ireland, the alliance at Kilkenny lacked outside assistants.

By 1652, with the surrender of the strongholds of Limerick and Galway on the west coast, reconquest was virtually complete. In the interval since Ulster rose in 1641, much had changed. In England, the king had been executed, monarchy abolished and a republic created: changes which strained relations with Scotland, involved in the joint enterprise of regaining Ireland. Neither France nor Spain had provided the expected help for the insurgents. The foreign powers, locked in a protracted and seemingly unending struggle of their own, although not uninterested in what was happening in Ireland and Britain, concerned themselves only intermittently with those distant places. During the 1640s, substantial Catholics in Ireland recovered much of what they and their ancestors had lost in the previous century, and resumed the government of localities and nation. These gains had not been free of discords: among the notables at Kilkenny over tactics; in the localities, over heavy taxes, oppressive government, overbearing priests and potentates, and soldiers on the march. All shared defeat. Soon enough, the backbiters would snap at each other with accusations of wrong-headed policies. However, the immediate aftermath of war brought more urgent problems.

Cromwell, by 1649 the most renowned cavalry commander in parliament's New Model Army, needed rapid successes. In the past, famed commanders like Queen Elizabeth's favourite Essex, lost their reputations in the defiles and bogs of Ireland. Cromwell had to reassure his paymaster, the Westminster parliament, senior partner in the infant English republic, that its heavy spending on the Irish expedition was doing the trick. He had also to hurry to Scotland, where, in 1650, the friends of the king of the Scots, Charles II (Charles I's heir), were preparing an offensive against the new regime. Cromwell, in taking two strongholds on the east coast – Drogheda and Wexford – used a savagery seen in England only during the closing phase of the Second Civil War. Otherwise, the killings reminded more of The Thirty Years War in continental Europe than of soldiering in Britain. In letters to the Speaker of the English parliament, Cromwell gloated over what had happened. Not just the garrisons, but civilians in the towns, had been killed. It looked as if military discipline, for which elsewhere Cromwell was famed, had broken down and his men had run amok. However, indiscipline was not the impression that Cromwell wished to convey. He wrote immediately after storming Drogheda: 'I am persuaded that this is a righteous judgement of God upon these barbarous wretches who have imbrued their hands in so much innocent blood, and that it will tend to prevent the effusion of blood for the future.'[51]

It was possible to argue that exemplary savagery of this kind would shorten the task of reconquering Ireland. In the longer term, it would save money, and repay more quickly those in England who had invested during the 1640s in the recapture of Ireland. At the same time, Cromwell expressed vengeful feelings towards the Catholics and Irish, groups now seen as synonymous. They had massacred Protestants and begun the rebellion. Elated by a string of victories in England, he – and others – cast the New Model Army as divine agents. These emotions fortified existing feelings that the Protestants of England were a, perhaps *the*, chosen people, with a God-given mission to bring their brand of Christianity and civility to a benighted Ireland. The lurid propaganda generated by the uprising of 1641 deepened religious and ethnic animosities towards the Irish Catholics. The English, bent on taking over the island, demonized the Irish. The Catholicism of the Irish was fused with earlier images of primitivism, even of savagery. Cromwell did no more than air the prejudices common among his compatriots. However, by publicizing and apparently rejoicing in the killing, Cromwell provided much of the evidence, which determined and darkened his subsequent reputation.

Cromwell's adversaries had only limited access to print. Their unflattering picture of him was fashioned and communicated chiefly through oral traditions. In the demonology of Catholic Ireland, Cromwell competed against more local villains, such as Ormond, often seen as the betrayer of Irish interests, and William of Orange, who completed what Cromwell had begun. Polemicists adopted a tit-for-tat approach. The distinct ethnic and confessional communities argued over which had committed the worst crimes. During the next centuries, Protestant partisans expatiated on the number of their forebears who had suffered at Catholic hands in the 1640s. Catholics lingered over the gory details of Drogheda, Wexford and their subsequent losses. They, as much as their Protestant supplanters, viewed themselves as a chosen people whose present sufferings would eventually be forgotten in a triumphant restoration. The contradictory uses of distinct pasts and essentially similar readings of Old Testament history and prophecy deepened the differences within the island arising from faith and ethnicity. In the shorter term, they comforted the dejected and emboldened the victors.

After 1641 and again after 1688, the Protestants magnified what they had suffered. Indeed, in the 1640s, a black legend took hold. Catholic rebels were accused of slaughtering 154,000 Protestants: many more than Ireland then contained. This myth, as intended, determined English policy, justifying a retributive element. It convinced Cromwell, and helped to account for, if not to excuse, his conduct at Drogheda and Wexford. In the longer term, the stories inflamed and perpetuated anti-Catholic and anti-Irish feelings both in England and Scotland, and also among later generations of Protestants in Ireland. Through writings and rituals, the notion that there was an irreconcilable opposition between the fundamentals of Catholicism and Protestantism infected the institutions and culture of English Ireland.[52] More immediately, this sombre reading of recent events led to acts of self-defence and revenge. The supposed perpetrators of the uprising and subsequent 'massacres' were easily identified as the groups traditionally powerful in Irish society: the clergy, the landed magnates, soldiers returned from continental Europe, and the lawyers. All were singled out for punishment. Catholic priests and monks were exiled. If they evaded the bans, they were to be rounded up and held in inhospitable locations, such as islands off the west coast, or executed.[53] Only Protestants were to be permitted to practise in the law courts. Landed Catholics lost their property, and with it any likelihood of resuming their accustomed places in local and national government. Catholic freeholders in Connacht were said to have voted in 1661.[54] Thereafter, with neither freeholds nor freedom of municipal corporations, the Catholics were disenfranchized. These exclusions were an augury of the more comprehensive bans enacted after 1691.

During and after 1649 disease and famine ran through the population. Mortality was high: maybe as much as 20 per cent of the population died in the aftermath of the war. The catastrophe added to the practical and psychological impact of the defeats.[55] It cast long shadows over both the victors – 18 per cent of the invading soldiery may have died – and the vanquished.[56] The former entered onto a depopulated country, denuded of livestock, buildings and crops. Those representing the puny English republic after 1649, mostly strangers arrived recently from England, came with presuppositions about what they would find and what they should do. Few of these ideas boded well for the surviving population. The island had long been seen as backward, even barbaric. Evident underdevelopment combined with, and was explained by, the pervasive Catholicism. Both economy and religious ideology cried out for change. The methods now to be employed recalled in essentials those which had been tried repeatedly by the English in Ireland. The latest reverse for the Irish Catholics allowed familiar palliatives to be resumed. In particular, the confiscation of rebels' property and its transfer to malleable Protestants from Britain, the basis of the smaller settlements of Ulster and Munster, would be extended into much of the island. A process already in train, the banishment of the indigenous Catholics to remoter and poorer lands, either in the uplands or on the western side of the country, would be accelerated. In 1653, it was planned to corral the remaining Catholic owners west of the River Shannon, either in the province of Connacht or in the neighbouring county of Clare.[57]

Two and a quarter million acres were to be redistributed.[58] The fresh settlement continued the principles and processes long favoured in England. Lands would go to the soldiers who had recently recovered Ireland and the civilians who, since 1642, invested money to finance the recovery. If the bare lineaments recalled earlier plantations, the scale of the confiscations of the 1650s surpassed them. For this reason, the importance of the Cromwellian land settlement in creating the substructure on which Protestant dominance was based is entirely justified. It is shown most clearly in the simple statistic that, whereas in 1641, 59 per cent of the profitable lands in Ireland had been owned by Catholics, by 1688, the Catholic share had dropped to 22 per cent. An incipient Irish Protestant ascendancy came into being during the 1650s.

Resettlement and Restoration, 1653–1685

A vacuum had been created by the removal of so many. It was hoped that Protestant immigrants would fill it. The numbers of newcomers envisaged – upwards of 36,000 – failed to arrive. Many soldiers stationed in Ireland traded their rights to small portions of land and returned eagerly to Britain. Similarly, the officers, impatient to receive their entitlements and then disappointed when the grants often proved to be meagre, infertile and unprofitable, disengaged themselves. Few of the 1043 civilians who were recompensed for their investments of the 1640s with grants in Ireland took up residence on the properties. Instead, they deputed management to others on the spot. In some cases, they sold the holdings. In 1670, of the notional 36,043 new proprietors from the Interregnum, only 8000 had their grants of Irish property confirmed. Not all of them then settled in Ireland.[59]

The non-arrival of many intended beneficiaries of the Cromwellian land settlement left the field to Protestants already in Ireland. At first, the planters established before 1649, often termed the 'ancient' or 'Old' Protestants, feared that they might be swamped by the pushy agents of the English republic. Quickly, the revolutionary regime, fragile even in England, recognized that any likelihood of its making itself permanent was remote so long as it relied on an expensive and obtrusive army of occupation and a few headstrong administrators from England. It needed support from the local communities, and so turned increasingly to the settlers in and around Dublin, the midlands, Ulster and Munster. In the balmier climate prevailing from 1655, Old Protestants climbed into much that had been vacated by the longer established Catholic grandees: seats in parliament, the running of counties and boroughs, the professions, notably law, and trade, especially in ports such as Dublin, Cork, Waterford and Limerick hitherto dominated by Catholic merchants. What is more, fortunate Protestants acquired lands taken from the defeated Catholics, either by outright purchase at bargain prices or through long leases at low rents.

The Old Protestant successes were displayed when Ireland, briefly united with England and Scotland, had to send 30 members to the Westminster parliament. Two-thirds of those elected in 1654 and 1656 came from the Protestant community established before 1649. A yet clearer sign of the new dominance of the Old Protestants was the composition of the representative body – the General Convention – summoned to Dublin early in 1660. Its brief was to watch over Irish Protestant interests in a dangerous interlude when it was unclear how soon and on what terms the Cromwellian protectorate would give way to a restored Stuart monarchy. One hundred and forty-four delegates from the Irish provinces assembled. All were Protestant. Of those who can be identified, 98 sprang from families which had come to Ireland before 1649. Only 40 had arrived more recently. Of that minority of 40, 27 had soldiered in the recent Irish campaigns.[60] The new Protestant monopoly over power and public offices was clearly visible. The Protestant interest had been fortified and, in time, would evolve into a Protestant ascendancy.

The Protestants' control, so lately won, was endangered by the return of Charles II in May 1660. He, and his brother and eventual successor, James VII and II, reverted to the stance of their father, Charles I. None of the trio subscribed to the adage beloved by militant Protestants throughout their three kingdoms: that Catholics were, by their very faith, imperfect subjects. The hostile contended that the Catholics' fealty to the pope overmastered and might cancel their allegiance to the Stuart king. Both Charles II and James VII and II saw concrete advantages in using Catholics to rule Ireland. The Protestants there were a small minority, inadequate in numbers and local influence for the multiplying tasks of government. Moreover, their record was one of tergiversation or outright disloyalty. In addition, the royal brothers, in exile during the 1650s, encountered some from Catholic Ireland, such as Richard Talbot, later earl of Tyrconnell, and Theobald Taaffe, earl of Carlingford, and appreciated their sacrifices for the Stuarts. In the event, regal inclinations to recompense the Irish Catholics were translated into occasional and erratic gestures. After 1660, a few were helped, recovering lost lands and positions; more were disappointed. Soon disappointment turned to disgruntlement. The disgruntled rediscovered their predecessors' stance of watching and waiting at the Stuarts' and continental monarchs' courts. The patient believed that a moment would come when the Stuarts, again desperate for Irish support against other adversaries, would grant what the Irish Catholics craved.

The cautious tactics continued traits evident in the politics of Catholic Ireland earlier in the century and during the Confederation of the 1640s. The Old English, adamant about their loyalty and their standing as 'the English of Ireland', were chagrined not always to be believed by English politicians or their monarch. The loyalists contended that the débâcle of the 1640s discredited those who had turned away from the English king to others. According to this thinking, defeat after 1649 proved the folly of cutting the ties binding Ireland to the English monarchy.

After 1660, the apparent sympathy of the Stuarts and the access to them enjoyed by notables such as Talbot recommended a return to the 'Old English' strategy. So far as the English government was concerned, calculus more than sentiment approved a policy of basing English rule in Ireland on well-disposed Catholics. Some Protestant loyalists within Ireland supported the more inclusive approach. Typical of the stance were Sir Maurice Eustace, the Irish lord chancellor from 1660 to 1665, and the first duke of Ormond, lord lieutenant between 1661 and 1669 and again from 1677 to 1685. Both descended from Old English families, many of whose members remained Catholic. Others, including Eustace's successor as lord chancellor, Michael Boyle, also in turn archbishop of Dublin and of Armagh, were suspected of affection for the Catholics because they had married into their families. Archbishop Boyle indeed had allied with the Old Irish O'Briens, now anglicized enough to be ennobled as earls of Inchiquin and Thomond.

So far as the Stuart monarchs were concerned, sharing power with reliable Catholics would ease their problems of ruling the kingdom. Catholics, therefore, were commissioned as magistrates and army officers, and appointed as sheriffs of counties and judges in the four central courts in Dublin. Such concessions were loudly opposed by Irish Protestants. Self-interest made the latter clamour for the maintenance of the monopoly that they had only lately acquired. They played on anxieties over the continuing peril of 'popery' and 'papists', shared by Protestants in Scotland, England and beyond. The uprising of the 1640s and the ultramontanes' seeming willingness to switch rulers, lent plausibility to these accusations. In Ireland, the effects of debarring Catholics from public offices on grounds of their alleged untrustworthiness differed sharply from the impact of the same exclusions in Britain. It reduced the pool from which place-holders were drawn to maybe 15 or 20 per cent of the total Irish population, rather than the 95 per cent who were Protestant in Britain.

Irish Protestants' strictures about the disloyalty of the Catholics sat oddly with their own wavering allegiances. Many had abandoned the defeated Stuarts and rallied to the Cromwellian conquerors: an opportunism which would be repeated when they speedily jettisoned James VII and II and embraced William of Orange. After 1660, Irish Protestants were perturbed by the pro-French and pro-Catholic orientations of Charles and James. The worried in Ireland allied with the kings' English critics. A few Irish Protestant grandees, such as Lords Anglesey and Orrery, dividing their time between Ireland and London, were well-placed to connect the opposition in the two kingdoms. Such links were important to Irish politics throughout the seventeenth and eighteenth centuries. When Irish politicians adopted the rhetoric and tactics of the parliamentary – and indeed extra-parliamentary – opposition in England, it was no accident. As in the 1630s, so in the 1670s and 1680s, what was happening in Ireland warned of what the Stuarts might try in Scotland and England. Monarchs, less trammelled in Ireland by the need to summon parliament and with an overwhelmingly Catholic population, used their prerogative uninhibitedly to bring Catholics back into full membership of the state. Opponents in Ireland, powerless to stop these initiatives, relied on sympathizers in the Westminster parliament or in the courts and streets of London to question and thwart the schemes. As early as 1672, the corporation of Dublin, fearful that its character as a Protestant monopoly would be diluted, mimicked Londoners' opposition to Stuart rule.[61]

The Reign of James VII and II, 1685–1691

Protestants were unnerved by the pace with which their precarious ascendancy was weakened. Catholics, naturally, were heartened. The calculations of the Old English, guided by Richard Talbot, were vindicated. James, ascending the throne in 1685, rapidly dismantled the Protestant dominance. Catholics were appointed to the privy council, the judicial bench, the magistracy and other county offices. Above all, two appointments symbolized the Catholic resurgence. Tyrconnell was appointed lieutenant-general of the army in Ireland. He cashiered Protestants and commissioned and promoted his fellow Catholics. Early in 1687 the king made him lord deputy, and so head of the civil administration. The return of local offices to Catholics prepared for a parliament in Dublin, which, like its English counterpart, was expected to approve James's measures. The 117 boroughs, which elected the majority of members to the Commons, were put into reliable hands. As in England, Protestant dissenters as well as Catholics were favoured. The former no less than the latter, it was maintained, would benefit from the king's more inclusive approach, and so would endorse his measures. Those Irish Protestants, out of favour during the heyday of Ormond and the returned cavaliers during the 1660s and early 1680s, looked for better times under James. Most soon realised that they would be outnumbered by the emboldened Catholics, but hesitated openly to oppose the king.

A second harbinger of the ending of this precarious Protestant ascendancy was the intrusion of two Catholics into fellowships at the Protestant seminary of Dublin University, Trinity College. This echoed the furore when James appointed a Catholic to head Magdalen College in Oxford. Trinity College, Dublin, a much smaller institution than either Oxford or Cambridge universities, could not mobilize the same extensive network of alumni and allies. Nevertheless, the interference, resolutely resisted by the college, presaged an assault on the privileged position of the Church of Ireland, with which it was intimately linked. The anxieties were increased when a recent convert to Rome, Peter Manby, was installed as dean of the cathedral of Derry.[62] As yet, this was an isolated episode. More ominous was an inclination not to fill vacant bishoprics: inaction which brought the episcopal revenues into the royal coffers and would in time deprive the established Protestant church of its leaders. Equally unsettling was the encouragement to Catholic parishioners to withhold the payment of tithes: the principal income of the Protestant clergy. There were also hints that a target of the Catholics in the 1640s – the physical repossession of pre-Reformation church buildings – was once more sought by the militants.[63]

Isolated incidents warned of a popular hostility to the personnel and property of the Church of Ireland. At Kilmallock in County Limerick, an officiating minister of the established Church, was killed in the graveyard.[64] Episodes of this sort brought predictions of more widespread violence reminiscent of the bloodshed in and after 1641. Trinity College as a precaution tried to transport 4000 ounces of its silver plate to England on the pretext that it needed to be refashioned, but in reality to guard against the possible depredations of rivals. The shipment was blocked by Tyrconnell.[65] Private landowners found it equally difficult to convey their valuables back to Britain. Remitting rents from Ireland to England became increasingly troublesome. Protestants in Ireland, chary about quixotic gestures of opposition, sullenly acquiesced in the royal measures. Those able to do so removed themselves from Ireland to the England, Wales or Scotland whence they (or their forebears) had come.[66] A few, despairing of making careers in the new Catholic Ireland, relocated themselves in the Low Countries, happy to soldier with William of Orange.

Charles II and more particularly his openly Catholic successor, James, reversed many of the disabilities under which substantial Catholics had laboured. However, in two matters they proceeded more cautiously than impatient Catholics wished. Protestants granted land in the 1640s and 1650s were not summarily stripped of the new possessions. Tortuous legal processes between 1663 and 1667, overseen by a Court of Claims in Dublin, obliged Protestant proprietors to disgorge as much as a third of the recent grants. Others would be required to exchange attractive portions for lands in remoter and infertile regions. Ardent Protestants contended that the nascent Protestant interest would be weakened and the pacification and enrichment of the kingdom – rather than of themselves – would be retarded. The Dublin authorities, charged with implementing the proposals during the 1660s, resorted to subterfuge, intimidation and cajolery to overcome the opposition. In particular, the lord lieutenant, Ormond, deputed the management of parliament to others: a herald of tactics that became common in the next century. Chief among the managers was the earl of Orrery, younger son of the most important settler family in Munster, the Boyles, whose head was earl of Cork. Orrery saw himself as more attuned to the worries of fellow Protestants than Ormond. Personal jealousy towards Ormond was rational-ized by Orrery, who contended that Ormond, although unswervingly loyal to the Stuarts throughout the 1640s and 1650s, had too many ties of blood, friendship and interest with the Irish Catholics to be a reliable English governor for Ireland. Orrery, through his dexterity first in exciting and then quieting Irish Protestant fears, hoped not only to make himself indispensable to Ormond as a political fixer, but also to demonstrate to the king and his ministers in London that he would make a better viceroy than the indolent Ormond.[67]

Orrery never persuaded English rulers to let him govern Ireland. Yet, his ambitions destabilized government as he looked constantly for ways to belittle and besmirch Ormond. In this, Orrery prefigured the factiousness which regularly unsettled Protestant Ireland. More con-structively, Orrery, in pursuit of his own aggrandisement, articulated an idea of Protestant Ireland which proved tenacious over the next century. Self-interest obliged Protestants to guard against any possible recovery in Catholic fortunes, which, from the 1650s, must be at the expense of the Protestants' possessions and power. It also recommended watchfulness and cunning to grab opportunities to enlarge the holdings and extend influence. The shakiness of the Protestants' position, few in number and ultimately dependent on measures devised in England, recommended flexibility. The assertion that as the English in Ireland they followed meekly wherever England led was contradicted by a readiness to back whoever best protected them. Loyalty to England seldom translated into a supine docility. Above all, it did not produce unquestioning obedience to the Stuarts.

In the 1640s, as the inability and unwillingness of Charles I to assist his endangered Protestant subjects in Ireland was vividly revealed, many withdrew their support. At first it was transferred to the Westminster parliament; then to the Cromwellian regime. Soon, the favours of Charles II and James VII and II towards the Catholic majority dismayed the Protestants. Once William III landed in Ireland and showed his ability to beat the Catholics, the Irish Protestants – with few exceptions – rallied enthusiastically to his cause. In time, William, hailed as 'a hero of the first class' and the deliverer, would disappoint fervent Irish Protestants by his eagerness to conciliate some of the Catholics.[68] All too soon, the new monarch adopted the habit of treating Ireland as a means to reward favourites and to help with his more urgent concerns, of defeating the French king, Louis XIV, in continental Europe. Thereafter, Irish Protestants, for all their professed devotion to the Protestant monarchy embodied first in William and Mary and then in the Hanoverians, had a notion of allegiance at odds with that expected of them by their English (and Dutch and German) rulers. The resulting dissonances grew louder as Britain tried more strenuously to subject Ireland to the same disciplines as England, Wales, Scotland and – by the mid-eighteenth century – the North American colonies.

The Protestants' insistence that only they, as the English of Ireland, could be trusted with its government conflicted directly with the similar attestations of the Catholic Old English. The clashing claims overthrew ethnicity as the criterion on which place and power were allocated. In any case, perceived ethnic origins, the much vaunted Englishness, were difficult to prove as the peoples of Ireland intermarried and adopted the habits of their neighbours. Instead, confession was made the key to privilege. This development was masked in the later stages of Charles II's reign, when his inclination to treat the Catholics favourably was translated into concrete measures. New commissions of enquiry, set up to appease discontented Catholics headed by Tyrconnell, revived anxieties that more land would be taken from the Protestants. Even so, James VII and II, who had been expected to speed the process, did not. The king hesitated to estrange the powerful Protestants by approving a wholesale resumption of their estates. In 1689, having quit England, James arrived in Ireland, summoned a Parliament and sought to rally his mainly Catholic subjects. Even then, he failed to ingratiate himself by sanctioning the immediate restoration of former possessions to the Catholics. His hesitancy was widely interpreted as an unwelcome reminder that James viewed Ireland from an English perspective and saw it principally as a means through which he might repossess the lost crowns of Scotland and England. Nor did James, for all his vaunted zeal, transfer the assets of the state church in Ireland to the Catholics. In time, with bishoprics and other livings in the crown's gift kept vacant, the Protestant church might be starved of sustenance and so collapse. In one matter of practical and symbolic import, it was left to Catholics in their localities to seize the buildings which before the Reformation had been theirs and to worship again in the pre-Reformation churches. Such seizures, sometimes effected through violence, unnerved Protestants. However, the episodes, although numerous, did not constitute the systematic terror which edgy Protestants had prophesied. Nor did the unrest of 1688 to 1691 approach the events of 1641, either in surprise or ferocity.[69]

What particularly disconcerted Irish Protestants was the ease with which the Catholics moved back into their old places. Throughout the late 1660s and 1670s, rumours abounded that Catholics were regaining offices as sheriffs and justices of the peace in the counties. Also, in the larger boroughs, such as Limerick and Galway, the king waived prohibitions and permitted Catholics to trade again, if not yet to govern the towns.[70] A shadowy organization of Catholic notables clubbed together to pay agents who would plead their cause in the courts of law and at the royal court in England. Reports of clandestine meetings did nothing to quiet Protestant misgivings. In the spring of 1686, uneasy Protestant clergy heard that their Catholic counterparts were gathering secretly. The priests were said to have been instructed by Tyrconnell to make returns of the number of able-bodied in each parish. A total of 52,000 was rumoured. Furthermore, it was whispered that once the Catholics had taken over the army, they would next seize church livings from the Protestant conformists and then regain the lands currently held by the Protestants.[71] Worrying, too, were signs of coordination among another group traditionally active in the leadership of Catholic Ireland: the lawyers.[72]

James, like his father, was first and foremost king of England, then king of the Scots (where he had governed in person between 1679 and 1681), and only thereafter aware of his third kingdom. Unlike his parent, or indeed any English king since the unfortunate Richard II at the end of the fourteenth century, James came to Ireland. In the summer of 1689, bells peeled from the cathedral of Christ Church in Dublin, where Catholic rites were again celebrated. Despite jubilation in the capital and provinces, little that happened endeared Ireland to him (or him to it). Instead, it was the humiliating rebuff at the Boyne (1 July 1690) and his precipitate departure, as undignified as his hasty exit from London in December 1688, which left the strongest recollections of Ireland. So far as his subjects were concerned, once the euphoria of having their monarch in their midst abated, his many shortcomings were kept in remembrance.

William's victory at the Boyne in 1690 was treated – in retrospect – as the decisive engagement. In practice, the war was far from won for William with that early success. Among James's Irish supporters, the destructive rivalries between Old English and Old Irish that had punctuated the 1640s, although not altogether missing, did not seriously damage the Jacobite offensives. Disagreements between Jacobite commanders, such as Tyrconnell, Sarsfield and Mountcashel, were about tactics not political philosophies. This may be a sign of an emerging Irish Catholic nationalism in which ethnicity was subsumed in their shared sufferings as Catholics. It could be, too, that the presence of French commanders, such as St Ruth, and troops obliged the Irish to unite lest they be brushed aside. As in the Cromwellian campaign, so in 1690–1, eastern regions, more accessible and better assimilated to England, fell more quickly to the invaders. Irish strength was concentrated in the west. There, at Limerick, Patrick Sarsfield resisted. In defence of this stronghold, the Jacobite forces prepared to repel their adversaries who had crossed the main natural frontier, the wide River Shannon. At Aughrim on 12 July 1691, despite early signs of a Jacobite victory, William's army triumphed. The French commander, St Ruth, was killed; soon afterwards Tyrconnell died: further blows to drooping morale. Irish Catholic resistance was shortened – not as in 1649 by savagery, but by concessions to the garrisons of Galway and Limerick. Yet, the victors were quick to attribute their successes to the justness of the Protestant cause. As one wrote after the fall of one stronghold, 'in a manner, 'tis a miracle, the hand of God was visibly seen in the attack'.[73] This providentialism echoed interpretations of the earlier deliverance in the 1640s and cast William, as before him the English New Model Army and Oliver Cromwell, as the agent of the divine plan.

Warfare expelled James from Ireland and delivered it back to English rule, now in the guise of the monarchy of William and Mary. Fighting killed thousands. But it was brief in comparison with the Confederate Wars. Nor was it followed by massive mortality. The economy recovered swiftly, only to be hit by the embargoes arising from William's wars with France and by the fresh inhibitions devised by the English parliament. Another striking difference from the war of the 1640s was that, although both belonged to a Britannic and international conflict, the Williamite war in Ireland was not conducted against a background of protracted fighting in Scotland and England. In 1689, the other two kingdoms succumbed almost bloodlessly to James's Dutch son-in-law. Events in Scotland and England undoubtedly influenced what happened in Ireland. Strategy for Ireland was laid down in London. There, as in the 1640s, Protestant refugees were well-placed to argue about the best responses. Representative of different provinces, they bid for money and soldiers for their own regions. But they hardly determined the priorities of the Dutch and English. It was, for example, an act of the English parliament, not any measure in Ireland, which made William and Mary rulers of Ireland as well as of England.

As France seconded James's attempt to regain what he had lost, Ireland became the principal theatre of operations. Briefly forces from several European countries competed on Irish soil. At stake was mastery, not just of Ireland and Britain, but of Europe and the European world. The outcome checked, for a season, the aggression of Louis XIV, and confirmed – in perpetuity – James's loss of his three kingdoms. Irish supporters were ruined with the Stuarts. The failures in Ireland bequeathed animosity and hurt. The war was marked by less blatant meddling by papal and clerical agents than in the 1640s. The pope, at loggerheads with Louis, was not going to venerate Louis's stooge, James. Just as martyrdom silenced doubts about Charles I's commitment to Catholic Ireland, so the Stuarts's lengthening exile swung many Irish Catholics behind them. The cautious reverted to the fabian tactics which had earlier been regarded as the speciality of the Old English. Catholics from Ireland, with few entries to the official worlds of Dublin and London after 1714, cultivated foreign rulers: in Madrid, Paris, Vienna, Brussels and Rome. In time, attitudes among a minority of one-time Catholic notables diverged from those of the lower orders. The former pondered the wisdom of their Stuart affiliations and concluded that accommodation with the new Protestant order was more prudent. The commonalty, with little to lose, chafed but did not – until the 1790s – rebel against Hanoverian rule.[74]

During the Williamite War, Irish Protestants, although stalwart in defending the besieged city of Derry or Enniskillen, were elbowed aside by the commanders who accompanied the new king to Ireland. Because William's itinerary passed mainly through Ulster and the Pale around Dublin, it was notables in these areas who formed the closest personal bonds. This contrasted with Cromwell who had lingered longest in

Munster and who assisted its Protestant grandees. Yet, if William's image was burnished most brightly in Ulster and in locations like Derry City, Enniskillen and around the Boyne, he was lionized throughout Protestant Ireland. William, less controversial than the regicide and republican usurper, Cromwell, became the focus of a cult of 'Williamitism', which the cynical supposed might rival Christianity itself.[75] A statue of William on horseback was erected in the centre of Dublin on College Green. It was alternately venerated and desecrated.[76] The victory at the Boyne, not the Cromwellian successes, was treated as inaugurating 'the great era' from which the Protestants dated their good fortune.[77] Protestants' properties and livelihoods were secured thanks to William's intervention and the providential assistance that he had seemingly enjoyed.

William King, a church of Ireland cleric who rose to be archbishop of Dublin, emerged during the war as chief celebrant of Irish Protestant interests. He warned a sceptic that the gentlemen of Ireland, having been reinstated thanks to the Williamite intervention, 'can't with patience bear any doubt to be made of the lawfulness of it'.[78] During the crisis, King had stayed in his Dublin parish, eventually suffering imprisonment by the Catholic authorities. His fortitude contrasted with the prudence and pusillanimity of many, including Protestant clerics, who removed themselves to Britain. By 1689, the western ports from Minehead and Bristol and on up the coast to Chester, Liverpool, Whitehaven and Ayr were thronged with refugees. As in the 1640s, the well-connected and well-to-do gravitated to London. There they lobbied to influence future policy once the island was restored to English and Protestant control. At the same time, they aspersed the Protestants – such as King – who remained in Ireland. The Protestant bishops received writs of summons to attend James's parliament in 1689. The few in Ireland, who obeyed, like Anthony Dopping of Meath, were reviled as collaborators. So were the steadfast, such as Edward Wetenhall, who shepherded his flock in Cork. These new differences, between those who had fled and those who remained, further embittered Irish Protestant relationships during the 1690s, and affected attitudes towards the Catholics once they had been vanquished.

The allegation that the Protestant collaborators were Jacobites was generally wide of the mark. Few Protestants in Ireland persisted in their loyalty to the deposed James after 1691. King, advanced first to the bishopric of Derry and then (in 1703) to the archbishopric of Dublin, emerged as an articulate apologist of the new Williamite order. Jacobitism, the cause of the dispossessed James and his heirs, appealed chiefly to the dispossessed – like the Stuarts themselves – rather than to those in possession of property and power. Protestant followers of the exiled Stuarts were rare: odd Protestants out of favour with the incumbent regime, such as the second duke of Ormonde and the earls of Barrymore and Orrery. James, during his brief reign, had welcomed and sometimes rewarded Protestant supporters, so Protestant Jacobites might plan to negotiate favourable terms for assisting a restoration. The strongest disincentive to active Jacobitism among Irish Protestants was the unlikelihood of the plots succeeding. Because the Stuarts's cause appealed chiefly to Irish Catholics, most Protestants in Ireland attached themselves first to the Dutch William, and then to the Hanoverians. Again Archbishop King expressed the prevalent pragmatism that 'not only our religion and liberties, but property also' depended on the unruffled succession of Protestants to the crown of Ireland.[79]

Chapter 3: Governing Ireland, 1692–1760

Settlement and Self-Protection

After 1690, the triumphant Protestants of Ireland had to attend to familiar tasks. They needed to complete the pacification of the island and ensure that it was not again disturbed by Catholic insurgency. Mundane but vital matters of administration, ensuring that the writ of Dublin ran into the remotest districts, and the interlocking issues of taxation and defence, dominated the deliberations of the victors. At the same time, the relationships of the minority with their near neighbour, England, which had ensured victory, and with those – the Irish Catholics – whom they had lately defeated (only with English and Dutch help) had to be renegotiated.

Leading Protestants in Ireland circled those sent from England to rule them like feral beasts trying to mark out their respective territories. Only after protracted skirmishing were the frontiers defined. Even then, the boundaries could still be disputed and moved. Recent history, and especially the wars of the mid-century and James II's reign, taught that Protestant Ireland could not long survive without sustenance from Britain. Again, though, the conditions on which Britain would give the essential aid had to be fixed. In essence, Britain wanted more from Ireland. To this end, the autonomy of institutions, such as the Irish parliament, law courts, administration and army, was further curtailed. The economy was to be more rigorously subordinated to that of England, by stopping the export from Ireland, first of live cattle and then, in 1699, of woollens. The tense relationship defined much of the public politics of Protestant Ireland between 1690 and 1760. Occasionally it degenerated into bitter recrimination, and popular protest. It stimulated the growth of a distinctive and sometimes contradictory Irish Protestant patriotism. It also encouraged ingenuity, inventiveness and subterfuges to evade the worst damage from English (or – after the Treaty of Union between Scotland and England of 1707 – British) interference.

The Protestants eyed their Catholic neighbours, tenants and employees, not altogether persuaded of their passivity. The triumph of Protestant arms in the Williamite War encouraged some of the victors to avenge themselves. Self-interest and self-protection recommended severe measures, which would definitively disable the Catholic majority from any further bids to regain power and property in Ireland. It was soon discovered that England, the principal architect of victory and the essential prop of the Protestant order in Ireland, took a more relaxed view of the Irish Catholics. So, the question of how best to treat the majority of the Irish population was added to the list of contentious matters over which the Irish Protestant élite and English government regularly quarrelled. Critics in Ireland felt that British approaches were determined by the smaller proportion of Catholics in England (no more than 5 per cent of the population) and by the imperatives of international diplomacy, and were inappropriate for Ireland. Similar feelings that Britain did not fully comprehend the peculiarities of the Irish situation (and specifically of the Irish Protestants' position) would complicate dealings over trade, taxes and the military.

The need of the Irish Protestants simultaneously to protect themselves against any Catholic insurgence and irksome interventions by England explained much that was done by the Irish Parliament during the next three reigns: of William, with Mary until 1694 and thereafter on his own until 1702; Anne (1702–14); and George I (1714–27). The preoccupations did not altogether vanish after George II ascended the thrones of Britain and Ireland in 1727. Some, dismayed that the defensive measures against Catholicism had failed to weaken it, called for the better enforcement of existing laws and the passage of new ones. Nevertheless, although older concerns endured, legislators and projectors increasingly urged schemes of practical improvement. Parliament gradually turned its attention away from the negative to the constructive. It would be too crude to divide the years between 1692 and 1760 into two phases: one of repression and a second of regeneration. Yet, emphases undoubtedly changed during the period, as this and the next chapter will show.

The aftermath of the Williamite campaigns resembled that of the Cromwellian reconquest in the vengefulness of the elated Protestants.

The mood led not to massacres but to measures. England had paid for much of the reconquest, as it had between 1641 and 1653, and so expected to dictate the future. The earlier conflict was reckoned to have cost England at least £2,000,000; the later one, £754,571.[80] 'Traditionally, the defeated must pay. By 1691, less land was left to confiscate. Few were now tempted to Ireland by the promise of extensive estates on easy terms. During the 1650s Ireland was united with England. This did not happen after 1690. Instead, the Irish parliament, hitherto an irregular and rare event, assumed a new importance. The reasons were the same as in England. In 1661, the members of the Irish parliament had been generous in voting revenues for life to Charles II: so generous, indeed, that he had no need to summon it after 1666. Early in the 1690s, there was an urgent requirement for Ireland to contribute more to its own costs. Irish MPs turned this unpromising prospect, of having to tax the country more heavily, to their advantage. By making only modest and short-lived grants to the distant sovereign, the latter could be kept on a short leash. Additional taxes had to be voted to supplement the now inadequate hereditary revenues granted to the monarch. Thus, at the very moment when England had decided that William and Mary should rule Ireland in the place of James, the representatives of Protestant Ireland gained control over the purse and through it over local decisions. This paradox, dependency on England but independency in most day-to-day affairs, underlay the developing Irish Protestant supremacy.

When the Dublin parliament assembled in 1692, its members quickly unsheathed their claws. Three issues particularly concerned them: the powers of parliament itself to vote taxes; the form and detail of the coming settlement of the kingdom; and the related matter of how best to guard against future trouble, notably from the defeated but still defiant Catholics. Irish Protestants felt that their sacrifices and predicament were not fully understood by either their new Dutch ruler or the Protestants of England. Accordingly, they approached the parliament of 1692 tetchily. So far as the English rulers were concerned, its principal business was to be financial. But, it was usual in the aftermath of war for parliament, often at Westminster but sometimes in Dublin, to decide other aspects of post-war reconstruction. In addition, a backlog of business had accumulated among the Irish Protestants, frustrated by the disappearance of their own assembly after 1666 and the failure to summon a new one in the late 1670s.

The most pressing matter arose from the concessions granted in 1691 by William's commander, Ginkel, to a section of the Catholic population.

The agreement – the Treaty of Limerick – was intended to shorten the war. It was immediately criticized for conceding too much. Combatants, if they surrendered under the terms of the treaty, would keep their property and the freedom to practise their religion. Members of the 1692 parliament jibbed at ratifying the Treaty. Their intransigence recalled responses to Charles I when he had proposed pleasing the Confederate Catholics. Whereas Charles's proposals had been general and far-reaching, those in the Treaty of Limerick were modest and helped relatively few. Yet, the stubborn MPs rejected the generosity, invented (it seemed) by those ignorant of Irish conditions. Scarred by numerous reverses, they vowed to stop their Catholic rivals from ever again overthrowing the Protestant interest in Ireland. Their obstinacy showed a new resolution on the part of the Irish Protestants, and their ability to exploit their bargaining power, especially when assembled in parliament. The resultant manoeuvres ushered in the accommodations, which, over the next 70 years, had to be made between the locals and their rulers in England.

Only in 1697 did parliament pass the Treaty of Limerick, in a version omitting some original clauses. MPs belatedly consented to the measure because its modest concessions had been outweighed by fresh penalties. From 1695, a series of laws (often referred to as 'the penal laws') greatly curtailed the religious and civil freedoms of the Catholic majority. In many Protestant minds, extra penalties made it safe to agree to the Treaty of Limerick, from which in any case some of the original concessions had been deleted. The weakening of the treaty between 1691 and 1697 turned it into an emblem of English and Irish Protestant perfidy for some Irish Catholics.

A second issue – money – revealed the dexterity with which the leaders of Protestant Ireland made Parliament serve their turns. By 1692, few members possessed parliamentary experience. The session of 1661 to 1666 was too distant to have been experienced by more than a handful. The more recent assembly of 1689, although it had contained Protestants, was now accounted no true parliament and its transactions erased from the official record. Irish MPs studied the methods at Westminster and recollections of how earlier Irish assemblies had operated, and soon invented their own procedures. The sittings between 1661 and 1666 hinted at a potential for the sophisticated conduct of business, but it had been stunted. Regular meetings after 1692 served as the incubator. In 1692, members confronted the executive, headed by a clumsy lord deputy from England, Sydney. They alleged that the Commons possessed the 'sole right' to initiate money bills.[81] The Commons' claim was hardly justified by the sparse constitutional precedents of the previous century. Understandably, the Dublin government was surprised by the determined stand. The assertion questioned the arrangements enshrined since 1494 in Poynings's Act. The statute decreed that bills drafted by the Irish council had to be approved by the English council before being introduced into the Irish parliament. Members had either to approve or reject them; they could not amend the bills. The cumbersome mechanism had been devised originally to hobble independently minded viceroys in Dublin. By the late seventeenth century, potentially over-mighty subjects no longer graced the viceroyalty, and so the reason for the constraint had gone. But the rigmarole survived. It prevented any swift response to events in Ireland. It also seemed to rob both the executive in the Castle and the members in parliament of the chance to shape legislation.

By the 1690s, the worst inconveniences were removed by allowing bills to be drafted in Dublin, as 'heads of bills'. The drafts, forwarded from the Parliament, were then scrutinized by the Irish council and transmitted for approval, amendment or rejection by the English privy council. The English scrutineers did not hesitate to suppress proposed measures, sometimes because they had been badly framed, but also because they were unwelcome to the English ministry. Measures endorsed in London were sent back to Dublin and went through three readings in each of the two chambers of the House. Still England decided what should or should not be enacted. The arrangement rankled; it also entailed awkward delays. In time, Irish MPs grew more adept at circumventing the inconveniences. A higher proportion of bills that had originated with the members themselves were sent to and then returned from London. By the 1730s, indeed, more than 70 per cent of the heads prepared in the Dublin parliament came back for discussion as bills. Moreover, a larger proportion of the successful bills had begun in parliament itself. The increasing confidence and control of the Irish legislators were revealed.[82]

On occasion, the English administration amended what it had been sent, tacking on controversial clauses which had then either to be agreed or the entire bill to be rejected. In this way, Irish MPs were obliged to agree to provisions at which they might otherwise have jibbed. Conspicuous among the examples was one in 1703, when councillors in London tacked an extra clause on to a bill to stop the further growth of popery. The addition required all entering into crown or civic offices in Ireland to certify communion according to Church of Ireland rites within the previous year. MPs in Ireland, faced with a choice between rejecting the clause and so losing the entire measure or acquiescing, did the latter, albeit reluctantly. By doing so they enacted the test which came to embody the exclusive nature of the new Protestant state in Ireland. Victims now encompassed both Catholics and Protestant dissenters, particularly the numerous contingent of Presbyterians in the towns of Ulster.

The insistence in 1692 that the Commons alone could give life to supply bills was ominous in both its theoretical and practical implications. The resulting impasse led parliament to be dissolved prematurely. Many bills were lost. The imbroglio cautioned the ministry in London and its agents in Dublin to take greater care in future. Sydney was replaced as lord deputy. His successor, the more emollient Lord Capell, resurrected a tactic used to good effect in 1662 when Irish Protestant disquiet had disturbed that parliament. Then the incoming lord lieutenant, Ormond, had deputed management of parliamentary business to locals, notably Orrery, who seemed more alert to the mood of the restive members. In 1695, Capell used some of the troublemakers from the previous parliament, especially the lawyer Richard Rochfort, who was chosen as Speaker, and the brothers Alan and Thomas Brodrick, members of parliament from south Munster: the same soil that had nurtured Orrery. A compromise was negotiated through which the royal prerogative and English control were upheld. The first money bill to be enacted had originated in England. However, room was left for the members to frame heads of bills for supplementary – but essential – supply. Also, members won considerable control over how moneys were raised and spent. Through committees of supply and accounts, government spending was audited and sums appropriated to specified purposes. By 1703, parliamentary supervision was well-established, both in principle and practice. MPs gained useful employment and a say in how the money that they voted was spent. Furthermore, by stinting the taxes authorized by each parliament, members guaranteed that it met regularly. Some hoped that it would assemble every year. In the event, from 1703 until 1783, it sat every second year.

Taxes

This regimen more than compensated for any notional loss of control to England.[83] The arrangements also necessitated decisions about how

Ireland should be taxed. If the essentials of the system were fashioned in England, details were settled in Ireland. The Dublin parliament blocked unpopular means of raising funds. After his restoration, Charles II and his successors were granted hereditary revenues. They included customs duties on imports and exports and the inland excise, levied primarily on alcohol. The rates on specific items could be varied and new articles were made liable to the tax. By taxing, and so raising the price of, luxuries – tea, coffee, silks, velvet, silver plate and coaches – the customs duties distressed those enslaved to fashion. Exactions on staples like alcoholic drinks, although irksome to the prosperous, bore most heavily on the poor. Parliament retained greater control over supplements to the hereditary revenues. Decisions about how extra money was to be found were more likely to be taken in London than in Dublin, but could not entirely ignore Irish conditions. Throughout the 1650s, assessments had been collected, similar to those required from English and Welsh counties. In 1660 and 1661, poll taxes were sanctioned; they were reintroduced in 1695 and 1697. For much of this period, a hearth tax, calculated on the number of chimneys in a dwelling, was preferred. This levy – first adopted in Ireland in 1662 – bore a loose relation to the income of a tax-payer. However, set at the rate of two shillings for every hearth, it was proportionately much heavier on the owner of a house of one or two hearths, with an annual income perhaps between £4 and £10, than the £1 10s demanded of the squire with a residence with 15 chimneys and a yearly revenue approaching £1500. The lightness of the liabilities on the wealthy can be illustrated from the O'Haras, a family of squires from County Sligo. The enlargement of their country residence saw the amount that the O'Haras paid in hearth money rise from a mere 16 shillings in 1747 to £1 16s by 1758.[84]

In 1698, the mulct favoured in England – a land tax – was introduced into Ireland. Proprietors found themselves obliged to pay at least half the liability, even on lands leased to others. This was interpreted as a sign that the Irish Commons contained more affluent tenants (head tenants) than nominal owners of the land. The former shifted part of the burden from themselves on to the often-absent proprietors.[85] Further evidence of self-interest among MPs was their stopping schemes to make the tax permanent. On numerous later occasions, the English government and governors warned the recalcitrant gentry of Protestant Ireland that they would again be forced to pay the tax.[86] In 1749, wild stories circulated that a larger military establishment would have to be financed by a new land tax: a story put about to increase opposition to the proposal.[87]

However, MPs averted the threat. Just how they did so, and what arguments and tactics dissuaded the English administration, are not yet clear. What is evident is this triumph: an important one, which left the mainly Protestant proprietors, such as the O'Haras, lightly taxed. It is true that many landowners had also to find sums to pay yearly charges – quit rents – on their estates to the crown, from which they had been granted, and to meet the cesses levied by the grand juries of counties, the urban corporations and vestries of Protestant parishes. But these were not large sums, and easily within the purses of the prospering. The O'Haras maintained a house in Dublin. The annual rent amounted to £50. Local taxes, designed to support the established Church and to pay for lighting, policing and poor relief, cost another £5.[88] The small exactions may have offset the higher prices that were paid by Irish consumers for imports and the generally modest incomes that they drew from their lands. The O'Haras certainly ran heavily into debt owing to their gusto for novel products and life away from Sligo, and indeed away from Ireland. From a wider perspective, the success of the Irish Commons in preventing unwelcome taxes matched the skill with which it won control over the money bills and over the spending of taxes.

A notable example of how adroitly the emerging Protestant ascendancy deflected potentially harmful developments was in staffing the revenue commission. By the 1690s, a board of commissioners oversaw the collection of the customs, excise and hearth money. Salaried agents of the revenue spread throughout the country and steadily increased in numbers. By 1715, they totalled more than 1100; by the 1750s, perhaps 1600.[89] The stated salaries usually ranged from £20 to £60. However, profits frequently exceeded recorded emoluments. Office-holders were expected to be communicant members of the established Church of Ireland. Despite prohibitions, many functionaries had other employments. The posts conferred local status and power, and were sought eagerly. The entire structure was supervised by a board of seven commissioners based at the Customs House by the River Liffey in Dublin. A place as a commissioner, worth first £800 and then £1000, was one of the most lucrative in the Irish establishment. English ministers, eager to annexe the Irish administration and appreciating the attractions of these morsels of patronage, appointed their own clients. One Englishman made a commissioner was a son of John Evelyn, the diarist, courtier and gardening guru. The junior John Evelyn sailed to Dublin in 1693 in order to attend to his duties as revenue commissioner. He attested to the burdens. Not all his English colleagues were as conscientious. The habitual absence of some among the seven commissioners allowed the diligent to dominate the Board. The regulars tended to be the Irish members. In 1697, a place as a commissioner rewarded Sir Thomas Southwell, a local hero of the recent wars. In 1709, he was joined by a weightier political figure, William Conolly. An attorney originally from the north-west, Conolly emerged as a leading politician in the first decade of the eighteenth century. In 1707 and 1709 he chaired the inquisitorial public accounts committee in the Commons.[90] Conolly was purged from the Revenue Board by the Tories in 1710, but returned with the Hanoverians. In 1715, Conolly, staunch as a Whig in support of the Hanoverian succession, was chosen as Speaker of the Commons and became the parliamentary manager on whom English lords lieutenant relied for the smooth despatch of business. Conolly's dominance in the Commons owed much to his command over the Revenue Board, on which he was the strongest personality. It gave him abundant opportunities to gratify his dependants and allies, and so to solidify his following.

Functionaries of the customs and revenue, although servants of the British state in Ireland, acquired little sense of obligation to that distant abstraction. Self-interest had to be kept within decent bounds, and too conspicuous a feathering of nests was likely to bring the unsympathetic scrutiny of the Revenue Board. The negligent and corrupt were disciplined and sometimes sacked. By 1720, Sir John Eccles, collector of the port of Dublin and eminent in the society and trade of the capital, owed his employers £5000. He was dismissed shortly afterwards. Later, Henry Cust, who had built up a valuable stake in County Armagh through service in the revenue and administration of the barracks, resigned rather than face enquiries as to why he had failed to account to his superiors.[91]

Appointments tended to tighten the bonds between the officers and their patrons, rather than between the functionaries and the ministers and king in London. Searchers in ports and collectors of the excise and customs sometimes had difficulty in reconciling their duties with amicable relations with locals. The board in Dublin had regularly to remove officers who had become too intimate with the traders in their jurisdiction. In 1747, for example, it was decreed that the entire establishment of tide-waiters and revenue boatmen in Sligo should be changed, 'they having been long employed in that place and contracted such acquaintance and interest with the inhabitants as renders them incapable of serving in their several stations'. Fifteen years later, a similar purge of all except two excise surveyors and gaugers was wanted at Cork, and for the same reasons.[92] At the other extreme, officious collectors, hated as 'merciless cheats and oppressors', upset locals.[93]

When trying to seize smuggled goods or to locate and destroy illicit stills, the functionaries of the revenue might be met with violence. In such circumstances, increasingly common from the 1740s, the revenue-men appealed to the army for help. Military commanders were unwilling to do such work unless explicitly authorized by the Dublin government. Orders were issued, especially in the turbulent 1750s and 1760s. A prospect opened that more of the routines of civil government in Ireland would be militarized. It brought with it a danger that many civilians would be estranged when both soldiers and customs and revenue officials discharged unpopular duties on behalf of the Hanoverian regime. Furthermore, the vigorous prosecution of regulatory offences, such as unlicensed distillation and smuggling, criminalized otherwise respectable members of society. Merchants were said routinely to deal in contraband, in order to steal a march on competitors. Piracy was sometimes excused as an expedient of an impoverished island to evade the economic penalties heaped on it by Britain.[94]

Penal Laws

The third urgent problem for members of parliament in the 1690s was how to treat the Catholic majority. Approaches had long varied between severity and generosity. Also, the ultimate goal of policy was conceived by some as repression and by others as enlightenment and reformation. The differences continued into the 1690s, and beyond. Restrictions imposed during the Cromwellian Interregnum of the 1650s and mooted in advance of a projected parliament in 1679 were resurrected. Bills passed between 1695 and 1709 aimed to deprive the Catholics of their religious, intellectual, social and military leaders. In particular, the supply of clergy would be interrupted and, it was hoped, ruptured permanently. Bishops, monks and friars were banned from Ireland. Those in the country were to be banished; fresh recruits were inhibited from exercising their priestly functions by severe penalties. Only parish priests, thought to be more biddable than the regulars (the members of the religious orders like Jesuits, Franciscans, Augustinians and Carmelites), were permitted if they registered with the authorities. Investigations revealed almost 400 who were to be expelled, and 838 secular (or parish) priests whose presence was allowed for the moment. In 1705, the number of seculars recorded had risen to 892.[95] Any inclination to comply was weakened when, in 1709, the parish clergy were also required to abjure the Stuart dynasty. Only 13 did so. The remainder, by refusing to swear the oath, rendered themselves liable to imprisonment and banishment. Some did indeed suffer, but many more survived. However, the survivors were at the mercy of magistrates, landlords and parishioners, who, from anti-Catholic fervour or in response to rumours of Jacobite and foreign designs, rescinded the tacit toleration. The Catholic clergy, under continual threat of disclosure and seizure, had often to conceal their identities and activities. Yet, enough evaded the restrictions to ensure that religious services continued.[96]

By the 1720s, devotees of the established Church of Ireland confessed that the Catholic Church, so far from being enfeebled, appeared stronger than ever. Some Protestants responded by demanding that the existing prohibitions be enforced more stringently; others clamoured to have extra restrictions enacted in order to close loopholes. In 1719 and 1723, such requests failed because the English council refused to return the proposed bills to the Dublin parliament. On occasion, too, pressure from Britain's continental allies, notably the Austrian empire, ensured that extreme measures demanded by Irish MPs were dropped. A different reaction within Protestant Ireland was to question the efficacy of persecution and instead to request a return to persuasion. Isolated voices, such as that of Edward Synge, a future bishop, expressed this opinion in the 1720s, and later.[97] The evident failure of the repressive strategy was interpreted by the thoughtful not only as a sign that the laws were misconceived, but that the failings of the Protestants themselves prevented the Catholics of Ireland from converting to Protestantism.

The Catholic laity also suffered from the penal laws. They were no longer to be educated overseas. Concurrently, other statutes intensified the pressures on prominent laymen to abandon their faith. The hope was that the traditional leaders of the Catholic community, if not already dispossessed, exiled or killed, would forswear their creed. In 1704, a sacramental test was required of all entrants into national and many local offices. This qualification hurt Protestants who dissented from the state church as well as Catholics. It turned much of national and local government into a Church of Ireland preserve, and thereby built the foundations for what became known as the Protestant Ascendancy. So far as Catholics were concerned, it completed a process in train since the late sixteenth century, but briefly reversed during the 1640s and 1680s. Except in the lowliest levels of local administration, Catholics were not used. Additional laws aimed to turn legal practice into a Protestant monopoly.

The landed interest became a special target. Catholics were debarred from the acquisition of freehold land or from leasing estates for more than 31 years. Those already possessed of estates were forced at their deaths to divide them between their male heirs, if all remained Catholic, or to pass them to any son who conformed to the established confession. The partition of properties in this manner, known as gavelling, reversed the system of descent by primogeniture to the first-born son, which had long been favoured by the English conquerors in Ireland. Paradoxically, it reinstated partible inheritance, dividing it between siblings, which the English had disliked as a relic of indigenous Irish customs. The hope was that when incentives to convert failed, Catholics, finding their estates fragmented into miniscule particles, would lack the wherewithal to lead their traditional followers either in peace or into war. Other, seemingly trivial but humiliating bans prohibited Catholics from possessing horses worth more than £5 or from wearing swords and keeping firearms. The first act, more demeaning than destructive, inconvenienced only the grandees, since it was rare for anything other than thoroughbred racers, hunters or carriage-horses to cost more than £5. Furthermore, some were exempted from the ban.[98] Also, when the law damaged the developing bloodstock industry in Ireland, breeders, even when Catholic, were absolved from its application.

The laws affected only a small proportion of the Catholic community: priests, lawyers and gentlemen or would-be gentlemen. The statutes were not applied rigorously and continuously. Yet, when aggregated, they amounted to an attack on Irish Catholicism. The purpose of the acts was to destroy the Catholic Church. In this objective, the laws failed. However, they did complete the elaborate legal substructure on which the Protestants' dominance was built. Some supporters of the penalties portrayed them as simple precautions. Recent experience of Catholic assertiveness convinced many Protestants that the Catholics, unless crippled, would scheme to recover what they had forfeited. Others in the Protestant camp were open about the self-interest which impelled them to grab more property and power from the Catholics and then to guarantee that they hang on to them.

Revenge drove some of the victors. In the 1690s, cursory reviews of recent Irish history indicated the frequency of rebellion in Ireland. Clearly, the inadequacy and relaxation of earlier penalties explained this depressing (to the Protestants) situation. The Catholics, although penalized throughout the 1650s, had not been emasculated. Indeed, they had shown an alarming resilience, fully capable of resuming the government of the kingdom in the later 1680s. Severe Protestants felt that the prohibitions of the Interregnum should be revived and refined. A parliament was planned in Dublin late in the 1670s, until the Popish Plot made it too risky. Had it met, anti-Catholic laws would have been passed.[99] In the event, the implementation of the programme was delayed until the 1690s. Now the Protestants, for the first time masters of the forum, turned it to their own ends. The resulting statutes attested to the conviction that Catholicism was inimical to true Christian principles; indeed was profoundly antichristian. Also, the creed was believed to endanger political stability and civil society. The less sophisticated forwarded and welcomed the anti-Catholic laws as expressions of atavistic hatreds and as handicaps to competitors for land, jobs and influence.

A number of recent scholars have denied that the measures amounted to a comprehensive scheme: a penal 'code'. Instead, they have emphasized how haphazard and piecemeal the decrees were.[100] Their enactment stretched over several parliaments. As late as 1729 and 1733 new restrictions were added, when Catholics were explicitly stopped from voting in parliamentary elections and from working even in the lower branches of the law as attorneys and solicitors. In 1745, marriages between Catholics and Protestants were outlawed, but not ended. More restrictions continued to be requested, as Catholic vitality and even expansionism were observed. The tenacity of the creed startled and depressed Protestants who had supposed that the numerous penalties would first sap and then kill it. Official enquiries in 1731 measured the Catholics' strength. The personnel of the Catholic Church easily outnumbered those of the Protestant churches. Catholic schools not only survived but flourished, especially in the larger towns. Protestants enjoyed numerical superiority only in six of the nine counties of Ulster and in the city of Dublin. In the Ulster counties with the densest concentrations – Antrim and Down – the Protestants split, probably equally, between conformists and nonconformists. Fresh surveys in 1766 yielded equally dispiriting information.

Defences

After 1690, the Irish Protestants owed their precarious eminence to military help from others. New laws were to shield them from any future Catholic menace. Soldiers would also defend them. The belief that a substantial garrison should be stationed in Ireland was a rare instance of convergence in the thinking of the Irish Protestants and of their new Dutch ruler. Since the twelfth century, Ireland hosted numerous troops. Soldiers from England (and elsewhere) fought to keep Ireland under English authority or to re-establish that authority when it was thrown off. Hopes recurred regularly that the number might be reduced and that Ireland would pay the army. English ministers were entranced by a vision of an Ireland able to send its own soldiers to serve anywhere in the Stuarts's empire and to subsidize some of the costs. It was not altogether a mirage. Late in the 1630s, Lord Deputy Wentworth planned that Irish troops should assist his master, Charles I, in suppressing the uprising in Scotland and then maybe overawe his critics in England. During the 1640s, similar hopes of regiments from Ireland reinforcing the royalist armies in Britain enticed Charles into talks, truces and treaties with the Confederates.

The notion recurred in the 1680s when regiments from a reliable Catholic army remodelled by Tyrconnell were sent to aid James in England. The reinforcements were temporary, small and even counter-productive, given English terror at the presence of allegedly wild Irish soldiery. Moreover, the brief intervals when Ireland supplemented English supplies were overshadowed by the longer spells, as between 1649 and 1660 or 1689 to 1692, during which England maintained, largely at its own cost, huge forces to repossess and retain Ireland. By 1692, an army of 36,520 cost an annual £1,285,000.[101] The expense, and the regularity with which it was incurred, led sceptics to question whether it was worthwhile. Even more widespread, and frequently expressed, was the feeling that England should recompense itself from Ireland. In this spirit, estates confiscated from the defeated were conferred on the conquering soldiers, royal favourites and on the investors who had financed the reconquest. In a more positive mood, optimists looked forward to a time when Ireland, pacified and prospering, hardly needing itself to be garrisoned, would again send its men into the British forces and pay for any continuing military presence.

William III, once Ireland had been brought back into his fold, wanted to remove his forces for more urgent operations in continental Europe. The ambition necessitated the incorporation of Ireland into his larger military plans. In outline, his scheme continued Charles II's and James II's. The earlier monarchs had treated Ireland as a component in an integrated military and naval establishment which encompassed all their possessions. Forces were moved regularly between the separate territories, with Irish regiments sent to unhealthy Tangiers, while Scottish or English contingents were stationed in Ireland.[102] In the 1690s, William pushed this approach harder. Knowing that his English subjects would gag on the presence of a standing army of 12,000 on their soil, he had the force quartered in and paid by Ireland. The defence of Protestant Ireland was not the main aim. The army was frequently depleted, sometimes to dangerously low levels, to deal with emergencies in Europe, regardless of the indignation of the Irish. The last were, nevertheless, placated, first by agreeing that these forces would not be billeted among the civilian population as they had been during the recent war and its aftermath. Instead, a chain of barracks was built.

Towns and landlords competed eagerly for one of the planned 150 barracks, since they believed the garrisons would enrich their neighbourhoods. By the 1730s, the barracks in Sligo were thought to bring an extra £7000 annually into the town. In remoter areas, especially those where Protestants were outnumbered massively by the Catholics, barracks were desired.[103] They increased the amenities of a district. Locals courted military officers: the latter diverted an otherwise dull society and were identified as possible husbands for dowdy daughters. The ordinary troopers were similarly welcomed, although in some places it was felt that they had worsened social and economic tensions by fathering bastards or abandoning wives and children when they were posted away from Ireland. The barracks themselves made work for contractors and suppliers. The quarters were overseen by functionaries, the barrack-masters, loosely controlled by a central barrack-board. The posts of barrack-master – 27 in all – promised attractive profits, both legitimate and illicit, and so became an office much sought by the civilians of Protestant Ireland.[104] Even more desirable was a place as one of the seven members of the supervisory Barrack Board. It resembled a seat on the other official agencies – the Linen Board, the Board for Inland Navigation or the many turnpike trusts – in opening up chances to assist allies and neighbours.[105]

The military, although they usually fell well below the notional total of 12,000, coloured and complicated Protestant Ireland. The presence of a substantial garrison distinguished Ireland from the North American territories in the early eighteenth century.[106] The aim of the English authorities was that none from Ireland should serve on the island. In theory, then, the soldiery were strangers from Britain. This could add to the appeal of individual soldiers. Collectively, origins outside Ireland brought friction. Officers sometimes espoused provocative politics and causes. When, towards the end of Queen's Anne's reign, Whiggish officers in Waterford and Limerick paraded their opinions in defiance of the perfervid Tory bishops who lived in the cities, the urban ponds were ruffled. Army officers, conscious of the larger British state which they served, took the lead in celebrating its high days and holidays. They engineered festivities on the king's or queen's birth- and accession days, and prodded the sometimes reluctant civilians to join in. Similarly, they were to the fore in organizing junkets for feats of Hanoverian arms outside Ireland, and were irritated when all did not rejoice.[107] Indiscipline during dull tours of duty in the Irish provinces was increased by the differences in confession, speech and outlook between the garrisons and their hosts. In time, Irish Protestant civilians voiced fears about a standing army. The misbehaviour of one commander had helped persuade Irish MPs of the need for barracks.[108] Later, in 1726, it was alleged that the unruly garrison of Limerick had threatened to lock the city gates and plunder the citizens.[109] In the 1750s, the officers' partisanship during a parliamentary by-election provoked strictures against a force which acted like 'mercenaries in the pay of a despotic government and not in a country of freedom and liberty'. A more favourable attitude towards the soldiery was shown by a magistrate in County Clare in 1742, who wrote plaintively that, 'our poor country [meaning, county] is left defenceless, without one red coat in it'.[110]

Irish patriots periodically protested against a situation in which they paid for an army of occupation over which they had scant control and which yielded doubtful benefits. Yet, as one cynic noted in 1748, an augmentation of the army, although financed by Irish taxes, would increase the money spent in the kingdom. Also, 'there will be more frequent opportunities for the gentlemen who reside here [in Ireland] to get their children and friends provided for by the government', which in turn would strengthen the administration.[111] The theoretical ban on those from Ireland serving in the forces deployed in Ireland seems often to have been broken, especially when regiments were transferred from overseas service to an Irish posting. Even without these breaches, Irish Protestants were recruited in large numbers into the forces, both military and naval, stationed away from Ireland. As the British 'fiscal–military state' expanded rapidly, so too did the opportunities open to the Protestants of Ireland. Access to the benefits, together with the effective control exercised over the military machine in Ireland, reconciled many Irish patriots to the garrisons within Ireland.

The exodus of able-bodied and ambitious Protestants from Ireland paralleled that of Catholics to serve in the armies of European monarchs, often the adversaries of the English. Since the 1650s, when the authorities permitted recruitment in Ireland for overseas service, the gain – removing potential trouble-makers from the kingdom – had been thought to outweigh any risks. More than 1000 are reckoned to have left Ireland each year in the early eighteenth century for this reason. Protestants within Ireland were more conscious of the dangers: that their local enemies would be trained in warfare and would eventually apply their skills against those who had supplanted them as owners of Ireland. The predictions seemed to be proved by the fighting during the 1640s and late 1680s. Despite the cautionary lessons, the British government took a pragmatic view, thereby demonstrating – yet again – how little it sympathized with the predicament of the Irish Protestants.

Civilians in Protestant Ireland overcame some of these disadvantages by improvising their own defences. They revealed their readiness to act as true citizens and protect what they held by enlisting in militia troops. In 1745, during the alarm over the possible descent of the Young Pretender on to Ireland, 835 Protestant men, aged between 16 and 60, were arrayed in the small county of Louth. Eleven years later, during a fresh emergency, there were said to be 984 Protestants fit to bear arms in the county, although not all appeared at a muster. These returns compared with 897 Protestant households noted in Louth in 1732. On paper, at least, few Protestant families escaped liability for defending the island.[112] However, in remoter parts of the kingdom, the scarcity of Protestants together with the weakness of local administration produced unsatisfactory responses to military alerts. Deputy governors and militia officers failed to appear at the appointed times in the chief towns of some baronies in County Clare during the emergency of 1756. In consequence, would-be militia men could not be enlisted.[113] The irregulars, fond of display but apparently ill prepared for action, became a butt for the derision of the regulars. Strutting in their finery, the amateur soldiers were rarely tested in action. A commander worried that 'we can't be of either ornament or service to the country'.[114] In 1760, when a French force landed at Carrickfergus, the shambling local militia left the invaders unchecked and its own reputation at a new low.

Relations with England, Britain and Europe

Reconquest between 1690 and 1691 led to the resettlement of Ireland, generally along lines that had become familiar over the previous century. By 1685, the Catholics had already lost so much land that, when they were again defeated in 1691, there was too little to be forfeited to create fresh plantations of English and Scottish immigrants. At first, the new monarch, William III, planned to give the confiscated estates to his own favourites, army commanders and the useful in England and Holland. The English parliament, increasingly irritated by William's arbitrary behaviour, cancelled many of his grants and, in 1700, appointed its own trustees to distribute the Irish lands. To Protestants in Ireland, hopeful of securing the forfeitures for themselves, this English interference was as resented as the king's high-handedness. It looked another – and especially blatant – interference in Ireland's domestic affairs by the ignorant and unsympathetic English. Irish Protestants were mobilized to resist the English trustees in a show of coordination and strength, which prefigured, in their arguments and tactics, political campaigns later in the century. The campaign succeeded: Protestant landowners and town-dwellers resident in Ireland did best from the redistributions.

The Irish Protestants had won the war only with external help: not just from England, but also from the European alliance behind William of Orange. Given these circumstances, it was understandable that England (after 1707, Britain) should watch vigilantly over its western kingdom. It was feared that Ireland might offer a bridgehead for England's continental adversaries. France had become the chief enemy, although Spain, once the main threat, could still cause alarm, as in 1740.[115] Despite repeated scares, Ireland did not rise: at least, not until 1798. However, neither the Protestants within Ireland, lately and still precariously installed in power, nor the English government were confident that peace would last. The survival in exile of the Stuarts – first James II (until 1701), then his son, James Edward (the Old Pretender) and the latter's offspring (Charles Edward, the Young Pretender) – caused anxiety about the likelihood of fresh risings. The Catholics of Ireland, like the Stuarts dispossessed and sharing their faith, were suspected of sympathizing with their former rulers: a sympathy which, in propitious conditions, would be turned into military aid. Anxieties among those governing Ireland after 1690 were worsened by the strengthened ties between the Catholics there and co-religionists and compatriots who opted for life in France, Spain and the Habsburg Empire. Abroad, priests were trained to mission in Irish parishes; there, merchants and craft-workers established themselves and sometimes prospered; there, too, the uprooted and desperate soldiered, occasionally rising to high commands and honours, but more frequently dying in obscurity and poverty. All in the diaspora were thought to retain links in Ireland. Along a variety of routes, most only dimly discerned by the authorities, ideas, funds and arms were supposed to travel, arming the Irish Catholics – both ideologically and physically – for another insurrection.

The scale and imminence of the threat could only be guessed, but knowledge of the multiplicity of connections between Catholics within and outside Ireland induced a wariness among Protestants. From time to time, the edginess toppled into panic. Alarms, and the responses to them, were clearest in 1715 and 1745–6, when, after a Stuart landed in Scotland and invaded England, it was uncertain how the Irish Catholics would behave or, indeed, whether Ireland itself might beckon to the Jacobites. Rumoured invasions sent jitters through Protestant Ireland in 1708, 1719, 1729, 1740, 1744, 1755–6 and 1760. Only once, in 1760, did the feared landing happen. A French contingent disembarked at Carrickfergus, unsettling far beyond the immediate vicinity of Ulster. The repeated alarms, certainly not groundless given the movements of the Stuarts, warfare between Britain and France, and the adamantine Catholicism of most living in Ireland led to a dual response. One element was to repress the obstinate Catholics so that they would be too weak to rise anew. The second approach, often in conjunction with coercion but sometimes as a clear alternative, was to cajole and caress. These options had long been the poles around which English policy for Ireland was organized. The decades after 1690 saw frequent resort to both types of measure, but with the positive slowly displacing the purely restrictive.

The ascendant Protestants within Ireland alternated between gloom and glee. According to the inclination of the observer, current policies were represented as triumphs or failures. Judged by the rudimentary test of keeping the peace within Ireland, the medley of measures succeeded. Furthermore, a modest prosperity was diffused, although most conceded that the benefits were spread unevenly. Visible results included the growth and embellishment of Dublin and larger towns like Cork, Derry, Kilkenny, Limerick, Newry and Waterford, the construction of roads and canals, the spread of tree-planting, flax-growing and linen-making, and a move away from 'lazy' pastoralism to intensive corn-growing. The indigenous Irish were more likely to dress, speak and behave like the English and Scots. The vaunted improvements were patchy and rested on flimsy foundations. In the southern province of Munster, for example, it was alleged in 1753 that the continuing prevalence of livestock as the main crop left the terrain, 'wild and horrid, their people slothful and uncultivated as the soil'. Sheep and cattle were said to 'eat up more men than all the wolves of the earth'. Moreover, the changes were too fragile to free the majority of the population from recession, disease and famine. Poverty doomed most labourers and their families to being housed, clad and fed in ways that contradicted optimistic assertions that the bulk of the Irish were coming to resemble their counterparts in Britain. The vulnerability to the vagaries of climate and to epidemics was shown at the opening of the century, between 1701 and 1706, and regularly thereafter. To the cruelty of nature were added damaging English interventions in the Irish economy. Hardships intensified during the 1720s and – grimmest of all – in 1740–1, when, in some regions, between 13 and 20 per cent of the population died. Thereafter, fresh crises of subsistence in the mid-1740s and mid-1750s, particularly in the north and north-west, warned how fragile livelihoods remained. In Munster, 'the wretched tenants' were likened to 'so many Hottentots', owing to the scarcity of tillage and consequent absence of steady employments.[116]

The wish of England (and Scotland) to subordinate the Irish economy to their own remained a popular explanation for the woes of Ireland. In addition, throughout the eighteenth century, Protestant partisans still traced the economic underdevelopment to the religion of the commonalty. According to this interpretation, the Catholic Church discouraged industry. First, it exacted numerous dues for the support of its priesthood, which effectively beggared laypeople. (The same charge was sometimes levelled at the established Church, the clergy of which were supported by tithes paid by all regardless of their confession.) Also, it was said that the many holy days in the Catholic calendar stopped the development of disciplined habits of regular labour.[117] Thinking of this sort, insisting that only Protestantism inculcated satisfactory habits of work, justified those who wished to redouble efforts to convert the local populations to Protestantism. From 1692, a familiar combination of goading and rewarding sought to prise the indigenes away from Catholicism. The Dublin parliament assisted the campaign – more by repressing than caressing. It left to others the more constructive programme to improve society and economy. However, even in parliament, by 1729 the emphasis was shifting towards subsidizing schemes of improvement.

Commentators noted and lamented the economic backwardness of much of Ireland – 'at this day [1738] less cultivated and improved than any other country in Europe'.[118] With about 86 per cent of potentially profitable land now in Protestant ownership and with the Catholics traditionally derided as a brake on development – proprietors, priests, lawyers and military captains – either exiled or neutered, fresh culprits were identified. Yet, the incumbent Protestants were tempted to deflect criticism from themselves back to the dispossessed Catholics, many of whom seemed (to their adversaries) depressingly buoyant. Because restrictions were either not applied or evaded, there were demands in the Dublin parliament, that the current laws against Catholics be better enforced or that new ones be added. Nevertheless, perceptions of danger from the Catholics fluctuated. Complaints that legislators and magistrates in Ireland were too sanguine about the good affection or feebleness of Irish Catholics shaded into the recurrent feeling that Britain failed to take the Catholic threat seriously enough. Such strictures joined others in an indictment of British misunderstanding of Ireland. Frequent meddling in Irish affairs by the London government – over trade, manufactures, the coinage, legal processes and how to treat Catholics and the Protestant dissenters – inflamed anti-English senti- ments. Strident Irish protests in 1698–9, 1719–20, 1723–5, 1753 and 1759–60 could never altogether mask the truth that the Protestants of Ireland had no sustainable future other than in a constitutional and commercial relationship with England, whence so many of them (or their ancestors) had come.

The essential community of interest between the Protestants of Ireland and Britain was not always acknowledged openly. Alarmists in Britain took the Irish impatience literally and accused the intemperate patriots of seeking independence, so recalling the offence of some insurgent Catholics during the 1640s. To counter the rhetoric of separatism, the idea that Ireland should be united with England was explored. An irk- some form of union had been forced on a beaten Ireland during the 1650s, as on Scotland, and left neither country with much taste for repeating the experiment. Nevertheless, as memories of the woeful episode faded and as the benefits to Scotland of its union in 1707 were predicted, a few in Protestant Ireland toyed with the possibility. In Britain, there was little interest in any benefits that union might bestow on Ireland. Rather, it was seen as a device by which the apparently incurable restlessness of the Irish, Protestant as well as Catholic, could be checked. When, after fresh bursts of Irish insubordination in the 1750s, an enforced union was mooted, rioters invaded the Parliament House in Dublin to make clear their disapproval.

Legal fetters could achieve only so much in binding the seemingly ungrateful Irish more tightly to an imperious Britain. In 1698, a new act stopped the legal export of Irish woollens, as earlier (1667) of live cattle. Soon, other measures insisted on the role of the British House of Lords as the final authority in appeals from the Irish courts of law and, in 1720, on Ireland's constitutional dependency on Britain. A more persistent irritation was the ease with which profitable offices in Ireland – from the lord lieutenancy, through the judiciary, the bench of bishops to the upper and middling reaches of the administration – were incorporated into the patronage empires of the monarch and his (or her) chief ministers in London. Irish Protestants received little compensation. Throughout the eighteenth century, few from Ireland ascended into the higher levels of the British government, Church of England or judicial bench. For the ambitious, industrious, well-connected and lucky from Ireland there were undoubted advantages in the intimate tie with Britain. Thereby they gained access to the expanding apparatus of the fiscal–military state of the Hanoverians. Enlarging, defending and running the overseas empire gave profitable employment to growing numbers from Protestant (and by the end of the century, Catholic) Ireland, as also to the Scots. The eagerness with which the Irish took service in remote British possessions told of the limited opportunities for advancement within Ireland itself or in metropolitan England. The Irish never broke into the closed worlds of the Scottish administration and professions.

The presence of English administrators in Ireland, the easy traffic between the sister kingdoms, and a shared language meant that, among the Protestant and English-speaking and reading communities, much of the grammar and vocabulary of English public life was adopted. But, just as the English language in Ireland was spoken with distinctive accents – the brogue – so too when English political terminology – Whigs and Tories, court and country, placemen, independents and patriots – arrived (briefly in the early 1680s and then more permanently in the 1690s), it soon acquired particular Irish intonations. At first glance, the easy adoption of an English political vocabulary suggested the imitative qualities not the originality of the Irish Protestants. Imitation – an intention behind English policy since the twelfth century – showed too in the alacrity with which the Protestants of Ireland took to the institution of parliament. It had long existed in Ireland as part of the luggage of law courts, local administration, land tenure and inheritance practices which early English administrators had unloaded. The same issues which agitated public life in England and embittered relations between the crown and its subjects excited the Irish. In each country, the growing confusion after Cromwell died in 1658 led many of the propertied to hanker after and secure the return of Charles II. Soon, the wish of the restored Charles to assist the Catholics back into local power and property unsettled passionate Protestants. In the 1670s and 1680s, Protestant partisans in England and Ireland (and in Scotland) tried to coordinate opposition to the Stuarts's projects. Already, though, there were signs that the concerns of the Protestants in Ireland diverged from those of their counterparts in Britain. The Irish Protestants, because so much fewer in numbers and so much smaller as a proportion of the population, faced greater dangers and were obliged to protest more stridently against royal policies. As has been stressed, they were too feeble to thwart a Catholic recovery or, indeed, to defeat the Catholic alliance backing James VII and II without help from Britain.

Throughout the eighteenth century, the dominant political culture continued to be oriented towards Britain. The Irish Protestants borrowed terms and tactics from England even when most strident in their denunciations of British incompetence and incomprehension. The majority in Ireland, who neither read English nor routinely spoke the English language, was less absorbed in the polemics. However, Catholics, even when illiterate or unversed in the English tongue, were not untouched by Britain. It had decreed and enforced their extrusion from power and property, and now maintained the exclusions. Moreover, England's dealings with Ireland and continental Europe helped to determine the conditions in which Irish Catholics dwelt. So unfavourable were conditions during much of the seventeenth and eighteenth centuries, that many Catholics abandoned the unequal struggle to wrest a livelihood from Ireland. English responsibility for the hostile atmosphere meant that numerous Catholics regarded England as their enemy.

Irish Catholics, estranged from England, especially once it was no longer ruled by the Stuarts, befriended England's enemies. Other factors complicated the responses of the Catholics to their predicament. Debarred first from sitting in Parliament, soon Catholics were also prevented from voting in parliamentary and municipal elections. In addition, the Test of 1704 confirmed and completed the Catholics' exclusion from national and local government. Unconcerned in the work of running Ireland, other than in the humblest capacities as constables and petty jurors, Catholics might perceive the British state as distant and hostile. The determined and ingenious could still devise means to influence elections in the localities and decisions in Dublin and London. Between 1704 and the 1770s, the methods were laborious and subterranean, and seldom leave clear traces or achieved great success.

Catholic activists, unwelcome in the counsels of the Irish and English governments, understandably transferred their efforts to the Catholic kingdoms of western and central Europe. There, in Vienna, Paris, Brussels, Rome and Madrid, exiles and the dispossessed were more likely to secure a hearing. Many compatriots and co-religionists exchanged the trials of life in Protestant Ireland for the opportunities in Catholic Europe. The successes of the few as soldiers, merchants, clerics and administrators drew more from Ireland. The expatriates formulated ideas and fashioned systems, which offered alternatives to the prevalent doctrines of the British state in eighteenth-century Ireland. The exiles helped to sustain their kindred who had stayed in Ireland, and prevented the latter from reconciling themselves to their degraded condition. The state, by stopping the full assistance of Catholics and Protestant noncon- formists, wilfully weakened itself. Just as much of the Presbyterians' civic sense had to be satisfied outside the structures of English Ireland, so too Catholics found alternatives.

The damage was twofold. By debarring so large a proportion of the inhabitants from the institutional and political life of the country, Britain in effect created in Ireland a narrow, confessional state: one, moreover, which could only be maintained artificially. When Britain decided to withdraw the props which had maintained the Church of Ireland minority in power, then the flimsy construct rapidly collapsed. The second problem arose from the alternatives created by the excluded. At the lowliest levels, Catholic parishes and the Presbyterian kirk sessions existed alongside the Church of Ireland vestries. Humdrum duties required by these entities schooled the participants in administration, sociability and civility, and so prepared them for more elevated roles. Catholics and Protestant dissenters received their preparation, but mostly in their own confessional bodies. Once trained for citizenship, those outside the established church had no obvious outlets. Baulked in their hopes of applying their skills and ideas, the excluded had several options. They might reason their fellows into submission to the powers set over them. Alternatively, the frustrated were equipped to criticize the prevailing system and to plot its downfall. In time, but only after 1760, the fabric of Church of Ireland privilege was eroded by those who had, of necessity, learnt civic virtue in different schools.

Chapter 4:   Parliament, Improvement and Patriotism, 1692–1760

Fears that a death-knell had been tolled for an independent Irish legislature, with the growing propensity of England to intervene in Irish affairs after 1690, were confounded. From 1692, the Dublin parliament not only retained but enlarged its role. Haughty Irish MPs responded to English slights by rehousing themselves. In 1729, a virtuoso from the emerging Protestant Ascendancy, Edward Lovett Pearce, well-connected and well-travelled in continental Europe, was commissioned to design a new parliament house on College Green, opposite Trinity College. Grand in scale and conception, the building proclaimed the arrival in Ireland of a sophisticated and modern classicism learnt directly from Italy and nowhere to be found in the secular public buildings of London or Edinburgh. This commission could be seen as a gesture, costly and permanent, which matched the rhetorical flights of the Irish patriots in parliamentary debates. It was equalled in grandeur and modishness only by the mansion of Castletown, which the Speaker of the Commons, William Conolly, was erecting in County Kildare during the 1720s.[119]

   In parallel, the assembly first devised and then refined procedures to ensure that it was heeded by English policy-makers. In the seventeenth century before 1692, it was convened five times. The most recent occasion was in 1689, when James VII and II appeared in Ireland. That assembly briefly reversed the process by which Parliament was becoming an entirely Protestant body. In 1661, no Catholics sat in the House of Commons. The exclusion of Catholics was formalized in 1692 when an act of the English parliament obliged the tendering to members of an oath which was unacceptable to Catholics. Membership of the Irish Commons numbered 300. Sixty-four members sat for the counties; two for the University of Dublin; the remainder for boroughs. The Upper House, designed to be a replica of the Westminster original, contained lay peers and the 22 bishops of the Protestant Church of Ireland. The spiritual peers, unequivocally Protestant and appointed to their bishoprics by the government, often attended assiduously and supported the government's programme.

During the seventeenth century, lay peers looked less attached to the new English and Protestant orders.[120] In 1661, a few had not taken their seats in the Lords because still outlawed for joining the uprising of 1641. Others, sometimes recently ennobled and living permanently in Britain, seldom or never attended sittings in Dublin. The absences of many enhanced the importance of the minority – such as the bishops – prepared to attend the Lords regularly.[121] By the 1690s, the Upper Chamber, like the Lower, had also become a wholly Protestant assembly. Unyielding Catholic peers went into exile after 1691, and were then (in 1716) formally excluded on account of their faith. As a result of the anti-Catholic laws, such as that of 1704, economic and social pressures increased. Great landowners, unless they became Protestants, would see their estates divided among several heirs or pass to Protestants. By the 1720s, it was estimated that fewer than ten of approximately 130 lay peers remained Catholic. However, although the majority were now Protestants, they were not necessarily keen to participate in the drudgery of the House of Lords.

In the Lower House, a large proportion of its 300 members turned up to important votes, especially near the opening of the session. In 1713, when members had to choose a Speaker, 258 voted. The hard-fought division over the money bill in December 1753, a scarcely concealed censure of English meddling, mustered 241 members. But in the dog days of long sessions attendance could drop to 40 (the size of the quorum).[122] Small numbers favoured the diligent. The regulars were not always those in the pay of the government and wedded to its cause, so that the outcome of debates could not be predicted accurately. In addition, the startling fluctuations in numbers who attended warn that for the majority of members, a place in the House, although keenly sought – even bought – did not then end other ambitions or dwarf alternative activities. The full-dress occasions, when the lord lieutenant opened or closed proceedings or when weighty matters were discussed, were rare. More frequent were the tedious sittings of committees or of the House to consider bills clause by clause. A willingness to shoulder such burdens differentiated a few from the many who professed civic mindedness. The limited importance of parliament is suggested by the small number of days on which it sat. Parliament in Dublin, when compared with Westminster, met for only 37 per cent of the time. Inevitably, it passed fewer measures. Normally, it convened every second year, and then for the months between late autumn and early summer: not too hectic a schedule.[123] Even zealots, eager to promote their own, their neighbourhood's and the general good, were left with plenty of time to work elsewhere. Often more was achieved by local and voluntary bodies than by the House of Commons.

There may be a danger of exaggerating the public spirit of MPs and the impact of parliament. Yet, what it did interested a larger audience than its own members or even the electors. Visitors flocked to the house to hear the lord lieutenant open and close proceedings.[124] Undergraduates from nearby Trinity College were said to frequent debates more than their own lectures.[125] Members were pressed to vote on the correct side and upbraided if they did not. Occasionally, 'mobs' intimidated MPs who failed to take a populist line. But these days were few in comparison with the soporiphic sittings. Orators used parliament as a platform, and wits made it a target for their invective. In 1723, Wood, a licensee from England, was authorized by the British government to coin copper money for Ireland. Small change was much wanted. However, onlookers in Ireland represented the project – Wood's halfpence – as a fresh device to remove their hard-earned wealth into England. The controversy spread far beyond the chambers of parliament: notables in the counties petitioned against the scheme; traders and craftsmen in Dublin demonstrated; pamphleteers, led by the awkward dean of St Patrick's cathedral in Dublin, Jonathan Swift, lampooned Wood and the ministers who had approved the design. The orchestrated hostility obliged the English government to replace the viceroy and then cancel the plan. Campaigns to press members to vote for or against specific bills recurred. Demagogues and reformers willingly appealed through print and speeches to those apparently outside conventional politics, and so contributed to the process by which the disenfranchized were transformed into political actors.

Politics

Throughout the heyday of the Irish Protestants' mastery, many of the same issues which divided the English, both from their sovereign and among themselves, appeared in Ireland. One fundamental of the new order – monarchs chosen by the English and then foisted on the Irish – William and Mary in 1689; the Elector of Hanover in 1714 – excited few qualms among Protestants. Catholics were less accepting. In the public arena, many echoes of English contentions were heard. But most acquired a distinctive Irish tone, sometimes amounting to cacophony. This characteristic showed in Queen Anne's reign, when Tory hysteria over Protestant dissent afflicted Ireland. There, from the 1690s, the Presbyterians, mainly emigrants from Scotland, grew rapidly in numbers and in assertiveness. The reality of the dangers of dissent put it high on the Irish political agenda. Two measures were directed against the Protestant nonconformists, the Test Act of 1704 and the Schism Act of 1713. Each expressed the vindictiveness of staunch adherents of the established Church of Ireland towards rivals; each copied measures already enacted in England.

The Test obliged all entering into crown and civic offices to certify that they had received communion according to the rites of the Church of Ireland during the previous year. It belatedly introduced a restriction, which had first appeared in England in 1673. Directed primarily against the larger contingent of Catholics in Ireland, it denied Protestant dissenters full participation in public life. The extension of the penalties under the Schism Act from England into Ireland told of the brief surrender of Irish Protestants to the High Church frenzy gripping England. Yet, the cry of 'The Church in Danger' – from the forces of dissent, irreligion and unorthodox doctrines – sounded more loudly in England than in Ireland.

Makers of policy for Ireland, faced with the twin challenges of Catholicism and Protestant nonconformity, tried to weaken both. In practice, neither the state nor the established church had the resources to proceed simultaneously against both enemies. As a result, the main target of official action changed according to perceptions of local and international dangers, and of whether the Catholics or Protestant dissenters were the more likely to unsettle Ireland. Behind the responses to topical difficulties lay differences in thinking about the two rival confessions. Each was feared as much for its political significance as for its theology. A few adherents of the Church of Ireland conceded that the Catholic Church was a true one, so that its sacraments – notably that of marriage – should be recognized whereas those of the dissenters were not to be. Some in Protestant Ireland felt that the Catholic priesthood and laity had been sufficiently weakened by recent laws – or in time would be – to transfer attention to the Presbyterian challenge. Others within the Church of Ireland disgreed, insisting on fundamentals shared between it and the orthodox forms of Protestant dissent such as Presbyterianism, religious Independency (later known as Congregationalism) and even the Quakers and Baptists. Accordingly, the fragmented Protestant confessions should unite against the Catholics. Thinking of this sort, more influential in official quarters in both England and Ireland after 1714 with the accession of the Hanoverians and the installation of the Whigs in power, brought the repeal of the Schism Act and the belated passage in Ireland of the Toleration Act in 1719 (it had been enacted in England back in 1689). However, moderates and latitudinarians were unable to secure the abrogation of the Test Act, which remained in place until 1783. In consequence, the ideal of Protestant unity remained exactly that. Dissenters, because of their legal disabilities, were excluded from important aspects of public life.

This was a serious loss, both to the dissenters, whose energies were diverted into endeavours focused on their own churches rather than on the Protestant state in Ireland, and to Protestant Ireland. The exclusions resulted in a rather different outcome from the effect of the same laws in England. The Irish situation also differed strikingly from that of the dissenters in Scotland, with which the Presbyterians of Ireland were familiar. Indeed, in Scotland since 1689, the Presbyterians had been installed as the state church with the attendant privileges. Adherents of the same system in Ireland found themselves accorded a depressed second-class status and were even, from time to time, harassed and imprisoned by zealous magistrates. This was the more galling given the growing strength of the Presbyterians, especially in the northern province of Ulster, and what they had contributed to the preservation of a Protestant Ireland in the 1640s and between 1688 and 1691.

Presbyterians from Scotland, settled in Ulster during James VI and I's time, alternated between favour and harassment. Congregations, expanded during the Interregnum until by 1660 there were perhaps 74, faced persecution under the returned Stuarts and episcopalians.[126] A brief respite under James VII and II was quickly succeeded by new trials. Despite their heroism against the Jacobites and Catholics at Enniskillen and Derry in 1689, the Presbyterians of Ulster received neither the toleration accorded to their brethren in England nor the status of being the established church given to those in Scotland. Tribulations increased as the provisions of the Test were applied. Yet, the usefulness of the Presbyterians as a load-bearing beam in the rickety structure of Protestant Ireland was widely recognized. Indeed, from 1672, an annual subsidy – the king's gift or *regium donum* – acknowledged this.

How to treat the Presbyterians perplexed those in power no less than the question of dealings with the many more Catholics. The puzzle also brought fresh divisions between the attitudes current in England and those of the zealous adherents of the Protestant Church of Ireland. Catholics and Presbyterians were blamed, either separately or in tandem, for the rebellions of the 1640s and the execution of Charles I. The republicanism of some religious separatists was readily conflated with the subversive ideas of the Catholics. In this interpretation, the Presbyterians were either in league with or more dangerous than the Catholics.[127] So far from being tolerated or comprehended within an enlarged and relaxed Church of Ireland, they should be restrained. This intolerance, at its height in the later years of Queen Anne's reign when Tories were triumphant in both Ireland and England, led to the introduction of the Test into Ireland, a brief cancellation of the *regium donum* and prosecutions of dissenting pastors. After 1714, with the Tories and High Churchmen discredited for their extremism and tarnished by alleged association with the exiled Stuarts, policy towards the Protestant dissenters softened. Yet, those who accepted that a fundamental community of interest bound the episcopalians to the Presbyterians jibbed at any award of complete legal equality by repealing the Test. In 1719, a Toleration Act extended greater security to the dissenting congregations.[128] The concessions, opposed by many orthodox churchmen and only reluctantly agreed, did not give nonconformists equality with conformists. The separated congregations, particularly of Presbyterians, although essential to a strong and unified Protestant interest in Ireland, constituted a challenge and a threat.

Church of Ireland hostility was sometimes worsened by the dissenters' forwardness in promoting and profiting from useful industries, particularly the manufacture of textiles. Also, as fecklessness and idleness came to be attributed to Protestants as much as to Catholics, Quakers and Presbyterians with their thrift and industry seemed models of worthy endeavour. The vitality of nonconformity and the evident prosperity of some of its adherents, often exaggerated, unnerved members of the established church. In describing the triumphs of the dissenters, especially the Presbyterians, there was a tendency to write only of undifferentiated aggregations (as there was in characterizing the straits and traits of the Catholics). By the early eighteenth century, the pressures – legal, economic and social – to conform to the state church had virtually extinguished dissent among peers and squires.[129] Instead, Presbyterian congregations derived their strength from the towns, and the middle and lower orders.[130] Few were subjected to precise description or analysis.

How best to handle Protestant dissent was merely one of several questions common to both Ireland and England (and sometimes to Scotland as well), for which policies appropriate to Britain did not always suit Irish needs. Trade and defence caused further vexation. The knotty issues inflamed opinion, or at least the opinionated, within Ireland, since each reminded of the price that Ireland paid for its continuing connection with England. Even without the episodic eruptions over contentious policies, the structural interconnections between England and Ireland abraded the sensitive Irish. Chief ministers in England chose amenable deputies to govern Ireland and peopled the Irish administration with cronies and clients. The choices were seldom determined by any sensitivity to distinctive Irish requirements. If lords lieutenant in Dublin Castle were resented as agents of an intrusive British government, specific failures could be traced to the viceroys' connections with dominant English personalities, such as Walpole throughout the 1720s and 1730s and the Pelhams and elder Pitt during the 1750s.

Supporters of the English administration in Dublin tended to align themselves with the incumbent ministry in Britain. Conversely, those out of favour with or congenitally hostile to the governor of the day allied with English opponents of the court. Taking up tactics and arguments used in England, political life was conducted through pamphlets, squibs, petitions, harangues, demonstrations and even riots which often recalled and sometimes surpassed the ribaldry and inventiveness of their English originals. By the 1750s, widespread fears were voiced, not only that a growing luxury was enervating the prosperous, but also that the profits of commerce and empire were buying the subservience and silence of the once vociferous critics of the executive. In Ireland, similar misgivings were expressed. There, however, the doubts were given a patriotic flavour. Britain, thanks to the constitutional and commercial constraints with which it enfeebled Ireland – such as the cumbersome mechanism of Poynings's Law, the more recent Declaratory Act of 1720 and the series of embargoes on exports – depressed Ireland and sapped the spirit of its inhabitants. A deft sharing of places, pensions and lucrative contracts silenced some, otherwise tempted to repine against English mistreatment of Ireland. In consequence, the independently minded and those out of favour with the current governors felt that the vigour and independence of the Irish parliament were in jeopardy.

Members who dominated the Dublin parliament after 1714 all professed variants of Whiggery. Dominance arose from and then depended on an ability to articulate the anxieties and prejudices of the majority of less fluent members. In return for undertaking to deliver to the lord lieutenant and his administration stable parliamentary support, the leaders – on account of their prime function called 'undertakers' – expected rewards for themselves and their followers. The sweeteners took the forms of prestigious and modestly profitable posts, seldom with onerous duties, in central and local government, the revenue and customs administration, the armed forces and the Church of Ireland. The successive undertakers included Alan Brodrick (ennobled in 1715 as Lord Brodrick and advanced two years later to be Viscount Midleton), William Conolly, Henry Boyle, created earl of Shannon in 1756, and John Ponsonby. All served as Speaker of the Irish House of Commons; all enriched themselves, their families and their clients through serving the British ministry and crown. Occasionally, the undertakers differed in priorities and emphases. Conolly, for example, had an apparently quixotic wish to improve the lot of the Protestant dissenters. Deriving much of his following from Ulster, he may have calculated that further additions of Presbyterian support would assist him to defeat political rivals. After 1714, the leading parliamentarians rarely disagreed about the essentials of policy. Each strove to protect and, when possible, to strengthen the Protestants' domin- ance within Ireland, and to repel British intrusions. In some degree, each lifted his eyes from day-to-day management to a more distant vision of a prosperous, populous and peaceful Ireland. All sponsored structural and physical improvements on their own holdings and neigh- bourhoods, and also throughout the kingdom. None was prepared to introduce sizable legal concessions for the Catholics. Since so little of moment separated the leading players in parliament, their periodic spats are readily seen as inspired either by greed or by personal ambi- tion, or by both. Each commanded contingents linked by intricate regional, familial and social meshes; each was driven by competitiveness and even personal dislike of or attraction to the incumbent viceroy or rival politicians.

These characteristics made the political scene look venal and petty, with patriotism a rhetorical bromide to steady waverers and win add- itional supporters. They also suggested an introverted activity interesting to few outside the precincts of parliament or the clienteles of the leading players. Unfriendly charges of this kind are not always wide of the mark. However, what members of parliament did mattered to a wider constituency – wider, indeed, than the entirely male and Protestant electorate. Many of the disenfranchized felt unpleasant effects. The middling and poorer sorts were subjected to taxes approved by parliament; the many outside the established church had their religious and civic liberties docked. MPs, in taking up the defence of Irish concerns against insensitive and maladroit lords lieutenant or antagonistic English ministers and MPs, appealed to an audience larger than that formally involved in conventional politics.

A pedigree of extra-parliamentary protest, mainly by Protestants and Dubliners, reached back to 1659–60. Manifestations, at the time of the fall of the republican regime and the return of Charles II, drew in more than the 144 delegates to the General Convention. A genealogy of political mobilization might also include orchestrated opposition from the capital in 1672–3 to Charles II's scheme to loosen the Protestants' grip on civic power. The continuities become clearer between 1711 and 1714, with the angry protests against a Tory administration in Ireland, headed by the lord chancellor, Sir Constantine Phipps (an Englishman). Opposition, overt and covert, emanated from the Whiggish municipality of Dublin. Charles Lucas, a Dublin apothecary, developed the potential of the discontented within Dublin to a new pitch during the 1740s. Lucas adapted for local use contemporary arguments about the danger to ancient constitutions from exponents of absolutism or oligarchy and to civic virtue from luxury and greed.

By the eighteenth century, extra-parliamentary opinion was activated with increasing frequency. There existed channels, especially in Dublin and the bigger boroughs, by which the middling and respectable could be involved. Regular gatherings of parish vestries, trading guilds, societies of journeymen and convivial clubs allowed political opinions to be aired and action to be planned. These groups, academies of political under- standing, typically belonged to the towns, although they were not entirely unknown in the countryside. Rural protest, often directed at the live- stock and occasionally at the dwellings and persons of the proprietors, relied on more shadowy customs. Many of the traditions and rituals were associated with the Catholic populace, which, to an even greater degree than in the towns, predominated among labourers on the land.

The processes of political education and civic consciousness were forwarded by print. Throughout much of the seventeenth century, a single press in Dublin produced material to dull the restless. Imported material, in contrast, was often calculated to inflame. The government was wary of libels, either published clandestinely or smuggled into

Ireland. By the 1670s and 1680s, the skits and squibs were mocking policies dear to the king or to his agents in Dublin. The material, although embarrassing, was too sparse seriously to damage the regime within Ireland. In 1698, during the controversy arising from the latest English assertion of authority over Ireland, with a legal appeal decided by the English House of Lords and the English parliament ending a profitable Irish trade in wool and woollens, one Irish member of parliament, William Molyneux, set out in print the fundamental and historical objections. Molyneux, prominent in the intellectual and social life of Protestant Dublin, sounded a note that few immediately echoed and that many reprobated. It is noteworthy that, at this date, the paper battles over Irish policies still raged in England rather than in Ireland.[131] Soon, the readership within Ireland for both angry and calm statements of Irish grievances increased. The growth encouraged a modest increase in the number of printers in Ireland, first in Dublin and then, as the eighteenth century progressed, in the provinces, and of works aimed at the local market.[132]

Towards the end of Queen Anne's reign, the controversies between Tories and Whigs agitated Irish politics. Pamphleteers and printers joined the fray. Between 1723 and 1725, Wood's scheme to mint half-pennies provoked greater activity within the Dublin book trade. The government, by hauling printers and booksellers before the courts, risked even greater humiliation from juries unwilling to indict those responsible for what was widely seen as fun or fair comment. The pursuit of articulate adversaries such as Dean Swift exposed the regime to even greater ridicule. Swift, hailed as a hero for his lampoons, again challenged policy emanating from England in 1737. London decreed that the value of gold in Ireland be lowered. This threatened to reduce the worth of many fixed stipends. Swift had a black flag of defiance run up from the spire of his cathedral and its muffled bells tolled.[133] Swift was merely one contributor, albeit with a dangerous purchase on the Dublin populace, to a loud chorus. In the later 1720s, numerous pamphleteers, appalled by the recent economic and subsistence crises, advised how to avert them in future. Again print, now produced overwhelmingly in Dublin, widened the debate. These themes, as we shall see, were reprised throughout the 1740s and 1750s.

Pamphlets, petitions and parades drew more into the political arena. The Dublin parliament, the English administration in the Castle and the government in London never monopolized Irish politics. As so many more became involved, the authorities struggled to maintain a semblance of control over the unenfranchized, but politically aware majority. During the second half of the seventeenth century, there were hints of extra-parliamentary pressures. However, just as the Irish Parliament came of age only in 1692, so it was not until the eighteenth century that there are clear signs of a larger constituency following political debates. Voting was the most obvious action through which more might be drawn into the formal work of running the kingdom. Yet, it was a privilege enjoyed, even notionally, by few. As in England, so in Ireland, the franchise in the 32 counties was confined to possessors of freeholds worth more than 40 shillings annually. In the more numerous boroughs, the qualification varied from residence in the manor or payment of local rates to the more restrictive requirement of freedom of the municipal corporation or of the inner clique of burgesses. In a few towns, the voters amounted to hundreds; in many, they consisted of no more than 12 or 13. During the mid-eighteenth century, it has been suggested that the total electorate numbered between 40,000 and 45,000.[134] The voters, exclusively Protestant men, constituted perhaps 2 per cent of the total population. As a percentage of the Protestant community, it was more impressive: maybe 10 or 12 per cent.

Throughout the seventeenth century, only small numbers exercised the right by coming to vote on the rare occasions when elections were held. In 1697, a by-election for County Londonderry attracted 162 voters.[135] By the mid-eighteenth century, more electors were crowding the hustings. In a County Clare election of 1745, over 360 voted; at Armagh in 1753, 1181. The 1761 general election brought out at least 1157 in County Cavan; 565 in County Limerick; and 555 in Westmeath.[136] Parliamentary elections provoked as much excitement as horse-races and cock-fights, with rivals intimidated and hurt. Yet, the opportunities for electors to participate in national affairs by choosing between rival candidates remained rare. After 1713, general elections were occasioned only by the death of the sovereign: in 1715, 1727 and 1761. Even in these years, few parliamentary constituencies went to a poll. In 1727, perhaps 50 were contested; in 1761, it is reckoned that the total had dropped to only 26. The lack of contests can be interpreted as a sign of political apathy. It could be, too, that by 1761 the mounting costs of electioneering deterred all but the foolhardy and profligate from seeking a parliamentary seat. One who declined to offer himself for election in 1761 announced that he had 'no two thousand guineas to give away from myself and my family, no venal views to reimburse so much loss of property'.[137]

The representation for most seats was settled by deals among the leading families of the locality. Occasionally they were formalized. In 1727, three magnates in County Kerry agreed to alternate as the representatives for the county and for the borough of Tralee.[138] By-elections occurred unpredictably and could be fierce. Longer than a year might elapse between the death of a sitting member and the selection of a successor. Such an interlude allowed competitors ample scope to prepare the ground. Preparations included the creation of new freeholds in order to increase the numbers qualified to vote in the counties, the creation of more freemen to change the complexion of the voters in boroughs, and the election of partisans to the municipal offices which carried an entitlement to vote in the closed boroughs. The incorporated towns, numbering over a hundred, afforded annual opportunities to fill civic posts and to enfranchize more freemen. The occasions were more frequent and often more important than the sporadic parliamentary elections in educating Protestant men in the duties of citizenship, in nurturing political awareness, and in determining allegiances. Civic posts mattered, in themselves and for their influence over the outcome of parliamentary contests. Appointments as freeman, burgess, mayor, treasurer, town clerk or recorder in a town brought profits and power. So, too, in counties, did inclusion in the county magistracy and grand jury and appointment to the prestigious if sometimes irksome offices of sheriff, governor and deputy governor (the equivalent of lords lieutenant and deputy lieutenants in English shires).

Throughout the seventeenth and eighteenth centuries, commentators pontificated about dealings between Ireland and England, between Catholics and Protestants, between the different varieties of Protestants, and between governors and governed. A series of searching studies has lately reconstructed what happened in the Irish parliament between 1692 and 1760. These excellent analyses bring different dangers. The foibles of viceroys, the posturing, politicking and principles of MPs, the growing involvement of electors and even of the unenfranchized in the controversies in parliament undoubtedly affected how the peoples of Ireland lived, but sometimes assume a disproportionate prominence. Developments in the localities tend to be studied in so far as they amplify or modify the picture of national politics. Yet, many communities had a vitality independent of or only tangentially connected with the dynamos of Dublin Castle, the Irish parliament or the distant British government. Most in later Stuart and Hanoverian Ireland lived outside the ambit of the 300 Protestants who sat in the Commons, the 30 or 40 regulars on the benches of the Lords, the small secretariat and court in Dublin where the English lord lieutenant was closeted, or even the 3000 to 5000 substantial freeholders and freemen. For this majority, the deliberations of parliament and the institutions of the state, although not irrelevant to how they lived, appeared in a guise different from that seen by those who manned the institutions.

Improvement

Victory in 1690–1 emboldened triumphalists bent on retribution, at least for a season. The result was the repressive measures which so severely constrained (at least in theory) the lives of Catholics (discussed in Chapter 3). For the moment, softer voices were drowned, but not silenced. The quieter message, reflecting on what the Protestants in Ireland had lately endured and escaped, also built on what they had encountered repeatedly from the 1580s to the 1680s. Rebuffs abounded – had they not been driven from their homes twice in the century? Setbacks, when represented as divine rebukes, demanded contrition and penance. What forms repentance should take split Protestant ideologues and politicians. As in the past, the forceful gave priority to measures to repress Catholicism, particularly in its public manifestations. Optimism that the penalties introduced between 1695 and 1709 would create a climate conducive to mass conversions was soon confounded when only a trickle of important Catholics defected to Protestantism. One explanation of the disappointments was that the laws were not stringently and uniformly applied. Another was that they needed to be strengthened. The remedy, therefore, was not just to enforce the existing laws, but to add new ones. So, as late as the 1750s, parliament was invited to debate and approve fresh bills aimed against the Catholics. However, an alternative view gained ground: that criminalizing Catholicism and Catholics created defiance not submissiveness. Instead of coercion, it was time to try persuasion.

   This more generous approach had a long history – indeed, since the Protestant reformation began in Ireland. There was, too, a persistent argument that the Protestant community needed to show itself worthy of its divine mission, and amend what was amiss among its own. Already in the 1680s, the thoughtful surmised that God would punish them for running after worldly delights and for failing to take the gospel to the Irish. In this vein, the 'temporal plenty' enjoyed by the newly settled

Protestants was contrasted with the meagre 'spiritual advantages' allowed to 'the poor Irish'.[139] Such forebodings were borne out between 1685 and 1691 when Catholics regained mastery. Diligent pastors – William King, Nathaniel Foy and Anthony Dopping – who had ministered in Dublin during the taxing years of Catholic *revanche* under James II, urged positive courses. King, Foy and Dopping became bishops. In this capacity, from 1692 they used the House of Lords to strive for measures to fortify the Protestant Church of Ireland. Institutional and financial improvements were designed to underpin projects of spiritual education and regeneration. The activists, mindful of the sinfulness of their own flocks, gave top priority to Protestant sins. In endeavouring to mend manners, the reformers borrowed expedients used in England and by their dissenting brethren. The work – curbing drunkenness and swearing, closing brothels and spreading knowledge of the Christian gospels – rarely reached beyond Protestant congregations to Catholics, and, apparently concentrated in Dublin, had a very limited impact elsewhere.[140]

One scheme in particular aimed to reach more. A few within the Church of Ireland hoped that the rudiments of Christianity (in its approved Protestant forms) would be made available in the Irish vernacular. Such projects had been mooted over the last hundred years, and had always been contentious. As in the past, so in the early eighteenth century, the scheming produced little. The campaign exposed and accentuated the divisions among the clergy of the Church of Ireland.[141] The ambitious task of evangelizing the Catholic Irish in their own language was largely shelved after 1714. It was not that the champions of the Church of Ireland were content to rely only on repression. Nor was the established church keen solely to service its own, although this could be an onerous and often thankless job. Instead, it was felt better to concentrate on schooling the young, and in English, and thereby detach the impressionable from Catholicism. Modest resources and uncertain enthusiasm made it wise to target the vulnerable, among whom poor children seemed easy prey.[142]

A team of talented bishops ensured that their church was strengthened after 1692. Laws enjoined Church of Ireland incumbents to reside on their livings and rewarded them for rebuilding their houses and improving their lands. Bishops in their dioceses and rectors on their glebe-lands set an example by building, decorating, gardening and farming in novel ways. Through writing and preaching, they tried to spread the ideas and techniques to a larger constituency. Clerics, no matter how diligent, could achieve only so much. Frequently they were met with indifference if not hostility. This came not just from the mass of Catholics, but also – more disturbingly – from the Protestant laity, especially when assembled in parliament. During the 1730s, the bishops and parish clergy found themselves at odds with the powerful over efforts to extend the obligation of propertied laypeople to pay tithes (either a proportion of their agricultural produce – historically calculated at a tenth – or money in lieu) towards the support of the clergy. A vicious anticlericalism was never far beneath the surface of Protestant Ireland, and, when it appeared, it cautioned all but the most foolhardy churchmen against antagonizing the laity. Such reactions necessarily restricted what leaders of the Church of Ireland achieved. The conscientious sought, by exhortation and example, to popularize both physical and ethical improvements. They were to the fore in the scheme to establish a network of Protestant schools throughout the kingdom: a project copied from Britain in the 1690s and endorsed by a royal charter for the Incorporated Society in Ireland in 1733. Clergy were also active in establishing and sustaining the Dublin Society and Physico-Historical Society of the 1740s, both of which were intended as spurs to material and moral improvements.

Thoughtful laypeople shared the ideals of the clerical activists. A vein of practical piety pulsed through some who cooperated happily with the clergy's endeavours. Christian and humanist impulses underlay the activism of MPs prominent in promoting improvements and the dedicated who immersed themselves in the constructive tasks of local and national charities and voluntary associations. Many appeals for improvements were couched in terms that appealed as much to cupidity as conscience. Private profits as well as public benefits flowed from introducing novel techniques and crops. Other investments – constructing or reconstructing residences according to classical symmetry and reordering gardens and parks – catered to the owners' sense of themselves as the leaders of taste, conversant with what was approved by their counterparts in continental Europe and Britain. Other ventures, subsidizing flax-growing and linen-making, establishing new townships and endowing them with market-houses, assembly rooms, better roads and bridges, even paying for Protestant churches, promised to help more. These were matters taken up, encouraged and subsidized by the Irish Parliament in the eighteenth century. Parliament was neither the sole nor invariably the most important agency in underwriting this fashionable cult. Official bodies in the localities, notably the grand jury and magistracy of the county, had power to assist this work, and used it. Concurrently, voluntary organizations, such as Masonic lodges, societies, clubs and boards, subscribed to the same ideals. On occasion, projects were duplicated in several settings. Also, the promoters were often working through different bodies simultaneously. On the one hand, the activities showed the assiduity and ingenuity of the committed in exploiting all opportunities to forward the important business; on the other, it reminds of the limited group interested in these matters, and the limits to change in the economy and society of the time.

The Dublin parliament, potentially at least, was best situated to direct taxes into productive works. From 1703, its members did so. The ability to plough back into the country some of what had been extracted from it by taxation showed an assembly increasingly adept at manipulating its powers and procedures. The objects which were deemed worthy of financial support – the planting of trees useful alike in house- and boat-construction; building of canals, turnpike roads, bridges and harbours; better navigation on rivers such as the Shannon, Blackwater and Barrow; growing grain and flax, so ending the likelihood of fatal shortages of bread-corn, and bringing a more stable prosperity through the manufacture of linen – revealed the success of improvers in insinuating their ideas into the minds of men of influence. The results, at least in terms of bills passed, can be measured. Between 1731 and 1740, two-thirds of the bills coming before parliament related to schemes of social and economic regeneration.[143]

Members of parliament often channelled money into an assortment of subsidiary panels and local committees. They included the Trustees for the Linen Manufacture and the Trustees for Inland Navigation and the privately financed initiatives represented in organizations like the 28 turnpike trusts set up between 1729 and 1741. Many of those active as members of parliament in promoting constructive and ameliorative measures also sat on the very committees which received and disbursed the funds voted by Parliament. MPs were not alone, nor necessarily did they dominate, the subsidiaries. Yet, whatever the precise role of MPs in the dynamics and decisions of these state-supported bodies, there was a pleasing circularity about the operations. Small groups of voters were gratified to receive subsidies, which they then allocated to deserving causes, the benefits of which are clearer within than outside the circles of privilege. A contemporary commented caustically, that 'the public money passed fluent as water through so many sieves, though we may with reason presume that each vessel was sufficiently wet by the way'.[144]

Observers in mid-eighteenth-century Ireland attested to the vogue for these works. Yet, just how many in Irish Protestant society were gripped by the craze, or how far into society the benefits reached, may be questioned. The well-meaning congratulated themselves and their colleagues on their public spirit. The unkind might see the ventures as part of a system in which a few monopolized membership of parliament and the running of local government, then ensured that they were lightly taxed, and yet redirected taxation into their own favourite projects. Altruism and self-interest powered the improvers. In some, the ideals of practical Christianity and a wish to proclaim the superiority of Protestantism were uppermost; in others, the teachings of classical and humanist philosophers. More, perhaps, exploited mechanisms, which they controlled, to guarantee financial help for the settlements and lands that they owned. Rhetoric and the subsidies alike allowed Irish taxes to improve the private estates of a lucky minority, by easing communication by road and water, by delivering better strains of flax seed or extra spinning-wheels and looms, and by paying them to plant more trees and corn. One rare dissentient from the dominant credo in the 1750s saw the construction of turnpike roads as akin to the Romans' aim of uniting its sprawling empire by the device of an intricate network of thoroughfares. The critic, by linking it with another Roman institution, of standing armies, ingeniously connected the roads with a British ambition to subject Ireland as completely as the Romans in their heyday had their territories. The unconvinced suggested that traffic was too light to justify the extensive system of Irish roads, so that the project did little other than flatter the vanity of landlords and raise the value of their properties, now more easily accessible from the capital. It was suspected that venality and corruption were rife in the allocation of public moneys and the salaried posts connected with the turnpikes, canals, military barracks and textile manufactures. 'Knaves and mean-souled wretches' made the activities into 'base, filthy jobs'.[145]

The Irish parliament, either by its own acts or through encouragement, fostered improvement. Nevertheless, commentators routinely noted the backwardness of much of Ireland. Various explanations were then advanced. Some argued that any material improvements must wait upon the achievement of greater political stability. The victories of William and consequent measures to disable the Catholics satisfied that pre-condition. Yet, to the dismay of sensitive observers, depression, dearth and famine again hit parts of Ireland in the 1720s. Attention was once more focused on the incumbent Protestant proprietors, too many of whom were absent, rapacious or negligent. Printed palliatives exhorted the propertied to attend to their responsibilities. Some took the messages seriously. In and outside parliament, the concerned strove to translate their anxieties into constructive ventures.[146] In time, it was prophesied, the gains would be felt throughout the island. The young would learn useful skills; tenants were to be assisted towards more productive and innovative agriculture; commodities would be cheapened and made more widely available. Advantages to substantial proprietors are clear: increases in the yield and value of their lands, and the ability to demand higher rents from allegedly more numerous and prosperous tenants. Gains for the poor producer are harder to gauge. The route to the nearest market might be improved, but before it could be walked or ridden, tolls had to be paid at each stage (turnpike) on the road. The new dues added to those already payable to gatekeepers at the entries to towns and to clerks of the market for the right to sell produce in their spaces. More capital was required to farm in the currently approved modes. Those without it either incurred debts or allowed the more commercialized husbandry to pass them by.

Statutory encouragements and state subsidies were fruits of Irish Protestant consternation at recurring and seemingly worsening crises of subsistence. The responses avoided fatalism and passivity, and constituted a variety of patriotism.[147] Yet, even those Irish patriots resolved to improve their own kingdom did not always avoid the temptation to castigate Britain. Recessions and famines might still be explained as sent by an angry deity to punish the insouciant and sinful. Disasters were also used as sticks to beat their English overlords. Meddlesome measures were thought to have distorted and stunted profitable branches of the Irish economy, although it proved remarkably inventive in evading or overcoming the difficulties created by England. In addition, England exerted a dangerous magnetism, which drew people and money from Ireland towards it. Penalties, such as taxes on revenues sent from Ireland to absent landowners and office-holders in England, were proposed and intermittently imposed.

Alongside penalties, incentives were tried. More intensive agriculture – tillage instead of livestock – would employ more hands. So, too, would the creation or expansion of manufactures such as textile-making, building, metal-working and mining. Moreover, if both staples and novelties of greater quality and appeal could be made locally, imports and the attendant drain of money from Ireland would be reduced. A systematic assault on the problems was promised by the Dublin Society. Started in 1731, it owed more to the private exertions of the civic minded than to parliament. Neither of its creators – Thomas Prior, the angry publicist of the evils of absenteeism, and Samuel Madden, a squarson who divided his year between County Fermanagh and Dublin – sat in the Commons. Indeed, it looked as if parliament was happy to leave the tricky task of regenerating and diversifying the Irish economy to volunteers. The Society had precursors in an informal group of scientifically minded virtuosi during the 1650s and then the more substantial Dublin Philosophical Society of the 1680s. The two earlier associations had combined speculation with practical endeavour. The Dublin Society concentrated on the utilitarian. Its message was projected beyond a few squires who were already reading manuals about innovative crops and methods. It resolutely declared in 1737 that 'the poorer sort, the husbandman and manufacturer are the proper objects of instruction', and promised to 'bring practical and useful knowledge from the retirements of libraries and closets into the public view'.[148] The directors found it hard to sustain interest. The fresh disaster of the famine of 1740–1 warned how little agriculture and manufactures had changed. Madden, alive to the challenge, remodelled the organization. The Society received a charter; successive lords lieutenant patronized it; parliament voted it funds; it enjoyed a continuous existence and attracted as members, not always active, peers, prelates, squires, intellectuals and do-gooders. By the 1740s it flourished in an atmosphere in which collective enterprises aiming at the public weal were all the rage. It enjoyed a place as the senior among diverse societies and clubs bent on improvement.

How far the Dublin Society defeated the scourges of underdevelopment, dearth and distress may be doubted. Under Madden's inspired direction it shifted its emphasis to nurturing turnips, killing rats, weaving tapestries, fashioning statuary and pottery, and sending gifted artists to study in Rome. It fitted into and strengthened an élite conscious of the requirements of Christian and civic duty, eager for elegance and sophistication, and insatiably curious. Madden was astute in prodding producers around him to compete and excel. Yet, it has to be asked, even if it cannot be answered, how many novelties the Society introduced to Irish producers and consumers. Standards of design and craftsmanship were to be raised through rewarding innovators. The hope was that more would happily buy Irish goods. Silverwares, pottery, textiles and woodwork were raised to new levels of excellence. However, the caustic ridiculed the 'little huckstering society, with its two-penny rewards and three-penny premiums'.[149] Also, the prosperous, while they might buy the local, also craved foreign products. Moreover, two innovations which had the greatest practical effect on how many in Ireland lived – potatoes and flax – owed little to the Society. The potato was popularised without any official interventions and subsidies. One public act alone helped. In the 1690s, it was decided not to tax potatoes.[150]

Parliament did more to assist flax-growing and the making of linen. The activities had long enjoyed official approval, chiefly because they need not compete directly with English ones, as the Irish wool trade did. Scots, also promoting linen, were less happy about the developing Irish manufacture. Scattered support in Ireland was systematized from the 1690s when linen was promoted as an alternative to the woollen textiles. The Linen Board, created in 1711, disbursed small sums voted by parliament, and was answerable to it. Four committees, one for each province, oversaw the allocation of subsidized seed and wheels for spinning. Minimum standards were required. Success can be quantified in the recorded exports. From annual totals of less than one million yards at the start of the eighteenth century, the figure grew to 20 million by the 1770s.[151] Most was shipped from the port of Dublin. At the same time, the buoyant economy and complex social structure of parts of Ulster suggested its wider impact. The changes were not universally applauded. The Linen Board was berated for favouring Ulster and Leinster to the detriment of Munster and Connacht. Gradually, the bias lessened as the cultivation of flax spread more widely across the kingdom. Moreover, some effort was made to balance the interests of the separate provinces by having a panel of trustees for each of the four.[152]

The Ulster trustees included conspicuous private promoters of linen: Thomas Coote of Cootehill in County Cavan, William Brownlow and Samuel Waring, both from County Down.[153] The trustees, in handing out the small bounties, barrels of flax seed and spinning and weaving implements, mediated between the counties and the central government. Initially, efforts were made to prevent any one interest from engrossing too many benefits.[154] The allocations came to be viewed like other spoils, valued for more than their simple monetary worth. Notables jostled to be named as trustees on the Board, or solicited their friends and acquaintances among the trustees for its bounty. Once more, connections and cousinage in high places were announced when a few of the Board's spinning-wheels arrived on a remote estate. In 1753, William Crosbie from Ardfert in County Kerry cautioned his father about boasting of 'the large number you and I have got' – 90 wheels, a broadloom and two small ones – 'which was a condescension, being contrary to the rules'.[155] In contrast, one unsuccessful applicant was irritated to hear Lord Limerick, whose request for aid for his linen works at Dundalk had been granted, boast of his success when they shared a passage back to England on the government yacht.[156]

At the Linen Board's behest, inspectors enforced stricter standards for cloth and by doing so enhanced the reputation of Irish wares. Yet, perhaps inevitably, the trustees were indicted for partiality or neglect. The county inspectorate was similarly condemned as 'notoriously corrupt'. A few years later, the system of premiums for innovations in the industry, 'which was designed for a general good', was said to have degenerated into 'selfish, scandalous jobs'.[157] Despite periodic complaints, sponsors of the linen industry 'may justly be esteemed true patriots of their country'.[158] By the same token, reverses to the industry or shortcomings in the Linen Board betokened larger evils. In 1753, the rejection in its original version of a new linen bill by the English privy council was inflated into an attack on the liberty of the Irish Protestants. One pamphleteer ingeniously connected the parliamentary freedom which had hitherto flourished with the prosperity arising from the linen manufacture. The spirit of the Irish Protestants was on the verge of being broken and in its stead a 'yoke of personal domination actually clapped round the neck of its wretched inhabitants'.[159]

Flax-growing, spinning and linen-weaving, hailed as the universal panacea, were promoted by organizations such as the Linen Board and Dublin Society. The Society arranged the publication of treatises intended to advertise better techniques.[160] Another of the voluntary bodies under state patronage, the Incorporated Society, established in 1733 to provide the poor with Protestant schooling, became involved in the expanding manufacture. Pupils were taught to plant and prepare flax, and instructed by spinning mistresses. The charity schools were able to sell the labour and cloth of their inmates, who were later sent into the world with marketable skills as spinners and weavers. The adoption of flax as a crop and of linen as a product, first in Ulster, but soon outside the northern province, offered more certain work and better wages than those in most other branches of agriculture. The dream that the manufacture would employ tenants who might otherwise be idle, shiftless and unable to pay their rents, beguiled numerous proprietors. As far afield as Kerry, west Cork, Westmeath, south Wicklow and north Wexford, landlords were bewitched by the belief that linen would enrich them. One confessed that he 'was a little linen mad'.[161] The besotted, like the younger Sir Richard Cox at his Cork settlement of Dunmanway, sometimes seemed uncritical in their adoration.[162] An early enthusiast was Samuel Waring in County Down. Active in parliament between 1703 and 1727 and on the Linen Board, he brought technological inventions of his own tenants to the notice of trustees, who rewarded the ingenious in Waringstown.[163] The value of Waring's annual rentals rose. If he directed subsidies towards his own, his actions also enriched the neighbourhood and strengthened the Protestant interest. In common with similarly circumstanced contemporaries, he approved state subsidy through parliamentary grants to the Linen Board.

Lords lieutenant and patriotic politicians also did their bits. They commissioned elaborate designs woven into linen napkins and table clothes; decreed that linen or linen blends, such as poplin, should be worn on the days of public rejoicing; they sent gifts of Irish linen to connections elsewhere, supplementing and in the end supplanting the other popular exports from Ireland – wolfhounds and whiskey. Self-interest and public spirit happily united. Even more than tree-planting, another activity which was subsidized from taxes and which beautified and enriched private properties, the linen trade catered to the craze in Ireland for improvement. One visitor, touring the island at the end of George II's reign, recorded the enthusiasm.[164] Other notes of self-congratulation were heard in a survey of the official, semi-state and voluntary associations in Ireland. Yet, the pervasiveness of the industry was not universally welcomed.[165] Farmers, weavers, spinners, drapers, bleachers and traders emboldened by larger earnings and frequently adherents of the Presbyterian churches displayed an obstinacy and independence that were unforeseen fruits of the industry.[166] Furthermore, as had been hoped, the manufacture gave work to Catholics, who thereby were weaned from idleness but seemed only to be confirmed in their confessional alignment.

Another task taken in hand by MPs was the financing of canals. Money had long been sought to drain bogs and to make natural waterways navigable. Back in the 1690s, Samuel Waring and William Brownlow sketched a link between Lough Neagh and Newry and a design to drain the Glan bog. Waring also interested himself in connecting Lough Neagh with the sea. Nothing came of the proposals.[167] Nor did a plan to make the River Liffey navigable, although supported by parliament in 1723, fare better.[168] It took the shortages of grain in the 1720s to make parliament act. Advocates of canals contended that they would ease and cheapen the distribution of scarce necessities: first corn; but also coal. Thanks to a statute to encourage tillage in 1729, navigational schemes received public moneys. This was systematized under a Board for Inland

Navigation. As with the Linen and Barrack Boards, seats were eagerly sought.[169] Some works, long dreamt of, were at last started.

Between 1731 and 1742, Lough Neagh and Newry were connected by a canal, 18 miles long. As Newry's already considerable trade expanded, the gains were vividly illustrated. The Newry canal spawned many imitations. In 1752, an army officer quartered in Bandon (County Cork) urged the building of a two-mile canal to bring fuel into the town from the Bandon River. Support for these measures was urged as a patriotic duty.[170] In the 1750s, the idea of driving a canal through the Bog of Allen and thereby linking the River Shannon with Dublin was applauded as likely 'to remain to latest ages the most useful and ornamental improvement that ever was made in this kingdom, as well as a lasting monument to eternize the memories of those noble patriots' who supported the work.[171] The Grand Canal, begun in 1756, realized some of these ambitions. In 1755, the promoters of a bill to improve navigation on the River Blackwater sought the backing of those qualified 'by their merit, rank and fortunes to superintend the first moving springs ... of the machine of government'.[172]

Between 1730 and 1787 £900,000 of public funds was spent on canals. As with other aspects of public spending, whatever the supervisory board did, it was accused of partisanship if not jobbery. Like the Linen Board, the trustees for Inland Navigation were believed to favour Ulster, and so met opposition from proprietors in Leinster and Munster.[173] Meanwhile, on private estates, enthusiasts experimented. At Elphin in Roscommon, a watery spot, successive bishops dabbled in hydrostatics and hydraulics. Exertions inside and outside parliament frequently yielded disappointingly little. In east Tyrone, the glitter of profits from the collieries beguiled projectors into cutting a channel of four miles from Coalisland to the River Blackwater. Begun in 1732, it was finished only in 1787. The scheme revealed how tightly the public and private weal intermeshed, and the resulting problems. The lands on which the Tyrone collieries at Drumglass were developed belonged to the see of Armagh. Early in the eighteenth century, they had been leased to the son of a Dublin brewer, Thomas Pierson, himself an MP, who happened also to be closely related to the Speaker of the Commons, William Conolly. Such connections assisted the project to a handsome parliamentary grant of £4000. By the 1750s, extraction of the coal deposits was financed by a company in which the primate himself and Archbishop Ryder of Tuam had stakes. Ryder elaborated on how much of his own money he had poured into – and lost in – the venture. Public funds were also lavished on the work.[174]

The scarcity of commodities like coal, a patriotic imperative to lessen dependence on imports, curiosity about new technologies and their application, a restless itch to improve, and avarice: all prodded private proprietors to seek state subsidies for favourite schemes. The results were patchy: Newry might boom, but Ireland never dispensed with cargoes of coal from Britain.[175] The labour of projectors and engineers and the expenditure of committees and investors were seldom commensurate with the gains. Nevertheless, the Dublin parliament continued to apply taxes to motley ventures. Funds were allocated to semi-official bodies, to which were deputed many of the detailed schemes of improvement. By the 1740s, the endeavours of the Dublin Society were supplemented by those of the Physico-Historical Society. Also, the Incorporated Society, given a royal charter in 1733, united the diffuse efforts of the previous 30 years to found more schools, which would teach vocational skills. Under its auspices, the benevolent set up schools in their own localities, which were then supervised by a central committee of 15 based in Dublin. In addition, a corresponding society of well-wishers met in London. It consisted of some with residual Irish connections and the absent owners of Irish estates, who tried to drum up donations. They, like the parent body in Dublin, put faith in an economy of special sermons, annual dinners and collections. Such efforts exemplified a type of endeavour gaining ground among the prosperous and humane, to which the Dublin Society also catered. The plight of the poor led to the establishment of hospitals. Six were opened in Dublin between 1717 and 1758. Musical concerts held in the capital raised funds for the new hospitals and poor prisoners. Handel's oratorios became the standard fare. The fashionable – almost always members of the Protestant minority – crowded into churches for the regular performances. On 13 April 1742, the world première of Handel's *Messiah* was given in aid of a Dublin hospital.[176]

Patriots

The practical patriotism channelled into charity and improvement suddenly took noisier forms, especially during the 1740s and 1750s. Inept viceroys could provoke discords. Neither Lord Harrington (lord lieutenant from 1746 to 1750) nor the duke of Dorset (1750 to 1755) pleased locals as much as predecessors like Carteret (from 1724 until 1730), Devonshire (1737 to 1745) and Chesterfield (briefly in 1745 and 1746).

The main fault lay with the policies which the viceroys were charged with implementing, not with their personalities. The British government, burdened with the defence of an expanding empire and facing the enmity of other European powers, principally France, needed urgently to fit Ireland – and the North American territories – into a Britannic system. Jaundiced observers concluded that too much independence was allowed to the leaders of the Irish parliament in return for modest services. Profiteers from the devolved government, headed by Speaker Boyle, resisted any suggestions that they offer more or take less.

This more excitable phase of politics was inaugurated with an attack, launched late in the 1740s by the Dublin apothecary, Lucas. His target was what he deemed the oligarchy, which had taken over the running of the city corporation thereby overthrowing the 'ancient constitution' of the capital. Lucas, originally from County Clare, was rooted deeply in the professional and artisan cultures of Protestant Dublin. His power was based in his own guild – that of apothecaries, barber surgeons and wig-makers. He enthused over fraternity, which the guilds – at least notionally – still upheld. The liberties of Ireland, or (in Lucas's more restricted vision) of the 'free-born' English Protestants in Ireland, were endangered by a sinister coalition formed by the aldermen of Dublin, the government in Dublin Castle, and the ministry in England. The language in which Lucas couched his protests could be understood readily across the island and beyond. Lucas adroitly exploited print by writing and publishing a newspaper, *The Censor*. To maintain the momentum of his attack, he drew in assorted causes. Each reverberated in the crowded communities of Dublin: pollution caused by uncontrolled baking of bricks, as developers cashed in on the demand for new housing; the plight of poor prisoners for debt; the delays, uncertainties and expense of legal proceedings; or the damage done by bankers and paper money. The leading parliamentary politician of the day, Henry Boyle, Speaker of the House of Commons, conceded that Lucas 'is a very devil of a fellow, and writes well'.[177]

One aim of the campaign was to secure the return to parliament of Lucas and an ally in by-elections scheduled for Dublin in 1749. Thereby, Lucas subscribed to a contemporary axiom that parliament was the summit of political life. MPs unanimously designated him an enemy of the people, and he hopped into exile throughout the 1750s. In 1761, he was elected to the Commons as one of the members for Dublin. Belatedly steps were taken to break the aldermanic oligarchy over the running of the city, although it was hardly opened to democracy. Many of Lucas's preoccupations originated in and were sustained by the sociable and fractious life of the capital. Paradoxes abounded. Keen to mobilize the obscure, he still believed in the hierarchical structure of craft guilds and the need to preserve them as Protestant monopolies, with Catholics admitted at best to a second-class status. Lucas, as a beneficiary of Protestant privilege, sought adjustments in the way that those benefits were distributed, but not their cancellation. He opposed journeymen – the day labourers – who wanted the same freedoms to trade as were enjoyed by the full members of the guilds. His use of print resounded in the provinces. One connection of Lucas from County Clare, Charles Massy, wrestled with the oligarchs of Protestant Limerick, and used arguments of the kind advanced by Lucas.[178] But, like Lucas, Massy, a Church of Ireland dignitary, denied full citizenship to the Catholics on prudential grounds. Indeed, Massy's vigilance in tracing Catholics keen to enter the service of Britain's foreign enemies had earned his earlier appointment as a justice of the peace and dean of Limerick.[179]

The severity of famine and mortality, the resurgence of foreign dangers and the renewal of continental warfare all served to increase political volatility during the 1740s. Easy dealings between the Castle and parliament gave way to mutual suspicion and recriminations. Both individuals and matters of principle were caught in the turbulence. Henchmen of the administration in Dublin Castle, like Arthur Jones Nevill, holder of the office of surveyor-general, were harried, and – in Nevill's case in 1753 – toppled. They served as surrogates for their unpopular employers: in the early 1750s, the overbearing viceroy, Dorset. The controversies owed much to Lucas's demonstration of the potential of pamphleteering and popular protest. They also thrived on ideas of 'court' and 'country', primitive virtue and enervated luxury, and servility and independence, which had arrived from Britain. By 1753, the patriots' ire was aroused by the question of how the surplus from Irish taxes should be spent. The fervent denied the right of the monarch, in whose name the moneys had been collected, to remove them from Ireland. Inside and outside parliament passions rose. Numerous pamphlets rehearsed the arguments and spread them into the streets and provinces.[180] Supposed supporters of British interests were pilloried. A favourite villain was the English-born primate of the Church of Ireland, George Stone. Archbishop Stone was easily mocked, for he lived in 'Polish splendour' and gorged on succulent Périgord pie in his Dublin mansion. He was a known ally of Dorset; in the popular imagination he repeated the offence of an earlier prelate, Atherton, bishop of Waterford, executed in 1641 on a trumped-up charge of sodomy. Stone, 'metropolitan of Sodom' and 'Gomorrah's pontiff', was not alone in the catalogue of shame: the names of MPs and officials who swallowed the viceregal line were published and vilified across the country, and in England too.[181]

Patriots defended liberties apparently endangered by English rulers who were corrupting locals with gifts of offices and luxurious living. The ancient constitution of Ireland embodied in the independent Irish parliament had to be protected. Yet, not all interpreted the crisis as one conjured from lofty principles. Some blamed frustrated nobles, particularly the earl of Kildare. The cynicism deepened when, in 1756, Boyle quit the speakership and resigned the management of the Commons for an earldom (of Shannon) and an annual pension of £2000. Kildare, head of an Old English family important in Ireland throughout the later middle ages and under the early Tudors, when it had supplied king's deputies to rule Ireland, craved the pre-eminence which once his dynasty had enjoyed. Through hidden processes, the Kildares, eclipsed throughout much of the seventeenth century, thereafter recovered financially and resumed something of their traditional social supremacy. The recovery was advertised by the inclusion of the 19th earl as a lord justice in 1714, and his purchase in 1739 of the former residence of Tyrconnell at Carton in County Kildare. There the Kildares constructed a modern mansion, which, although not as startlingly innovative in style as the Conollys' nearby Castletown, proclaimed their grandeur. Even more assertive was the town house which the Kildares erected in the south-eastern sector of Dublin. Their lavish entertaining announced ambitions to rival and perhaps supplant the English-born lords lieutenant in their cramped quarters at Dublin Castle. Kildare eagerly rekindled memories of illustrious predecessors who had resisted the encroachments of Cardinal Wolsey in Henry VIII's time. It became apt to liken Archbishop Stone to Wolsey, the imperious son of the Ipswich butcher. But the uncommitted felt that Kildare was no less imperious: guilty of 'pride, obstinacy and folly'. His careerism was clothed in, but not concealed by pious talk of safeguarding 'the Irish interest'.[182]

Some of the damage inflicted by the arrogant Dorset, his son Lord George Sackville who served as his chief secretary and man of business, and the meddlesome Stone was repaired by Dorset's successor as lord lieutenant, Lord Hartington, who soon inherited the dukedom of Devonshire. Instead of closeting himself with a few confidants in the Castle and yearning only for the yacht which would carry him back to Chester and London, Hartington caressed members of the Dublin parliament. Thereby he hoped to create a more stable coalition than Dorset and Harrington had had. Hartington disarmed many critics and reintroduced greater harmony into dealings between the Castle and parliament. He entrusted parliamentary management to John Ponsonby, his brother-in-law, another important Irish landowner who had built up a powerful interest in the Commons and (like Conolly before him) was a revenue commissioner.

The suavity of the current lord lieutenant could not entirely dispel the underlying tensions. Control from London and the intrusion of interlopers from England into some of the best positions in the estab-lished church, judiciary and administration irked Irish Protestants. Furthermore, ministers in London, beset by the difficulties of foreign warfare on several fronts, had not abandoned hopes of imposing a more uniform administration on Ireland. Indeed, in 1759, talk revived of a legislative union, which would terminate the separate Dublin parliament in exchange for seats at Westminster. This option had been tried only once, during the Commonwealth and Protectorate in the 1650s. That experience had not commended union to Protestant (or Catholic) Ireland. At the earliest opportunity, with the General Convention in 1660, Protestant proprietors had resumed control of their own affairs. There-after, the idea of the union of Ireland and England resurfaced periodically, as when (before 1707) the Scottish treaty of union was on the anvil. Irish Protestants – and Catholics – knew that their interests were unlikely to prevail in a Westminster assembly dominated by the English.[183] Stories that union would be forced on a reluctant Ireland late in 1759 brought Dubliners on to the streets and crowds into the precincts of parliament. One spectator, a woman up from the west of Ireland, declared, 'all lovers of their country should be obliged to the mob. If the members would pass such an act it would ruin Ireland.' Her reactions warned of the limited backing for union outside a small circle and the readiness of the engaged or enraged to demonstrate.[184] In turn, the demonstrators, like the readers of topical pamphlets and the participants in urban excitements, remind of the reach of patriotism away from Dublin Castle and the nearby Parliament House.

Improvers and Patriots

How the fortunate in Protestant Ireland worked on several levels – the national and local, the public and domestic – can be demonstrated by

Richard Edgeworth. Inheritor of an estate (Edgeworthstown) in County Longford, qualified as a barrister and, from 1737, a member of parliament, Edgeworth showed the ways in which the conscientious attended to their multifarious duties. Edgeworth typified the civic minded. Otherwise he was wholly untypical in his obsessive accounting for time and money spent on his family, household, estate, in the discharge of local and national responsibilities, and on recreation. Edgeworth belonged to an élite, numbering fewer than 500, with an assured status and an income, rising from £1500 to £2400, sufficient to undertake public offices and fashionable relaxations.

Squire Edgeworth busied himself in his locality soon after he came to live with his new wife at his family seat. Two particular activities occupied him. The first, service as a justice of the peace, was a traditional obligation for esquires conformable to the Protestant Church and resident (at least intermittently) on their estates. The second, involvement in promoting turnpikes, was an obsession of the moment. Edgeworth was added to the commission of the peace for his county in 1734. Although a trained barrister, on appointment he equipped himself with Dalton's *Justice of the Peace* (for a hefty £1 16s). The manual, composed for English use, was popular in Ireland. Indeed, its utility there suggested how closely Irish systems were intended to replicate English originals.[185] In addition, Edgeworth did buy two guides designed for Ireland: Dutton's *Justice of the Peace* and *The Office of Sheriff*.[186] Accepting the unpaid office of justice of the peace cost money: nearly £10 in fees. The expense, trivial to a landowner of Edgeworth's means, stopped widespread participation.[187] Edgeworth, the new boy, on first appearing at the sessions, treated colleagues to supper.[188] This set a pattern of assisting at the county assizes and sessions – and the attendant sociability – when he was not away in Dublin or England.[189]

Promoting turnpikes dovetailed with his tasks as a county magistrate. Each of the 28 turnpikes authorized by statute between 1729 and 1739 was sponsored by a group of local landowners. The promoters not only guided bills through their several stages in the Dublin parliament, but also solicited in London to ensure that they were approved and returned intact and in time by the English privy council. Edgeworth, working for the road which would link Mullingar, the county town of Westmeath, and Longford town, sent £200 to a solicitor in London to hasten the bill there.[190] Once the enabling legislation was in place, landowners and town-dwellers wrestled over the exact route of the road. Estates or townships served by a new turnpike expected business to grow and property values to rise. Conversely, places ignored by the roads would be marooned and stagnate. Landowners knew how important it was to have themselves – or at least their agents – named as commissioners overseeing the road. In 1734, the identities of those supervising a turnpike traversing Westmeath caused a flutter. Most trustees were likely to be members and clients of the locally dominant Handcocks and Rochforts, 'in order to make the road according to their own liking'. Not being named as a commissioner was looked on 'as a kind of slur or public discredit'.[191]

By pushing a particular stretch of road energetically a public-spirited gentleman, such as Edgeworth, could help his locality.[192] Edgeworth was made a trustee of two turnpikes. Having busied himself to smooth the passage of the bill in Dublin and London, he joined others in Longford to sort out the route.[193] He attended special meetings. Like the gatherings of the county magistracy, they involved sleeping overnight in the county town of Longford and dining with other diligent trustees.[194] Since the line of the road ran beside his own demesne and through the small settlement of Edgeworthstown, which he largely owned, Edgeworth had much to gain. The turnpike seemed of a piece with other physical improvements which he initiated. He rebuilt his mansion and the nearby Protestant church, and redesigned their surroundings. The road featured in an ensemble, which would give a stronger English flavour and increase the bustle of the neighbourhood. Edgeworth was not a member of parliament when first he involved himself with the road. By championing the road, he improved his credentials to represent the district when, in 1737, he did mount the hustings. Thereafter, as both member of parliament and turnpike commissioner, he laboured for the road. This work shaded into that with which, as magistrate, grand juror, arbitrator of neighbours' disputes or – for one year – as high sheriff of the county, he was concerned. The drudgery of board meetings was alleviated by good fellowship, music, performances by strolling actors, and card games at which modest sums were wagered.

Edgeworth, the ardent campaigner for turnpikes, wanted to enter parliament. Once elected to the Commons, he could try to direct some of its largesse towards his own kindred and neighbourhood. However, his eagerness went beyond a disinterested wish to serve his community. For him, as for many of his colleagues, membership was a means of distinguishing himself from neighbours, asserting pre-eminence in the district, and would enable him to cut the 'grand figure'. A sign of his anxiety to be an MP is his spending to win the parliamentary seat. The electorate in Longford town, like that of many other boroughs, was confined to the burgesses and freemen, who probably numbered fewer than 100. More than the electors had to be cultivated. In a pattern evident in numerous constituencies, candidates watched attentively for vacancies. Future success was thought to depend on filling empty places as burgesses and freemen with allies. Packing the corporation or, in the counties, creating new freeholds worth more than an annual 40 shillings so that the occupiers could vote, absorbed aspirant MPs and their adjutants. Edgeworth cajoled and flattered the electors of Longford. At the same time, he cultivated townspeople without votes, even the 'mob', likely to be overwhelmingly Catholic. The treats in local taverns for which he paid might suggest no more than a rampant venality, with votes sold and bought, and trouble-makers having to have their mouths stopped. Edgeworth was duly elected, but the pleasure lessened when an affronted neighbour dispersed scabrous and scatological verses against him. Edgeworth sought redress from the Dublin law courts, but to no avail.[195]

Edgeworth's care for a larger group than simply those qualified to vote hinted at the uncertain demarcations between the politically aware and unaware.[196] The uncertainties appear in details of elections in other parts of the island. In the Waterford borough of Tallow, wives and even the children were entertained in an effort to win over the male voters.[197] Such efforts, whether in Longford or elsewhere, suggested a political process less restricted than might be supposed: one, moreover, which took some notice of the Catholic population, although it was now disqualified from voting.

Edgeworth spent heavily in 1737. The investment was justified because, once returned to parliament, he added several cubits to his standing. Moreover, he was now secure for the duration of the parliament. It ended only with the life of the monarch in 1760. Once elected, he took his seat, went to debates and fraternized with the political bosses in Dublin.[198] From time to time he dined or supped with groups of MPs from the midlands, in order to orchestrate projects of value to the area.[199] In 1755, when the lord lieutenant, Hartington, was fashioning a stronger parliamentary footing for his administration, Edgeworth was one of numerous MPs bidden to dinner at the Castle.[200] Edgeworth was punctilious about his responsibilities, both private and public. Yet his duties as MP seldom dominated. He did not hesitate, for example, to remove himself and his family to Bath for a long stay. At home, he threw himself into tasks with clear relevance to his district, and which may have been more productive than attendance at parliamentary debates.

In 1761, with a general election in the offing after the death of George II, Edgeworth decided not to expose himself to a fresh contest, and retired from the Commons. Interested in a wide range of improving schemes, he may have realised that membership of parliament was not essential to advancing them. In this he resembled other public-spirited figures like William Smythe of Barbavilla, Samuel Waring in County Down, John Digby from Landestown in County Kildare or John Putland, a notable of Dublin city. Some spent spells in the Commons; others, none. However, all were active in schemes of improvement, often those driven forward by the Dublin Society. Edgeworth had been lucky in entering parliament when he did, and for a constituency with a small electorate. Costs, if not negligible, hardly compared with what some soon incurred. Winning counties, usually with electorates numbering 1000 to 2000, involved increasingly heavy expenditure. But so too did contests in some smaller boroughs. During the 1690s, when elections suddenly became frequent, a shortage of candidates ensured the return of the obscure – small-town lawyers, merchants and army officers – not within the palladium of landed society. After 1715, elections occurred infrequently, owing to the longevity of George I and George II. A seat in parliament, increasingly desirable, commanded a higher price. The minor gentry, professionals and merchants were deterred from entering the lists. The Commons was becoming a more exclusive club: an oligarchic tendency also discernible in county government. The ability of parliament adequately to mirror the diversity of Protestant Ireland, let alone of the whole population, diminished.

The example of Edgeworth illustrates several themes. Membership of the Dublin parliament was not detached from other public responsibilities, whether in the locality or the capital. The mundane routines of magistrates, grand jurors, freemasons and the members of organizations like the Dublin Society merit as much investigation as the daily drudging of MPs on committees. Second, although those who elected members were few, non-voters did not all stand passively aside. In return, conscientious members, such as Edgeworth, worked for what they saw as the public good. The vision was restricted, usually to the point of serious distortion. Too often, it seemed, the general welfare meant loading the Catholics with disabilities. Rather than condemning this attitude, the reasons for it need to be understood. Some have been suggested already. A further insight offered by Edgeworth is that he and his kind were not obsessed, as some later historians have been, with the narrow circuit of official Dublin. Edgeworth was no boorish country squire. Widely read and well travelled, he moved smoothly from country routines to life in Dublin or Bath. At the very least, his biography hints at the diversity of the ascendant élite. Contemporaries of Edgeworth certainly discerned a cultural gulf. On one side stood the prosperous such as Edgeworth, who travelled, read, conversed and reflected; on the other bank were those landlords who seldom ventured further than the nearest market town and then only to sell cattle and corn.[201]

Exemplary as some of Edgeworth's behaviour looked, it did not excite universal admiration. Politicians, if they were to command a following large enough to make them useful to the Dublin Castle administration as undertakers, needed to attract others than the prim like Edgeworth. The outstanding Irish parliamentarians – of whom Edgeworth was not one – pandered to Protestant prejudices. Between the 1650s and 1670s, Orrery had based his political mastery on a skill – and unscrupulousness – in articulating the fears and hopes of his lowlier Protestant neighbours.[202] In the 1710s and 1720s, William Conolly elevated into his credo a doughty Irish patriotism, which did not exclude close cooperation with and profit from England. Henry Boyle, Conolly's successor as Speaker and prime manager for the government, perfected the pose of bluff country gentleman, equally impatient with the tricks and treachery of Dublin, the wiles of Catholics and deceits of England. It was remarked that on becoming Speaker in 1733, Boyle read his acceptance speech 'with as much indifference and as little concern as if it had been at a tavern amongst a few of his friends'.[203] Boyle played the squire well, and, keeping in good repair his links with the provincial gentry, ruled the Commons for more than 20 years.[204] Prowess of this kind brought a measure of stability to the public politics of Protestant Ireland. Furthermore, by avoiding too much friction with Britain, the Irish Parliament enacted a series of useful bills. The statutes gave a stronger framework for those, such as Edgeworth, to busy themselves about enterprises which might bring better roads, canals, schools and hospitals, and ensure that markets, fairs and shops were more abundantly stocked. Flattering to the self-esteem of the diligent paterfamilias and landlord, it is less clear what Edgeworth's wife and children, let alone his servants, tenants and neighbours made of these works.

Chapter 5: Rulers and Ruled

The Viceroyalty

Because the king of Ireland was the most notable absentee from the kingdom, he required a deputy. Throughout the sixteenth and seventeenth centuries, the choice alternated between local magnates, usually descended from the Old English settlers of the middle ages, such as the Fitzgeralds, earls of Kildare, the Butlers, first and second dukes of Ormonde, and Richard Talbot, ennobled as earl of Tyrconnell, and generals or nobles despatched from England. Neither option avoided dangers: locals promoted themselves and their cronies; the imported seldom had much grasp of the personalities and nuances of Irish affairs. English ambitions to subordinate Ireland more fully required the more frequent use of Englishmen, to the chagrin of loyal locals. For a time this trend away from the employment of the Irish-born was masked by the long viceroyalties of the two dukes of Ormonde, which stretched, although not uninterruptedly, from 1643 to 1713. Thereafter, no one of Irish birth was appointed to this, the highest office in the English government of Ireland. Just as the lord lieutenancy told of the special character of the Ireland within the dominion of the English monarch, so too did other important posts on the official Irish establishment. Prizes in the Protestant Church, on the judicial bench and in the civil administration were conferred on strangers from Britain. The rationale was the wish to impose uniformity on a stubborn dependency. It contrasted sharply with the policy adopted in Scotland, where distinctive ecclesiastical and judicial systems survived and were staffed by locals. No English – let alone Irish – locusts descended on the plenty of Scotland.

The withholding of the viceroyalty from locals reminded of the low regard in which they were held. In return, the Irish, whether Catholic or Protestant, viewed both the institution and its occupants askance. In the intimate and critical world of official Dublin, the faults of lords lieutenant and their followers were magnified. The visitors found it hard to please their censorious hosts. The viceroys were severely circumscribed in what they could do by their instructions and by the priorities of the British government which they represented. Rulers unfamiliar with the minutiae of the Irish scene had urgently to find auxiliaries to handle the business of government. Much was delegated. From the 1660s, the lord lieutenant, aloof from the hurley-burley of parliamentary debates and intrigue, turned to undertakers. These surrogates, from the first earl of Orrery between 1661 and 1665, through the Brodricks in the 1690s, Conolly between 1715 and 1729 and Henry Boyle from the early 1730s until 1756, to the Ponsonbys in the later 1750s, varied in their effectiveness and so in the stability that they brought to public affairs. Each manager insisted that he and his followers should have a generous share of the pensions, places and perquisites in the gift of the crown and its deputy in Ireland.[205] Often the supplicants imagined that the cornucopia was more capacious than was the case. They did not always realize that many jobs on the Irish establishment, whether it be deaneries of cathedrals, military and naval commissions or appointments as customs officers in foggy inlets on the Atlantic seaboard, were not for the lord lieutenant to give.

The feebleness of viceroys as patrons diminished the respect in which they were held. Hopefuls from Ireland stampeded to England where, it was supposed, preferment was more easily gained. This situation, with so much important to Ireland decided elsewhere, again reminded of the subservience of Ireland to England. It also widened the gulf between the lucky with useful connections in England and the means to activate them, and the generality within Ireland who had to rely on intermediaries closer at hand. A vital function of the undertakers working to smooth the passage of bills through parliament was to connect provincials in Ireland with the distant distributors of patronage.

The lord lieutenancy was weakened as an agency of anglicization after 1713: first by the need of its occupants to rely on others to despatch so much work; and then by the lengthy absences of most viceroys. Usually they sailed over to Dublin only every second year, and stayed no longer than the duration of the parliamentary session. However, even when parliament was not sitting, there were ceremonial and substantive tasks that had to be performed. The custom was for deputies to be appointed. In the 1660s and 1680s, Ormond, preferring to spend time at court in England where he doubled as lord steward of Charles II's household, left Ireland to his comely sons, Ossory and Arran. By the eighteenth century, such cosy arrangements gave way to a practice whereby in the absence of the English lord lieutenant, figures of consequence in Dublin were commissioned to act as lords justice. A troika was favoured. The three were selected on the strength of the offices that they held – lord chancellor, Speaker of the Commons or primate of the Church of Ireland – and their political tractability. Practice was varied periodically by including other Irish notables whom the administration was keen to woo. In this way, the awkwardly patriotic archbishop of Dublin, William King, or the Tory nepotist, Archbishop John Vesey of Tuam, were at different times included. So, too, were motley Irish peers: Blessington (1696), Drogheda (1701–2), Mount Alexander (in 1701 and 1702) and Kildare (1714–15). Thanks to this device, Irish Protestants preened in showy plumage, but found that their clipped wings did not keep them aloft. Irish lords justice compared their modest powers with those of the English-born lords lieutenant. The contrast aggravated rather than allayed resentments.

The viceroys themselves were constricted by instructions from their English masters. Accordingly, they made their main impact through the scale and style of their hospitality. Courtesy towards others, accessibility and stamina in downing the bumpers of wine which circulated around the dinner table were either praised or censured. The lords lieutenant and their ladies took up seasonal fads. They dressed themselves and their tables in Irish manufactures, went to the races on the Curragh of Kildare and further afield, dozed through plays and charity concerts and subscribed to the societies devoted to improvement. Thus Devonshire dutifully presided over a meeting of the Dublin Society in 1737; the duchess of Bedford supported Irish crafts by buying a carpet imitating the Gobelins factory but made in Dublin.[206] As cultural innovators, they failed almost as completely as they did in popularizing British rule among the touchy Irish. Some, such as Grafton, Dorset, Bedford and Halifax, impatient with local ways, barely hid their disdain. Usually, the courtesies were observed on both sides. But the deference of the Irish, accepting invitations to bashes at the Castle, might be mistaken for contentment with Ireland's depressed standing. Many Irish Protestants happily exploited their membership of the Hanoverians' empire in order to make careers outside Ireland as soldiers, sailors, administrators and merchants, but without accepting that their own kingdom had been subsumed into, let alone subordinated to, a British monarchy. The periodic and sometimes strident reiterations of Ireland's standing as a distinct kingdom alongside England and Scotland rather than subservient to Britain startled viceroys and their masters in London.

Lords lieutenant had their advisers, some of whom they brought in their entourage. Others remained in London so that they could ease communication with the ministry there and protect their absent masters against detractors. Viceroys also struck up alliances with congenial and plausible insiders in Dublin. More formally they worked in conjunction with the Irish council: the counterpart of the privy council in London. The effectiveness of the Dublin council fluctuated with the competence and attentiveness of the governor himself and the identities of the councillors. Early in the 1640s, Ormond, struggling to reconcile the needs of the hard-pressed Charles I with those of the Protestants in Ireland, ran into opposition from a claque in his council. Four who opposed the proposed truce with the Confederate Catholics were arrested. During the 1650s, a small working council was beset by factions. Splits continued, apparently inherent in an unwieldy institution. Divisions in the 1670s repeated those of the 1640s. A minority of councillors advocated a militantly Protestant programme and resisted any generosity towards Catholics. Councillors were not divorced from parliamentary politics. Most sat in one or other of the Houses, and were privy to the coming debates. Moreover, they knew and shared the preoccupations of the other peers and MPs. Its size militated against the council evolving as an executive which relayed Irish Protestant opinion to an ignorant English administration. As earlier in England, large numbers brought factiousness and inefficiency. In 1714, the Irish council numbered 56; by 1723, 67.[207] Reasonably enough Archbishop Boulter in 1737 cautioned against enlarging it, complaining that 'many have been brought in there without any knowledge of business'.[208]

The problem was lessened by the small attendance at most meetings: a dozen to a score. As in so many organizations, the business was undertaken by a few. Councillors who came regularly to meetings in Dublin Castle possessed considerable leverage as arbiters and advisers. They had to respond to draft bills sent from London and to those emanating as heads of bills from the Dublin parliament. The council also evaluated the reports arriving from distant regions and, in emergencies, decided on appropriate action. Since 1672, the lord lieutenant and council were empowered to approve or reject the annual appointments of officers in the largest towns in the kingdom. Especially at moments of political passion, the choices were disputed, leaving the authorities in Dublin Castle to adjudicate. In 1726 and 1731, contested elections in the County Cork boroughs of Youghal and Kinsale saw strenuous efforts by partisans to secure the attendance of sympathetic councillors at decisive meetings.[209]

The functioning of the Irish council, other than in the rare but well-publicized disagreements, has hardly been investigated. Assertive lords lieutenant could try to remodel the body with new appointments of the reliable, but these additions were seldom numerous enough to overawe the troublesome. During the Confederate War, Ormond had had dissentients imprisoned. William Conolly and the two Brodricks were removed from the council by the Tories in 1711. As a result of their treatment, the victims were transformed into heroes. More characteristic was a covert opposition as councillors voiced patriotic sentiments and failed to back headstrong lords lieutenant. In 1759, some councillors were accused of sympathizing with, and even abetting, the rioters against a rumoured bill of union between Ireland and England.[210] In such episodes, the council reproduced the varieties of opinion found inside and beyond the parliament house.

Parish, Manor and Barony

Britain found willing collaborators in Protestant Ireland. They ranged from the parliamentary managers such as Conolly, Brodrick, Boyle and Ponsonby, through country gentlemen like Edgeworth, to the petty functionaries in towns and townlands across the kingdom. Collaboration conferred many benefits on the Protestants of Ireland. Britain on its side repented of the deal only when it wanted more money or soldiers than Ireland could supply, when it seemed vulnerable to invasion or internal insurrection, or when the reigning favourite in the Irish Commons no longer shepherded a majority through the right lobby. The political bosses in Dublin in order to keep their pre-eminence, had to humour and discipline their followers in the provinces. So far as the government was concerned, a docile parliament counted for little if the kingdom dissolved into disorder or defected to a foreign power.

One key to a securely British Ireland lay in Dublin. In the 1640s, the embattled Protestants, by hanging on to the capital, prevented the confederates securing the entire island. But dominance over Dublin, enough for medieval monarchs content to be no more than lords of Ireland, no longer sufficed by the seventeenth century. Mastery of the provinces required full exploitation of the networks of parishes, manors, townlands, baronies and counties. Until the reprisals of the 1650s, much of the system was manned by Catholics. Even in the unpropitious conditions of the 1690s, Catholics were not altogether supplanted. They survived alongside the newcomers, usually but not invariably in humbler roles, renting lands which once they had owned. For want of enough reliable Protestants, Catholics were retained in some of the lowliest offices and on juries. In addition, the dethroned potentates retained the affection of fellow Catholics. Exiles maintained Irish links. Priests, notwithstanding laws against them, presided over shadowy organizations of the faithful. By these devices and through distinctive confession, language and traditions, assimilation to the new British order was slowed and sometimes opposed.[211]

At all levels, the administration of Ireland copied that of England and Wales. The paraphernalia of juries, petty and grand constables, vestries, overseers of the poor, manorial courts, even informal committees of village worthies brought the relatively modest into government.[212] Indeed, this involvement may have reconciled many to the operations of the remote but increasingly assertive British state. Seventeenth-century villagers grumbled, but they willingly assessed, collected and – less joyfully – paid taxes. In doing so, they identified – at first hazily – with the state which they were serving.[213] Similar demands of the fiscal–military state touched Ireland. Agencies of enforcement, notably the revenue officers and the regular soldiers, were frequently resented.[214] Alongside them, although usually less conspicuous, the officials of vestry, ward, manor, barony and borough proliferated. In 1672, Ireland was said to have about 3500 working on behalf of the state. Of these, 2700 were thought to be Catholics. After 1690, more vigorous efforts attempted to lessen the number of Catholics. The Test Act of 1704 turned much of the bureaucracy into a Church of Ireland monopoly. However, shortages of conformists meant that the bans on Protestant dissenters and Catholics had often to be waived. The statute itself acknowledged the difficulty when it exempted high constables (responsible for baronies), petty constables, tithing men, head-boroughs, overseers of the poor, church wardens and surveyors of highways from the requirement of producing a certificate that they had taken communion according to the rites of the Church of Ireland.[215] In some rural parishes in Counties Dublin, Louth and Meath, Catholics are known to have filled the potentially important office of churchwarden.[216] At best, these tasks brought the relatively insignificant into the ambit of the state. Less welcome was the emergence of pseudo-gentry and middlemen as parochial tyrants. In 1762, one critic denounced the typical cock-of-the-walk as akin to a 'bashaw over the poor, an intriguer for injustice and oppression on grand juries, and a false neighbour', offering 'a shocking caricature of manliness'.[217]

By looking at the several levels of local government, it is possible to widen the angle from which Ireland is customarily viewed. The townland and parish were the smallest and most ubiquitous units. In Ireland, there were said to be 62,000 townlands, varying in extent from 2000 to five acres, and 2278 parishes.[218] Both had secular responsibilities, offering convenient bases on which to regulate and tax inhabitants. Another organization was the manor. Ideally, as in lowland Britain, parish church and manor should form a physical and administrative ensemble. More than simple buildings, both embodied the notions of civility, settlement, control and industry intrinsic to the English project for Ireland. Manors were included in the baggage which the Anglo-Normans unpacked after they had landed in 1169. Those living in settlements elevated into manors were obliged to offer suit and service at the manor court and to grind at the proprietor's mill. The jurisdiction made it easier to enforce conditions in tenants' leases. But manors were scattered unevenly across the medieval lordship and the more recent plantations.[219] They continued to be created to gratify important or importunate Protestant proprietors, such as Archbishop Vesey of Tuam early in the eighteenth century.[220]

In 1837, 204 manor courts were counted.[221] Many had dwindled into twilight existences. That at Ballymoney in County Antrim was chiefly occupied with choosing petty constables and inspectors of weights and measures.[222] Others continued to hold courts baron and courts leet. However, their jurisdictions competed with rival agencies. A ceiling of £10 limited the value of disputed property with which the manor courts dealt. The powers of the manor alone could not restrain unruly tenants. They had to be supplemented. In consequence, lords of manors had their agents commissioned as justices of the peace, so that they could more effectively discipline the tenantry, and repaired routinely to higher courts in the county and Dublin. So far as the state was concerned, while it did not regret delegating modest authority to the lords of Irish manors, increasingly it preferred to strengthen the regulatory functions of the parish and vestry.

Manor courts could aid aggrieved tenants. They adjudicated wrangles over boundaries, straying livestock, unneighbourly conduct or wills of modest worth. The processes, matched in the towns by those of borough courts, went some way to realizing the English boast that the poor in Ireland should feel the benison of a devolved and impartial system of justice.[223] In County Clare during Charles II's reign, on the earl of Thomond's manors of Kilrush and Cruoverghan, a multiplicity of economic and public order offences came before the manor court. Not only were tenants helped, but Old Irish exponents of the indigenous system of brehon law colonized the court.[224] Elsewhere, for want of other mechanisms, the manor expanded its functions. At Ennis in County Clare and Edenderry in King's County, the court leet evolved into the equivalent of a borough council. In 1725, 400 were said to have come to a manor court at Edenderry. It approved measures to enrich the town.[225] At Lismore, too, the court leet discharged municipal responsibilities. By presenting one ne'erdowell as a scandalous person, it was hoped to create a precedent whereby 'all the idle people that are a burden to the town … especially those that are strangers' would be expelled.[226]

Landlords' agents frequently ran the manor. Inevitably it expressed proprietorial philosophies. Where the institution was seen merely as a prop of landlordism, and of English and Protestant overlordship, it elicited contradictory responses.[227] In Kerry, the Herberts' manor court centred on Castleisland, meeting every three weeks in the 1680s, was disliked as 'partial and dilatory, and the fees exceeding'.[228] Tenants and jurors could sometimes turn the system of courts to their own advantage. At the start of the eighteenth century, Thomas Samson, seneschal to Lord Tyrone in County Waterford, reported how he had been threatened at a session of the manorial court. The locals habitually abused 'all English Protestant seneschals that come amongst them'.[229] In 1718, there was dismay in County Cork when Catholics were summoned to the manorial courts not just to answer presentments but also to act as jurors. It was thought 'a very ill precedent', but difficult to avoid. Just as owners had sometimes to accept Catholics as agents, so they were employed as seneschals. An agent deputed to convene a manor court at Castle Pollard (Westmeath) did not know what to do.[230] By 1730, the bishop of Down and Connor excused some of his tenants from service at his court leet, 'because I was afraid the use for them was little, but the burden upon the tenant much'. The bishop refreshed those who were still obliged to come with food and drink. In this way, the stated meetings of the manor courts came to be surrounded with some of the exhausting conviviality which, higher on the social scale, had gathered round the assizes and quarter sessions.[231] The innkeeper from Downpatrick who officiated as a seneschal presumably attended more to the hospitable than technical obligations of the position.[232] For the well-to-do, such as the Antrim clergyman, Andrew Rowan, attendance at the court leet at Galgorm was one among frequent events, ranging from quarter sessions, bishops' visitations, funerals and fairs, at which neighbours were encountered and business transacted.[233] Even this sociability was not universally enjoyed. In 1746, the Percevals's agent reported that the manor courts still assembled in the north of County Cork. However, he no longer obliged distant tenants to come, 'as they always complained of the expense of the dinner on that occasion'.[234]

Proprietors defended their manorial privileges against encroachments.[235] Challenges came from the sheriffs with their tourn courts in every barony and, along the coasts, from the agents of the distant English Admiralty.[236] Neighbours endowed with their own manorial jurisdictions were also a threat. In the port of Sligo, ownership was split between three families, which competed over who should have a manor court there.[237] In north Cork, the absent Percevals, like rutting stags, locked antlers with rivals, especially Lord Barrymore, in order to prove their seigneurial virility.[238] Manor courts distinguished their possessors from others in the vicinity. The jurisdiction had practical and monetary as well as symbolic value. Used systematically to police the terms of leases, the courts could deepen the imprint which the improver put on his estate. On the Herberts's Kerry estate, Edward Herbert, the chief agent and a distant kinsman of the owner, acted as seneschal. He deputed the work of chairing the manor courts, incumbent on a seneschal, to his brother. An incoming agent, bent on breaking this cosy arrangement, appreciated that he must himself capture the position.[239] In 1747, Henry Hatch took over the supervision of the Blundells's Irish concerns. He ousted the seneschal, himself annexed the seneschalship and then put in a deputy to preside over the courts at Dundrum.[240] In a similar way, a new agent on the Burlington estates in the 1740s assumed the office of seneschal at Dungarvan, and appointed a deputy who was still there more than a decade later. In this particular manor, coterminous with the parliamentary borough, the seneschal was of unusual importance since he acted as returning officer for parliamentary elections.[241] Nevertheless, the vigilant might nod on even the best run estates. By the 1750s, John Keane presided over five of the manors of the Burlingtons. Old and infirm, he did so laxly.[242]

Keane's collection of seneschalships suggested that they had a worth above their face value. It was claimed that £40 had been offered for the position at Dungarvan, although there were said to be no profits.[243] The Percevals throughout the 1730s and 1740s were deluged with applications whenever any office in their County Cork manors of Burton was vacated. In weighing the claims of competitors, Perceval candidly favoured one familiar with the area. If this suitor were not appointed, he added, 'perhaps the family may otherwise take it unkindly, for the profits are small, yet 'tis a feather in the cap'.[244] This, perhaps, was the reason why seneschalships, in common with other seemingly minor posts, were fought for so hotly. Clandestine profits and influence attached to the offices.[245]

County

The Church of Ireland parish touched many more than entered its buildings, as will be seen in the next chapter. Above the parish rose the barony, 117 incorporated boroughs, and the 32 counties. Even the cheerful conceded that in some remoter locations, principally in the south-west or north-west, although a simulacrum of English municipal and shire administration existed by the end of the seventeenth century, it did not always function like the original. Remoteness and a dearth of appropriately qualified functionaries retarded success. Sheriffs, grand jurors and the justices of the peace were needed to run the counties. They were assisted twice a year by judges on assize. The assizes, in addition to trying crimes, became social and political occasions. In 1686, the assizes at Cork city lasted 17 days; those in Wicklow at the start of George I's reign, six days.[246] The events attracted more than just magistrates, jurors, witnesses and miscreants. The confluence of notables from across the county allowed political planning. In 1724, the worthies of several shires signed petitions against Wood's Halfpence; later in 1745, they fell over one another to advertise loyalty to the Hanoverians threatened by a Jacobite insurrection.[247]

Other business was transacted. At Clonmel, the assizes were the occasion when the bulk of the wool from the flocks in County Tipperary would be traded.[248] At Wicklow, early in George I's reign, an industrious agent struck deals with timber merchants and tanners. In Limerick, the diocesan schoolmaster was visited by 'many gentlemen' in town for the proceedings, who expected 'to confer with me about their sons'.[249] Lobbyists rode their hobby-horses. Information for county histories was solicited, seldom successfully.[250] Individuals, like Edmund Spencer, pestered the grand jurors of Cork for subscriptions for a projected edition of his ancestor, Edmund Spenser's poems: again in vain.[251] An economy of amusements catered to the influx: race-meetings, assemblies, dances, military parades and auctions. In 1739, a female householder wrote from the county town of Down that, 'the assizes here makes such a noise that one can't do anything, one friend or other calling in to see me'.[252] Gentlemen from outlying parts of the county took lodgings for the duration of the sessions. So valuable was the custom from the visitors that towns competed to hold the courts.[253] By the eighteenth century, purpose-built court rooms were designed to despatch proceedings with greater solemnity and comfort.[254] Furthermore, the surrounding sociability demanded new market places with shelter for traders and assembly rooms, where balls, concerts and theatricals were staged.[255] Inns were opened or improved in order to refresh justices and jurors.[256]

As the town hummed, many outside the ruling orders – the middling sort, women or the 'mob' – were drawn in. Varied experiences left differing impressions on participants. Any identification with the county or sense of belonging to a county community had to compete against the feelings that the unit was an artificial one, imported moreover from England, and against other loyalties both more immediate – family, village or barony – or less constricted – geographical region, province, nation or confessional and social communities.[257] Despite the rival allegiances, some who lived in the Irish counties cared for them. Affection was commonest among the privileged engaged in county routines and able to buy the maps and histories which were defining the places more precisely. In 1660, the county of Cork served as the basis for collecting from its weightiest freeholders, 'knight of the shire money' to defray the expenses of the representative whom they had come together to choose.[258] Richard Cox, exiled in Dublin as lord chancellor, pined to be back in 'the sweet county of Cork'.[259] Similarly, the heir of Ardfert, in Kerry, sighed to be there rather than linger in Dublin.[260]

Sheriffs

It suited the English government to place the county at the centre of its schemes for Ireland. A system of county governors was extended from

thirteen shires in 1679 to all 32.[261] The governors, concerned primarily
with mustering and training the militia, corresponded with lords
lieutenant in English counties. They were assisted by deputies, also
drawn from the important and reliable among the resident Protestants.
At moments of danger, notably in 1715, 1745 and 1760, the governors
and deputy governors were heavily burdened with defensive tasks.[262]
Each county also had a high sheriff. Dublin, in the person of the Irish
lord chancellor and in consultation with the lord lieutenant, prepared
each year the lists from which the high sheriffs were picked, by having
their names pricked. The shrievalty, despite being held only for a year,
was shunned throughout much of the seventeenth century as physically
and financially burdensome. As in contemporary England and Wales,
appointment may have punished the awkward.[263] Roger Carew, threatened with being named sheriff of Waterford in 1684, declared that, at
the age of 70 and as a tenant of Lord Cork and Burlington, he was 'very
unfit for the employment'. The administration, with too few candidates,
overruled Carew's disclaimers. He was warned that he would not escape
'without making great interest'.[264]

Reluctance to serve persisted, but surprised some. In 1724, a former
high sheriff of County Down was amazed 'to find the gentlemen of this
county so backward in accepting so honourable a post when it can so well
defray the charge attending it'. But chances of profit had to be balanced
against the obligations to collect and account for taxes.[265] In Charles II's
reign, Robert Southwell's turn as sheriff of County Cork coincided with
harvesting the hearth money. Two years after he had left office, Southwell
had accounted for no more than 70 per cent of the expected receipts. In
order to be forgiven the remainder, he expended time and money in
Dublin, and mobilized friends there.[266] But Southwell was fortunate
in serving as sheriff when he was required to implement decrees of the
Dublin Court of Claims, for which he and his underlings received
fees.[267] As time passed, fewer taxes fell within the sheriff's purview.
What remained could still trouble. When George II ascended the
throne in 1727, it was reckoned that as many as 160 former sheriffs
had failed to clear their accounts. Of the defaulters, perhaps a
hundred had already died. As late as 1764, the departing sheriff of
Mayo was threatened with prosecution for his failure to account
promptly.[268] Largesse was expected from the sheriff: a burden which
deterred some from discharging the office. During the year when
Richard Edgeworth served as high sheriff of Longford (1741–2), he
invested heavily in his attire, equipage and entertaining the local

gentry. He even borrowed a showy coach, carriage horses and coachman from a grander kinsman.[269]

The sheriff possessed judicial powers. Sheriffs' courts, although limited in their competence, survived.[270] Southwell in 1663 required his deputies to convene tourn courts in each barony of the county. His court also sat on 13 recorded occasions in Cork city and once in his home town of Kinsale.[271] The sheriff, and his minions, enforced the decisions of the superior courts. On civil bills they received fees, but not in criminal suits.[272] This was said to be reason 'why the government always takes care to make choice of a man of good estate'.[273] The shrievalty, a hinge on which many doors turned, required oil if it was to open smoothly. How much and what sort of lubricants were harder to decide. Legitimate and illicit payments led to repeated complaints and efforts at regulation.[274] Especially in the seventeenth century, with much property granted to new owners, the sheriffs were vital to securing possession. After 1660, two recent recipients of estates, William Legge and Sir William Petty, discovered how officials could help or hinder. Legge, a courtier absent in England, relied on agents in Ireland, who from the start predicted difficulties. Legge's agent reported candidly in 1664, 'bribing and corruption in all places where money can prevail'. Legge was soon embroiled in a contest with Lady Mary Bourke, heiress to Lord Clanricarde, long a dominant figure in County Galway. The dispute was to be arbitrated by the governor of Galway City and the high sheriff of the county. When this strategy failed the law was tried. Legge's man of affairs in Ireland congratulated himself on making a good interest with the sub-sheriff, 'as that he has returned me a jury of the ablest men in the county (as I am informed by intelligible persons) are not allied or interested in the family [the Burkes]'. This optimism proved ill-founded, as the sheriff and his subordinates delayed proceedings. Lady Mary Bourke affected sorrow, but it was thought 'to be crocodile like, though she had a very great confidence in a jury of the country to carry the cause' against the stranger, Legge. The longer Legge's agent laboured, the glummer he grew. 'Indifferency', he concluded, was not to be expected from officials like sheriffs and their deputies or from juries empanelled by them.[275]

Some of these problems arose from local government and courts still staffed by Irish Catholics. They also impeded Petty's efforts to turn into reality his title to large stretches of Ireland, particularly in Kerry. Knowing the ways of those who governed in London, Dublin and the Irish provinces, he was contemptuous. He aimed to 'work upon the great men by fawning and whining and upon the small fools by bribery to the utmost of what they can'.[276] In 1671, he told his agent, 'because I know all trades must live', to give the sheriff in Kerry 'what you think fit for so small a matter'. Two guineas were deemed appropriate.[277] Earlier, Petty himself had delivered to the sheriff a legal order which he wanted to have executed, together with 'a good lump of money'. In his protracted campaign, Petty instructed his representative in Kerry to win over this officer and his men, 'for which spare nothing of charge or labour and obtain the best you can'.[278] Yet, avarice was not the whole explanation for the rebuffs. The former owner whom he was seeking to displace, Lieutenant-Colonel Donogh McGillicuddy, was related to several sheriffs in Kerry.[279] By 1685, Petty, wearied by the setbacks and realising that more were in prospect now that the Catholic James was king, groaned that 'no good can be done while O'Sullivan More's and McGillicuddy's relations are sheriffs'.[280]

The Protestant preponderance under Charles II, fragile in Dublin and feeble in the localities, was quickly overturned by James. The choice and conduct of high sheriffs remained contentious. For their part, the sheriffs' choice of jurors could determine title, possession and boundaries. Partiality was traced, as has been seen in Galway and Kerry, to ethnic or confessional alignment: Irish against English or Scot; Protestant against Catholic. Obligations to neighbours, kindred, patrons or dependants were thought – usually correctly – to lead office-holders into favouritism. Inevitably, those newly arrived in the localities lacked the intimacies enjoyed by the longer settled. Petty and Legge blamed setbacks on the misconduct of the sheriff and other officials, recruited from or sympathetic to the Irish Catholic community. Impartial justice was not to be expected from this quarter. But so jaundiced a view of the sheriffs perhaps revealed the common expectation of the time, based on observation of how Protestants themselves behaved when in office. Each confessional or ethnic group naturally aided its own. As a dispassionate observer stated in 1687, 'it is ill for any that have controversies at law, the courts and juries favouring one side now, as much as heretofore they did the other'.[281]

Sheriffs, although frequently accused of partiality, were rarely disciplined. In 1675, the retiring sheriff of Tipperary was unusual in being punished for his initiative in clearing the county of trouble-makers. Some prisoners had been transported to Barbados in order to rid the locality of 'the evil of a rogue and a vagabond'. The Dublin government concluded that he had exceeded his powers. The sheriff was fined £500, 'to deter the committing of the same offence'.[282] It was alleged that Sir Edward Tyrrell, sheriff of Meath in 1686–7, had been offered 20 guineas 'in hand', with the promise of another £300 or £400, if and when the Catholic Lord Dunsany regained his estates.[283] Tyrrell's counterpart in County Louth was pressed by the lord deputy, Tyrconnell, to favour one party in a forthcoming case.[284] In 1694, the high sheriff of Cork was himself the subject of a presentment by the county's grand jury for having bailed a suspected Jacobite. By this step, staunch Whigs flagged what they saw as undue indulgence towards Catholics and Jacobite fifth-columnists.[285]

Arbitrary sheriffs and their officers claimed victims at assorted social and economic levels. Thereby they were thought to undermine civility and good order, especially when a sheriff failed to keep track of deputies, whom he simply hired for the year.[286] In 1691, the bishop of Limerick was arrested in Dublin and was briefly incarcerated by zealous agents of one sheriff.[287] In 1737, the sheriff's men invaded the Dublin house of the newly dead physician, John van Leuwen, while his corpse still lay there, in order to seize goods in payment of a debt.[288] Similarly, in the 1740s, the faithful agent of a Limerick family secreted various of its possessions to prevent their being impounded by the sheriff's deputies.[289] In each of these three cases, the threat of arbitrary confiscations accompanied by excessive force was lifted only when the sheriff himself was summoned and called off his hounds. They were the lucky. In other incidents, the sheriff egged on his devils. In 1733, the sub-sheriffs of Westmeath assisted the followers of the long-established baronet, Sir Henry Tuite of Sonnagh, in levelling ditches and fences, and rode through the standing corn of a neighbour with whom Tuite was at loggerheads.[290]

Grandees battling for, or to defend, pre-eminence within their district valued the shrievalty. This was because sheriffs chose grand jurors and, in the counties, acted as returning officers at elections. In consequence, pashas like Lord Cork and Burlington in Counties Cork and Waterford, the Brodricks in County Cork, the Rochforts in Westmeath or the Hills in County Down, intrigued to have allies named as sheriffs.[291] In 1713, Robert Molesworth predicted that he could lose his election through opponents' 'making use of scoundrel sheriffs'. William Conolly was apprised routinely of the character of candidates for the Donegal shrievalty.[292] In 1740, the head of the Burtons of Buncraggy pleaded with the lord lieutenant to appoint his candidate as sheriff of County Clare. Only then, Francis Burton contended, would he be protected against the enmity of an older family, that of the earl of Thomond, who had vowed he would spend half his fortune 'to turn me out of the county'.[293]

Aspirants to the shrievalty piously promised to steer between partisans. In this mode, a contender to be next high sheriff of Limerick proclaimed, 'I am an honest man and have a fortune which puts me above dependence on any person in the county'.[294] In County Wexford, Caesar Colclough desired the shrievalty. His manifesto included 'making up all parties, quarrels and recommending peace and good neighbourhood'.[295] Colclough's professions were not altogether disinterested: as a convert suspected of Tory if not Jacobite leanings, appointment would rehabilitate him publicly.[296] Frequently, a better qualification for choice as sheriff was not neutrality but engagement. Remembering a sheriff's power over the composition of the grand jury and the conduct of county elections, it was seen as important to have a sympathizer inserted in the post if important matters were in the offing. Parliamentary elections, occasions when the affiliations of the sheriffs mattered, were rare. By-elections were sometimes held 18 months after the sitting member had died. The delay allowed the selection of a helpful sheriff.

On paper, what was to be done was clear, leaving little leeway. In practice, the sheriff, as presiding officer, could choose place, time and duration of the poll, and so assist a particular candidate. The sheriff decided when to adjourn or close the poll. He had also to judge who was or was not qualified to vote as a 40-shilling freeholder. Nor did the sheriff's work end once the polls had closed. If the return were challenged, he would be summoned by parliament to answer for his conduct. In 1761, the unlucky sheriff in King's County, having presided over an acrimonious election, was reproved for quitting the poll on the pretext of going outside to urinate.[297] More commonly levelled were charges of partiality in selecting grand jurors. Grand juries had to be empanelled twice yearly. Because the grand jury undertook multifarious regulatory, administrative and political functions, the choice of its members required care and could provoke controversy. Grand jurors decided through presentments how money was raised and spent in the county. They sifted through the indictments of prisoners to decide which were true bills and should proceed to trial.

Grand Jurors

The sheriff was free to pick the grand jurors – customarily 23. By the eighteenth century, he was expected to work from lists of the eligible compiled by the high constables in each barony. Stated qualifications were not onerous: a freehold worth more than £5 p.a. or a lease of £15 p.a. (or more) for terms of 61 years and longer. Protestant dissenters sometimes served, as in County Antrim.[298] Catholics were debarred: explicitly from 1708.[299] The grand jury was recruited from more families than supplied either the shrievalty or commission of the peace. With relatively few Protestants of substance in most counties outside Ulster and a need to distribute the load, parochial gentlemen, professionals, traders and clergy were enlisted from time to time. In the 1730s, the low standing of some grand jurors in County Waterford was deprecated.[300] Grand jurors, like other volunteers in the Hanoverians' territorial army, divided between those who appeared only fleetingly and the stalwarts who reappeared frequently. The dim, chosen once for the grand jury, vanished into the historical mists after the assizes closed. In 1749, a pamphleteer expressed the hope that grand juries, would be composed of men 'having substance,' so making them independent of any sinister bias. Such independence hung like a mirage before idealists.[301]

As the eighteenth century progressed, more powers were acquired by the grand jury, thereby increasing the attractions of service. Participation became the perquisite of fewer county families. In County Armagh between 1752 and 1767, it has been calculated that 83 individuals from 56 separate families were empanelled. This contrasted with the situation in the previous 16 years when 120 men from 84 families had sat in the grand jury room.[302] Nevertheless, the size of the grand jury, and the need to make fresh nominations twice yearly, ensured that more county families supplied grand jurors than county magistrates or sheriffs. In Donegal between 1753 and 1768, for example, 80 different men were named as grand jurors. The commission of the peace for the county totalled 34 in 1720, and 67 by 1760.[303] In Westmeath during George II's reign, 68 different men served on the grand jury. The total differed little from the number of justices of the peace: 61 at the start of the reign; 69 at the end.[304]

Even when grand juries were not packed deliberately by the sheriff, few on entering the jury room broke all ties with the rest of the county. They were subjected to strong pressures. Judges on circuit reminded them of their duties and the wishes of the Dublin administration. The grand jury also singled out urgent local issues, prodded sometimes by the sheriff or its own foreman. These worries varied from county to county: vagrants, Tories, Catholic schoolmasters and priests, as well as the ordinary law-breakers.[305] Grand jurors – in common with members of parliament – could direct public monies into schemes which benefited their neighbourhood and indeed their own properties. However, potential gains were balanced by risks. In County Down, the failure of the grand jury, early in George I's reign, to stop alleged frauds in the burning of seaweed to make fertiliser provoked complaints to parliament. In consequence, grand jurors were summoned to answer before a parliamentary committee. This obliged some to travel 80 miles to Dublin, with 'great fatigue, expense and loss of their own affairs'.[306] Grand juries, alert to local issues, were difficult to discipline even when they ignored or subverted the programmes of the Dublin or London governments. They represented another device by which Protestants in the Irish provinces took control of their own destinies.

Magistrates

Enthusiasts believed that the grand jury schooled the locally important in active citizenship. If this were so, it educated only a fragment of the population, and allowed no opportunities to Catholics, and few to Protestant dissenters. The unenthusiastic regarded the grand jury as venal: the protestations of zeal for the general good barely masked the rapacity of a self-serving clique. Similar shortcomings were adduced to the justices of the peace. The Dublin government, short of candidates for these county offices, insisted chiefly on political reliability. By the seventeenth century, it was most easily measured by religious tests. Catholics, unwilling to acknowledge the English monarch as head of the church, were debarred. Political reversals between 1641 and 1691 for a time suspended the oaths and so let Catholics back into local government. By the 1670s, of 900 justices of the peace, 300 were said to be 'Irish', and so either sympathetic to or themselves Catholics.[307] This permissiveness, appointing new magistrates 'upon their paying the fees of a new commission', was thought to have created a magistracy 'too many in number, mean in quality, and what is worst of all, they are generally men of ill principles'.[308] After 1685, Protestants aghast at their own loss of local power, supposed that 'there will be some more than ordinary difficulty to find out men of that [Irish] nation, either of sufficient parts, learning or estates to bear that office [of justice of the peace]'.[309] It was also noted apprehensively that in County Limerick where, by the summer of 1686, a dozen Catholics had been sworn as magistrates, they would not mingle with their Protestant colleagues, 'nor come to any public appearance, but herd by themselves, as if their business were to keep up a distinct interest', which obstructed 'the king's service'.[310] Allegations of incapacity were routinely levelled by the excluded, whether Protestant or Catholic.

The Williamite victories doomed the defeated Catholics to permanent exclusion from national, county and municipal offices. Initially, the more ruthless exclusion of Catholics and Jacobites left counties such as Galway with alarmingly few justices.[311] Fears persisted that Catholic fellow-travellers survived. In 1733, a new statute forbade converts and men with Catholic wives from serving in the county magistracy.[312] Such suspicions reminded of rivalries which splintered Protestant communities and turned institutions such as the grand jury, municipal corporations and the commission of the peace into battlegrounds. In 1663, Ormond asked the local Protestant bishop and two grandees with impeccable royalist credentials for advice about whom to include in the new commissions for Antrim and Down. At a time when the survival of republicanism and Presbyterianism in the area was dreaded, the advisers identified nine from the 25 in the Antrim commission and eight of the 26 in Down for dismissal. The trio were, nevertheless, conscious of the opprobrium if they were revealed as the executioners, and sought anonymity.[313] By the early eighteenth century, Protestant disunity expressed itself in the competition between Whigs and Tories. From 1711, the ascendant Tories excluded Whigs from the county commissions. In 1714, the tables were turned and about 72 Tories were struck from the county commissions. In some counties, such as westerly Clare, it was alleged that the purges had not gone far enough. Supporters of the ultra-Tory Lord Chancellor Phipps, recent converts from Catholicism and crypto-Jacobites were said to survive as magistrates. At the same time, the baleful effects attributed to purges elsewhere – the appointment of men 'of very slender fortune and interest in their country' – were observed in Clare.[314]

Any vendetta against the Tories soon abated. So long as they accepted the Hanoverian dynasty and disowned the exiled Stuarts, former Tories streamed back into parliament, office and favour.[315] In the localities, the Dublin administration was too desperate for willing work-horses to scrutinize credentials minutely. It depended on those with local knowledge for assessments of candidates. Unscrupulous patrons secured the appointment of allies, agents and dependents as magistrates, and thereby consolidated their local power. In 1682, the lord chancellor disclosed that only those vouched for by him personally or by a privy councillor, peer, judge or 'person of such eminent quality that as there can be no reason to doubt their recommendation' received commissions.[316] By 1732, signed testimonials were required for each suggested for the magistracy.[317] In 1750, a recommendation from the county governor was thought essential.[318] The need for this kind of endorsement brought the magistracy into a spoils system where connections and lobbying rather than capability or probity prevailed. In 1718, one reformer asked that the government stipulate that 'no man ought to be a justice of the peace who is not at least an housekeeper or has an estate in possession, or is eminent for some abilities extraordinary'.[319] In Ireland, as in England and Wales, few of those named to the commission sat regularly on the magisterial bench. With so many defaulters, the government was obliged to issue long commissions in the hope that enough would be active. In England, as the commission of the peace doubled in size between 1675 and 1720, lesser landed gentry and professionals had to be included.[320] In Ireland, with a much smaller stock of Protestant gentlemen and professionals, the likelihood of the modest being commissioned was great.

Magistrates, so far from curbing lawlessness, occasionally caused it. Extreme in this regard was an escapade in 1657. The servant of one justice belaboured a newcomer about to be sworn into the commission. The unlucky new magistrate had his mouth stopped with horse dung.[321] In 1695, the prospect of Sir Robert Gore being added to the Sligo magistracy was likened to putting 'a drawn sword in a madman's hand'.[322] The swearing of 'the young squire of Coole' as a County Cork magistrate in 1741 was greeted ironically. At a recent meeting, the squire had so misbehaved himself as to be handed over to the constable. An observer commented wryly, 'no doubt he'll discharge the office with great distinction'.[323] The general failings of arrogant and over-mighty magistrates were occasionally remarked. In 1707, a bill to stop extortion by justices of the peace failed in the House of Commons. Members of parliament, the majority of whom served in their own districts as magistrates, rejected the proposal as a libel on the justices.[324] In 1734 parliament again debated closer regulation of the commission of the peace, but eventually abandoned it.[325] In the city of Dublin during the 1720s, two aldermanic justices were disabled from office on account of their corruption.[326] The Reverend Francis Lauder was removed from the Kerry commission for colluding in the much publicized robbery of silver from a Danish ship wrecked on the coast.[327] In County Westmeath, justices were outraged when two of their number, Arthur Bowen, and his brother-in-law, Herbert Price, misused their powers.[328] In 1736, a censorious observer concluded of the justiceship of the peace that the 'office is much abused in Ireland'.[329]

The scope for the obsessive to hunt their favourite quarries was revealed by Arthur Rochfort, 'a very young gentleman', added to the commission of the peace for Westmeath. In 1737, Rochfort pursued Maguire, a Catholic and an officer in the imperial Austrian army on leave in the Irish midlands. Maguire was apprehended carrying a sword contrary to the law of 1695. He haughtily stated that he had worn the sword as 'an appendage to his habit, not only as he was an officer but a gentleman'. Rochfort, not a wit abashed, outraged another neighbour by accusing the latter's servant under the game laws of being a poacher. The Dublin government, disquieted by Rochfort's provocations, backed him in the hope of scotching a tendency 'among Protestants and Papists to insult magistrates for doing their duty'.[330]

Rochfort personified the supposedly impersonal operations of the law in Protestant Ireland: an unhappy situation. Justices enjoyed a degree of latitude in deciding which statutes should be enforced. Outside the quarter sessions and assizes, a brace of magistrates, acting in partnership, had wide powers.[331] The enthusiasms of a few in Dublin during the 1690s largely explained successful prosecutions of moral transgressors. Conversely, slackness in applying penal laws against the Catholics was traced back to reluctant magistrates.[332] In 1712 with agrarian violence in the form of maiming or 'houghing' cattle menacing parts of Connacht, Archbishop Vesey wanted local justices to act. However, when the assizes opened at Castlebar, only two justices of the peace appeared. Any hope of prosecuting the houghers had to be put off until the next month.[333] An agent in Kerry observed that justices of the peace were well named 'for holding their peace and doing nothing'.[334] An aim of the Dublin government was to spread justices so that every district possessed at least one. However, the uneven settlement of Protestants in many counties, such as Waterford and Cork, meant that some baronies were without a resident magistrate. In 1684, the quarter sessions in the small and remote county of Leitrim were attended by only two justices.[335] There were worries, too, about the absence of magistrates in towns, such as Edenderry and Newcastle in County Limerick, and even in industrial settlements like those at the Chapelizod textile works close to Dublin or the Enniscorthy iron manufacture.[336]

Delinquent magistrates and sheriffs attracted most attention, but – by the eighteenth century – were rarities. The merely absent, incompetent or somnolent are not easily traced; nor are the conscientious. Among the last – as was seen in the previous chapter – was Edgeworth, the County Longford squire. Magistrates customarily dined with the assize judge, supped with the sheriff, and then clubbed with their fellow justices for other meals. In 1711, a County Down magistrate wrote ruefully that he could recall nothing of the previous day's business at the assizes owing to libations of the last evening. Over the decanters of wine and pipes of tobacco, news was exchanged, deals struck and alliances negotiated or sundered. Thomas Pakenham, Edgeworth's nephew, on returning from a trip into Connacht, confessed that he had attended two assizes and an election and that all had been drunk continuously.[337]

Justice

Serving the state in Ireland brought tangible and intangible rewards, but also dangers. Justices, in tackling less serious 'created' or regulatory offences, had to pick targets from an ever-lengthening schedule. Magistrates and grand jurors immured in the court room discovered that the press of business was matched by the throng of people inside and outside the court houses.[338] The manifestations warned of the extensive followings of litigants and defendants. In 1748, Captain Stannard, carted off to gaol for a debt of £500, was freed through the intercession of his brother, the recorder of Dublin. The released captain 'was brought home in triumph, having been met by all the crew of Ballyhooley, with the mummers, pipers, &c'.[339] At the quarter sessions at Mullingar, 'a great mob' gathered before an indictment was thrown out. This force, headed by two pipers, marched up and down outside the sessions house shouting slogans.[340] As at elections, so in local affairs, jurors, witnesses and mere spectators enlarged the constricted circle of justices, counsel and grand jurymen. Those excluded from office by the confessional requirements participated in some of the routines. Nervous Protestants felt that Catholics as constables, petty jurors and witnesses negated many of the prohibitions and precautions. They failed to find true bills or to proceed with indictments, and acquitted many.

The English ambition to establish a national network of courts throughout Ireland had been accomplished by the eighteenth century. It failed to deliver all the expected boons. Parts of Ulster, because more densely planted with English and Scots, seemed amenable to the full reception of English laws. Yet, levels of recorded violence were higher there than in the counties around London. Modest prosperity, associated particularly with the linen industry, generated its own brands of lawlessness. However, the situation did not provoke severity equal to that known in England. Samples from the north of Ireland suggest that 55 per cent of those indicted for offences were then sent to be tried. This compared with 80 per cent in England. In the Ulster courts, no more than a third of the accused were convicted; in England the proportion was almost two-thirds.[341] The scale of prosecutions is not well documented in the remoter south and west of Ireland, where restlessness might persist longer.

The findings hint at a possible effect of the humble, including Catholics, acting as jurors and witnesses: an unwillingness to subject their neighbours to the full might of the English law. The very localized jurisdictions in manor and borough, together with the admiralty courts, were open to poorer Catholics. So, too, were the county courts. The resulting chances of participation may have reconciled the otherwise excluded to the legal system, and ultimately to British authority. Alternatively (and more probably), the ease with which the dispossessed adapted to and exploited the English-style courts suggested an ingenuity in devising strategies to survive worsening discrimination.

Low rates of conviction did not stampede the Irish parliament into legislating. Many fewer criminal statutes were enacted in early eighteenth-century Dublin than in London.[342] One reason may be a greater readiness to resort to alternatives. Some English rulers in Ireland argued that the kingdom, still at an earlier stage of development, should be handled more summarily.[343] A sign of the ruthlessness was the shipment of convicts and vagrants to distant colonies in greater numbers than from England and Wales. This practice built on an established habit of transporting the troublesome and destitute overseas. By the eighteenth century, it reduced pressure on scarce resources at times of dearth.[344] Other indications of summary processes were the regular use of proclamations, executive decree and the soldiery. Even so, the Dublin authorities showed reluctance in asking for and invoking emergency powers, other than in the aftermath of the seventeenth-century wars. Then, the dislocations created a type of brigand soon labelled as a 'tory'. The government in Dublin licensed the hunting of the despera-does by bands of Protestants. They also tried to force Catholic communi-ties to surrender them by imposing sanctions on entire settlements.[345] The phenomenon lessened although it never vanished, as the desperate opted for vagabondage, seasonal migration, or soldiering and life over-seas. In some cases, tories may have expressed political discontents as the grip of the Stuarts on Ireland was loosened. More often, it would seem, the uprooted were struggling to subsist.

By the eighteenth century, a multiplicity of laws made it easier to apprehend if not to convict those suspected of recruiting men for the Hanoverians' enemies or of harbouring the Catholic clergy. Despite the many garrisons situated across Ireland, there was considerable resistance to deploying soldiers to keep domestic peace and to enforce the law. Commanders refused to assist magistrates or revenue officers unless authorized explicitly to do so by the government. However, by the 1750s such orders were given more frequently.[346] Clashes with smugglers, illegal distillers and supposed incendiaries could culminate in bloodshed. The affrays hardly endeared the military to the bulk of the population, and may further have contributed to the indifference of civilians, regardless of confession, towards the British state as it was encountered in the Irish hinterlands.

Boroughs

A method to speed the assimilation of Ireland to English rule was to establish towns. They had long been regarded as a unique agent of anglicization since (it was said) the aboriginal Irish had not built them. Early in the seventeenth century, the campaign intensified. Forty-six parliamentary boroughs were incorporated under James VI and I, one during Charles I's reign and another 15 during Charles II's time. A powerful motive was to tip the balance in the House of Commons away from the Catholics and towards the Protestant newcomers. New boroughs rapidly achieved the objective. Some incorporations simply remained names on impressive skins of vellum. They stirred into life only when two members had to be sent to the Dublin parliament. However, about 55, although differing sharply in size, took on distinctive physical form. They also had economic, communal and cultural significance. Boroughs trained and restrained the inhabitants. They offered services, experi-ences and entertainments lacking throughout much of the countryside.

These ranged from participation as freemen, rate-payers and burgesses in both parliamentary and municipal elections through the work of vestries, borough courts and corporation committees, membership of masonic lodges and voluntary groups to shopping, processing and promenading through public spaces, relaxation at the bowling green, cockpit, racecourse or assembly room. Larger towns were designed to foster scarce skills. To this end, traders and craft-workers were organized in guilds. Dublin possessed 24, rising to 25 in 1747. Waterford had nine; and smaller places, fewer. Guild members ran their corporate affairs; as freemen, they governed their town. Thereby, fraternity was upheld and communal responsibilities discharged. At the same time, hierarchy and tendencies towards oligarchy characterized many eighteenth-century boroughs.[347]

During the 1650s, civic office became a Protestant monopoly. It was hoped that urban property and trade would also be engrossed by the Protestants, but this never happened. Indeed, in the 1670s, the government sought to revive depressed trade by reinstating Catholics in some ports like Limerick and Galway, the commerce of which they had dominated until recently. More rigorous prohibitions on Catholics were implemented in the 1690s. The Test Act of 1704 planned to make the principal boroughs into Church of Ireland cartels. Since Catholics had already been excluded from the government of the towns, the impact of the act was felt chiefly by Protestant dissenters. The nonconformists were removed from the corporations of Belfast, Carrickfergus, Coleraine and Derry.[348] Denied scope for public service, they diverted their talents into institutions of their own, to the detriment of the British state in Ireland.

Individual towns worked out compromises whereby Catholics shared some of the trade and work. Deals of this sort, struck in Dublin, Cork, Youghal and Waterford, offered Catholics outlets.[349] Critics of the concessions complained that they worsened a trend that arose from the ban on Catholics buying freeholds or leasing land for more than 31 years. Unable to prosper in the countryside, they plunged into commerce, enriched themselves and would soon pose a new danger to their Protestant neighbours. These anxieties rested on hearsay and imagination not facts.[350] Nevertheless, they revealed Protestant edginess when confronted with incontrovertible Catholic numbers and resilience. The place of Catholics in the guilds and trades of the towns, like the tacit toleration of Catholic worship, rested on the forbearance of the ascendant Protestants. It might be cancelled at any time. Catholics paid hefty 'quarterage' charges so that they could be admitted to trading companies as quarter brothers. Through this expedient they gained liberty to trade, but not the political rights which came automatically to Protestants with freedom of a guild. It is unclear whether these arrangements eased confessional tensions, encouraging those of the separate denominations to cooperate over trading questions and to mingle socially, or added to the resentments of those denied full citizenship.

Trading companies were only one of many urban institutions, which incubated a richer associational life than was available in the countryside. Sociability might arise from a shared profession, as with lawyers and attorneys, in craft associations or masonic lodges which proliferated from the 1720s. Many of these developments were clearest in, and in some instances confined to, Dublin. Smaller towns were not devoid of diversions. By the mid-eighteenth century, Bandon had a 'patriot club', which attracted weavers, wool-combers, shopkeepers, attorneys, blue-dyers and farmers. It met in an inn, levied subscriptions and followed local and national controversies avidly.[351] Already in Ballyjamesduff (County Cavan), a loose grouping of curate, excise collector, apothecary, the squire's agent and an innkeeper gathered in a tavern after church to discuss happenings in Dublin.[352] Haughty squires despised these stirrings of independence among the insignificant, and sought to stifle them.[353] Towns were too vibrant as nurseries to be silenced or suppressed. The urban became urbane, while their supposed betters among the squirearchy mouldered as uncouth rustics. However, the vitality of political life in the boroughs was sapped by the Newtown Act of 1748. The statute decreed that non-residents could swamp resident freemen in parliamentary elections. Despite this blow, convivial meetings and political discussions continued. What is not clear is whether or not these gatherings welcomed adherents of the different denominations. It seems possible that Protestant dissenters might mingle with relative ease, but not the Catholics. In this way, the boroughs, central to English and Protestant Ireland, reflected and intensified its sectarianism.

Chapter 6: Catholic Masses and Protestant Élites

Majorities

English policy aimed to eradicate Catholicism from sixteenth- and seventeenth-century Ireland. Failure quickly to do so led to a more limited although still ambitious scheme to remove its leaders. Government service was closed to those who would not profess Protestantism. Other openings – in the law, education and even skilled crafts – narrowed and sometimes closed. By the early eighteenth century, the only profession in Ireland open to Catholics was medicine.[354] However, the most important element in the leadership of Catholic Ireland, the priesthood, although harassed, survived. Even Protestant observers thought that the lack of priests was more damaging than their presence. Near Dublin, at Ballymore, parishioners, deprived of Catholic worship, were left 'without even the sense or thought of religion'. As a result, the people were said to 'die rather like beasts than Christians'.[355] In other places, such as County Kerry, the Catholic priesthood was more active than the established Protestant church. There the negligence of Protestant ministers made parishioners turn to Catholicism, 'and several are buried like swine for want of a parson, and others are forced to get popish priests to baptize their children or suffer 'em to die without baptism'.[356] Priests and schoolteachers worked – at different moments – under threat of imprisonment, banishment or even death. Yet, by 1731 enquiries uncovered more than 2300, both the regulars (members of religious orders like Franciscans, Capuchins and Dominicans) and secular (essentially parish) priests. In addition, 549 Catholic schools were noted. Probably the number was considerably larger.[357]

The Catholic Church, like its Protestant counterparts, wished to improve standards among its clergy. Intending priests, monks and nuns were trained in Catholic Europe, at seminaries scattered from Prague through Louvain and Paris to Salamanca and Lisbon.[358] A statute of 1695 aimed to cut the link; it failed. Substantial sums of money were needed to follow the required educational regimen. The cost put it beyond most, unless helped by bursaries. The resulting education, even the fact of literacy, separated the ordained from the many to whom they ministered. Their qualifications could make priests leaders of their communities, articulating ideas and ideals. Clerics, literate and with access to foreign presses, were to the fore in late seventeenth- and early eighteenth-century Ireland in framing and communicating memories of sufferings and loss. They nurtured defiance of English Protestantism through published recollections and exhortations. Officials failed to stop these sometimes inflammatory materials being imported into and read in Ireland. Yet more resistant to censorship were verse and song. The refrains, often in the Irish language, lamented losses, lampooned the conquerors, vilified traitors and cherished heroes. Most were handwritten or spread by word of mouth. Fables and parables kept alive expectations that the dispossessed might some day again enjoy their own. Stories in the vernacular, moreover, constantly belittled the system associated with Britain and manned by Protestants, and extolled alternatives.

No more than their Protestant counterparts did the Catholic clergy and poets speak in unison. Some vehemently supported the Stuarts and strengthened a traditional strain of royalism associated with the Old English of Ireland. Others, long absent from Ireland, out of touch with the realities of power within Britain and thankful for the backing of Catholic monarchs, urged the abandonment of heretical England and its rulers. These divergences, evident from the late sixteenth century, worsened the divisions among the Confederates during the 1640s. In particular, the uncompromising, sceptical of what Charles I could or was prepared to do for his Catholic subjects, found a leader in the pope's nuncio, Rinuccini. The ultramontane stance, contemptuous of compromise, persisted among some bishops and priests, especially those trained in Spanish territories. The reigns of the later Stuarts, apparently sympathetic to their Catholic subjects in Ireland, looked a propitious time to extort concessions. One group, led by Peter Walsh, tried throughout the 1660s to devise a formula through which Catholics could demonstrate unequivocally that, while wedded to their faith, they were obedient to their English monarchs. This bid to frame 'A Loyal

Formulary' reopened and widened the fissures. The quest would be renewed from time to time over the next century. It repeatedly split Catholics, and failed to persuade the authorities to repeal the anti-Catholic laws.

The brief periods during which the full panoply of Catholic ritual could be freely followed – in the 1650s and late 1680s – were succeeded by repression. After 1697, bishops and monks were obliged to choose between exile and extreme circumspection. After the initial alarms, the parish clergy continued in or returned to Ireland. Their presences, let alone the covert celebration of the sacraments, depended on the connivance of the Protestant authorities. Magistrates might activate the severe laws if Catholic priests obtruded themselves too much.[359] Accordingly, the caution of those striving to preserve the basics of regular Catholic worship in Ireland contrasted with the intemperance of exiles. Also the wish not to provoke official intervention added to existing differences between the secular and regular clergy.[360] The latter, less tied to parochial cures, tended not to compromise. The intransigence of the regulars led Protestants to try to banish them. In contrast, the seculars were required simply to register and to abjure the Stuart dynasty. The first step was much more easily taken than the second. Only 33 priests are known to have sworn the oath of abjuration after 1709. Paradoxically, the Protestant state accepted the validity of Catholic ordination: marriages performed by priests, unlike those by dissenting pastors, were treated as legal. However, the Church of Ireland still claimed a monopoly over other rites of passage and extorted fees for them. It was ironical that the fate of the mendicant friars in Ireland was settled not by British but by papal commands. In 1751, having hitherto been controlled only loosely, they were to be brought more firmly under the bishops' supervision. The decision, which curtailed freedom to wander and preach at will, may have assisted the emergence of the parish as the fixed centre of communal Catholic life.[361] The Catholics, with a greater number of ordained clergy, were able to serve more of the historic parishes than the Church of Ireland incumbents.[362]

The habit of Irish Catholics to look for relief to the Stuarts, still justified while James VII and II reigned, ossified into an alliance unhelpful alike to James's heirs and to the Irish. The exiled Stuarts continued, thanks to papal prescript, to nominate to vacant bishoprics. For this reason, the Catholic Church in Ireland could not be separated – at least in the minds of its opponents – from the Jacobite cause. The seemingly indelible taint of disloyalty defeated any suggestions that the disabilities of the Irish Catholics should be removed. Instead, it was argued that, so long as they remained committed to the overthrow of the incumbent Hanoverian state, they constituted a political peril. Protestants argued that elementary prudence decreed that the Catholics be denied full membership of the Irish state. The daring on each side of the confessional rift explored stratagems to bridge it. A formula was sought which might allow Catholics to enter fully into civil and civic society without having to abjure their religious beliefs. None emerged. Moreover, the attempts excited fierce controversy among both Catholics and Protestants, and may well have retarded any improvement in relationships between the separate religious confessions.

Catholic clergy remained at risk of vindictive attacks. As a result, they might be incarcerated, forced into foreign exile, or even brought to the gallows. Religious rites were performed, but often in degraded if not dangerous conditions, and without the public magnificence which had been possible during the ascendancy of the Confederation and of Tyrconnell and which was familiar to any who had seen Catholic Europe. Schools and convents were known to function in the larger towns of Dublin, Cork, Galway and Waterford. But, dimly discerned and rarely visited by the Protestants, they excited wild rumours. This ignorance nourished a crude anti-Catholicism which still demonized the entire Catholic community, and justified its exclusion from the freedoms and rights accorded to Protestants. Anti-Catholic feeling flared unpredictably, and added to the insecurities and uncertainties under which Catholics laboured.[363] Both convinced and unscrupulous Protestants fanned the embers of hatred. Yet, the ugly impulses coexisted with friendlier accommodations.[364]

At the zenith of retributive Protestant zeal in 1653, the Catholics of Ireland, when not doomed to harsher treatment, were to be exiled west of the River Shannon and expelled from all important towns and coastal regions. Such exclusions proved impracticable: inimical alike to the recovery of agriculture and industry, and so of government finances. Protestants, no matter how rabidly intolerant of the Catholics, needed them to tenant and till their lands, to serve in their houses and to supply the goods and services without which civilized life could not go on. Living cheek by jowl with numerous Catholics, some Protestants retained their prejudices. Terrors that the Catholics might rise at any moment were preserved and refreshed by powerful politicians, from Orrery in the 1670s to his grandson, Henry Boyle, Speaker of the Commons from 1733. The culture of Irish Protestantism, enshrined in the liturgy of the established church, in the commemorative rituals of the state and the municipalities, and through the histories and iconography of the Irish Protestants, perpetuated an almost Manichean opposition of good and evil, English and Irish, Protestant and Catholic. Sightings of Irish Catholic officers supposed to be soldiering abroad or enemy men-of-war off remote headlands, the swagger of local Catholics, the news from the courts and battlefields of mainland Europe, all aggravated anxieties arising from the undeniable fact of the Protestants' numerical inferiority in every county outside Ulster.[365]

Jumpy Protestants hardly exaggerated the strength and tenacity of Irish Catholicism. However, they predicted more trouble than materialized. History, which thoughtful Protestants studied, warned that rebellion seemed regular and endemic in Ireland. Suggestions that the pattern had been broken, encouraged by the passivity of Irish Catholics during the Jacobite risings of 1715 and 1745, were not universally believed.[366] Despite the public bombast, attitudes could be unexpectedly casual. During the alarms over the Young Pretender in Scotland, sympathizers were hauled before the Dublin courts. William Branagan, although convicted in 1745 of uttering the 'malicious and seditious words' that 'the whelps will be turned out and a Stewart is your lawful king', was sentenced only to two hours in the pillory. Fergus Gallagher, despite choosing the 5 November, to cry 'God damn King George and all his subjects and God bless the King of France and the young Pretender', was one of several brought before the Dublin magistrates and acquitted.[367] Alarmists never altogether trusted the seeming Catholic passivity, and interpreted it as evidence of guile. History abounded with precedents: the apparent harmony between the distinct confessional communities resembled that of the 1620s and 1630s. Then the 1641 uprising had followed, and might yet be repeated. The vigilant likened the Catholics to 'a lion chained', which though better than – as of old – 'a lion at liberty', remained a dangerous beast.[368]

This picture of latent Catholic might was not one that most Catholics in the 1650s or from the 1690s to the 1760s would have recognized. Between 1660 and 1688, the recovery of a few, drawn generally from the estated and professional families of the Pale and other areas of Old English settlement, was not shared with humbler victims of the Confederate Wars and Cromwellian settlement. The exiled streamed back across the River Shannon; others returned from their European refuges to resume their trades and crafts in Irish towns. The speed and apparent ease with which local administration was restored to Catholics in the

1680s revealed local élites in place and waiting. How they had managed to hang on financially until these brighter times can scarcely be gauged.[369] The respite was short. Fresh defeat completed the ruin of numerous houses, which had preserved a precarious gentility throughout the recent reverses. Far fewer weathered the new tempests. Those who did had usually to trim to the prevailing winds: most conspicuously and effectively by conversion from Catholicism. But few steered this course. Catholics, no less than their Protestant neighbours, comforted themselves through their readings of recent and Old Testament history. They confidently awaited 'the ever-flying tomorrow', when once more they would enjoy their own.[370] This hope, defying the dismal legal and economic prospects for Catholics of consequence, furnished further evidence in the Protestant prognosis of trouble to come. Catholic strategies of survival can seldom be identified with any precision: only the fact of survival apparently against the odds. Two branches of the Bellews, Old English Catholics who hung on in landed society in Galway and Louth, personify this tenacity. In the fertile county of Meath and in districts west of the River Shannon, the successes of Catholic survivors among the gentry were remarked.[371]

Although the government pressed Catholics to convert to Protestantism, conversions were not always applauded. In the legal profession, previously dominated by English-trained Catholics, many converts were thought to be doubtful supporters of the Protestant interest. Sir Toby Butler, a leading practitioner at the Irish bar at the end of the seventeenth century, was one of the gownsmen who worried the authorities. Butler spoke for the powerful Catholics who protested against the proposed penalties of 1704. His arguments failed, and he himself was now in danger of being silenced in the courts unless he qualified himself by yearly communion at a Church of Ireland service. Butler remained in practice, but it is unclear whether he had abandoned the old religion. He resolutely preserved the strong Irish brogue of his speech.[372] A successor at the bar, Anthony Malone, also prominent – like other barristers – in the House of Commons, was suspected covertly of favouring Catholicism.[373] The existence of this convert interest, and the fears that it aroused among the nervy Protestants, negated many predicted gains of the highly placed defections from the Church of Rome. Converts were required to go through the drama of a public recantation in a Church of Ireland building. Occasionally defectors were rewarded with pensions; sometimes, too, their speeches were published, with the intention of encouraging others to follow.[374] Often mercenary motives for conversion were stressed rather than the promptings of Protestant truth.[375]

Priests and monks who took the momentous step were reviled by those whom they had left. Nor were converts always feted by their new Protestant brethren. Defecting Catholic clergy tended to be pushed into poorer livings, or employed as curates and schoolmasters. Uncertainties about the motives of converts were generally allayed within a couple of generations, just as the unsightly glare of new wealth acquired the attractive patina of age. The Frenches, a prolific Old English tribe in County Galway, had branches keen to supplement landed incomes by legal practice. At Monivea, Patrick French obeyed the law of 1704 by renouncing his ancestral Catholicism. His son, also a qualified lawyer and in time a MP, wholeheartedly endorsed Protestantism. He married the daughter of a Protestant bishop and threw himself into founding and running Protestant schools. Similarly, another branch of the Frenches, located at French Park in County Roscommon, aroused no doubts about their adherence to Protestantism, as the head of the family was elected to parliament and then made a judge.[376]

Best documented of the Catholics after 1690 are the groups which forsook Ireland. Many built on foundations laid over many decades. In the preceding century, merchants, priests and swordsmen forced from a hostile Ireland had settled in the ports around the coasts of the north Atlantic and in congenial havens across Catholic Europe. Some even established themselves in the Americas and West Indies.[377] More joined the émigrés after 1691. They ranged from the impoverished soldiers of the Jacobite armies who, with their families, went to St Germain with James and his courtiers, to grandees such as the second duke of Ormonde, who, after rambling, dwelt in splendour at Avignon.[378] Others by dint of talents and connections prospered in foreign trade and armies. One group, settled in the Basque region around Bilbao, dominated the local tanning trade. Its cohesiveness was maintained by intermarriage, continuing use of the Irish and English languages, devotion to the cult of St Patrick, and extensive links with traders in Ireland, Bordeaux, Cadiz and the West Indies.[379] The diaspora, entrenched in Catholic Europe and beyond, sustained the demoralized Catholic community at home. Catholic Ireland, just as it thought of itself as including the dead, many of them martyrs to English oppression, encompassed the absent.

Ideals and ideas seemingly at odds with those of Hanoverian Britain unsettled Protestants. Converts might prove the Trojan horse through which the Protestant citadel would be stormed. Perhaps, after all, it was better to be surrounded by adversaries whose confessional allegiance was unequivocal. The government happily licensed defeated soldiers to leave Ireland and serve under other banners. But there remained the danger that military skills learnt overseas would in time be applied in Ireland, as they had been in the Confederate and Williamite campaigns. Links between the resident and the exiled Catholics were assumed but not always solidly documented. Along these channels travelled the people and money which enabled priests, monks and nuns to be trained on the continent and so sustained the Catholic Church within Ireland. Experienced officers, armaments, and rousing propaganda also used the same routes. As many as a thousand Irish each year joined foreign armies.[380] Protestants periodically fulminated against the recruitment of sturdy Irish for service with the Hanoverians' enemies.[381] Reports from County Kerry in 1729 told of one of the Mahonys – the dominant local sept – recently returned from France to recruit. He did so 'as publicly as if permitted by the government', marching the recruits through the local town and calling the roll there.[382] Such manifestations warned of elusive and seemingly indestructible bonds between Catholic Ireland and continental Europe, which the authorities were unable to sever. Fears recurred that veterans might return to head insurrections. More often, successful officers revisited Ireland on furlough. Promoted and sometimes ennobled through sterling service to Catholic princes, they enjoyed a standing that contrasted tellingly with the degradation of their kinsfolk and neighbours in Ireland, as Maguire's treatment at the hands of Rochfort in 1737 disclosed.

The unwillingness to trust Irish Catholics from Ireland to defend Hanoverian interests overseas belonged to the myopia, which prevented them from serving the state in other useful capacities. English monarchs, desperate for proficient officers and soldiers to fight their wars in and beyond Europe, forfeited helpers. Only after 1760 did shortages of manpower oblige Britain to rescind some of the prohibitions. Until then, no more than 10–15 per cent of the population was equipped by full membership of the state church to act for the Protestant state in Ireland. Natural increase of the conforming Protestant population ensured that by 1714 there were more competitors than places for them. Nevertheless, the pool was shallow, and left the government with little room to reject the small fry. Life for the members of the incipient ascendancy, although envied by their dispossessed rivals, was not always easy. Landed incomes measured acre for acre seldom matched those in lowland England. However, responsibilities and styles of living differed less, but had to be financed by lower incomes. Supplements – paid posts, military and naval service or careers in the professions – were desperately sought. Another option was to add to estates. This course, easy enough during the seventeenth century when large tracts were transferred from Catholic to Protestant ownership, and usually on generous terms, ended once the Williamite confiscations had been digested. Henceforward, those wishing to lengthen rentals had either to buy more on the land market or improve what they had.

Minorities

On occasion during the seventeenth century, Protestants encountered Catholics on the battlefields of Ireland. These occasional confrontations produced in some an almost reflexive hostility. More frequent, and indeed the norm between the 1690s and 1790s, were encounters in the townland and parish. Inequalities – legal and often economic – marked meetings at markets and fairs, and between landlords and tenants, employers and servants or customers and producers. The intimate space of the townland incubated amity and animosity. With no institutional existence, this, the most important of units, has left few records. Instead, the parish, the other framework which arched over townlands, affords some clues about everyday lives. When settlers from England and Wales disembarked in Ireland during the twelfth century, they found a parochial organization already in place.[383] By the sixteenth century, as evangelical reformers took over the state church, they commandeered a ready-made national network. However, the mesh was too holed to catch the entire population. Moreover, as Protestantism spread, parishes related badly to its densest concentrations. Sheer distance or derelict fabrics prevented many from appearing each Sunday for public worship, as required by statutes of 1560 and 1665.[384]

The established church, as a privileged corporation, advertised its dominance. In the larger towns, ambitious rebuilding increased its visibility. Catholics were keen to wrest church buildings from their Protestant occupants during the 1640s and late 1680s. Protestants soon recovered the churches, and edged the Catholics into improvised and surreptitious worship. Similarly, Protestant dissenters took care that their meeting-houses, legal if licensed after 1719, did not offend conformists through their scale and style. The privileges of the established Church of Ireland, evident in its control over marriages and burials, increased with the Test of 1704. Communion, an action central to private belief, was invested with public import.[385] In contrast to recantation of Catholicism, no special ritual surrounded this event; only formal certification was needed.[386] Yet, there was a sense of drama in the parish church of Kinsale shortly after George I's accession, when Edward Bradston, the surveyor of excise in the port, together with 14 colleagues in the customs administration, qualified themselves by receiving the sacrament.[387]

In England, the state had long treated the parish as a trusty workhorse. The Irish administration was slower to use it to control and relieve. Nevertheless, the parish in Ireland acquired secular responsibilities. Care of local roads, including the provision of labour for their repair and construction, fell to the parish, until transferred to county grand juries in 1765.[388] One bustling bishop suggested that parish officials should enforce the regulations about the size of filament permissible in fishing nets.[389] In this instance, the parishes contented themselves with being fishers of men. In 1698, the Irish parliament made parishes overseers of a programme of tree planting. Parish officials counted the trees and allotted quotas of saplings either already, or to be, planted.[390] In the same year, the legislature also decided that parishes, at least in Dublin, should manage the valuations and assessments for the land tax.[391]

More permanent and more likely to impinge on inhabitants was the role of the parish in caring for those within its bounds. The poor, old or feeble attracted the compassion of the parish; the unruly and dissolute, its ire. To relieve the deserving, money was raised. By the late seventeenth century, levying, collecting and distributing these rates preoccupied parish worthies.[392] Embryonic bureaucracies developed. Soon there was other work for the parish. More exacting standards meant that churches had not just to be made fast against the weather; they were to be decently flagged, ceiled, wainscoted and provided with fixed seating; graveyards were tidied to serve as promenades. Where once the incumbent or lay patron might have attended to these works, by the close of the seventeenth century, the congregation was likely to be involved.[393] An élite evolved: salaried parish and vestry clerks, annually chosen churchwardens, sidesmen, overseers of the poor, surveyors of highways, applotters and collectors of cesses.[394] Many of these positions rotated each year, so a substantial proportion of the male householders of the parish had to share the chores. Neither Catholics nor Protestant dissenters were debarred from the modest parochial jobs. Both groups, although non-participants in the religious services, were obliged to pay tithes to maintain the Church of Ireland pastorate. They had also to accept the authority of the church courts. By the 1690s, Presbyterians in Ulster paid substitutes to act on their behalf as constables, church wardens and overseers of the poor.[395] The expedients were regularized by law in 1719.[396] The diversion of Protestant nonconformists' energies from the Church of Ireland parish into their own system of kirk sessions, synods and general assembly warned of the separation of a substantial section of the Protestant population from the institutions of Hanoverian Ireland. It was paralleled by the Catholics' withdrawal from the Protestant parish into their own quarters.

Conscientious parishioners dealt with a heavier press of business. *Ad hoc* committees, which in the past had assisted or supervised incumbents and churchwardens, were now formalized into vestries. Dublin, with its crowded parishes, probably pioneered the innovation.[397] Vestry meetings, to which potentially the heads of all rate-paying households could come, proved too cumbersome for the efficient dispatch of business. An inner group of the active turned itself into the select vestry. In the 1660s and 1670s, the vestry of St Bride's in Dublin was attended by between 12 and 21 parishioners. Similarly, a vestry meeting at St John's in Dublin in 1719 attracted 20 laymen and the curate.[398] In provincial towns as far apart as Cork and Lurgan, the more substantial members of the Church of Ireland congregations ran the vestries.[399]

The vestry, in common with other corporate bodies of the Protestant state, tended towards oligarchy. Self-appointed and self-perpetuating worthies engrossed power rather than dispersing it among all adult male parishioners. A sense of the public-spirit animating churchwardens is conveyed by the emergence about 1725 of a society of churchwardens in Dublin. This group arose from common concerns over destitution, disorder and debauchery across metropolitan parishes.[400] It told at once of the ever-growing demands of the post and the assiduity with which – at least in the capital – it was discharged. In 1721, the newly consecrated bishop of Down and Connor appreciated that good order, especially in the towns, depended on the right choice of the churchwardens.[401] About the same time, that perpetual Jeremiah, Archbishop King of Dublin, feared that the burden was deterring the substantial from becoming churchwardens. He repeated a warning that 'these are employments that are either not so honourable or not so easy as to invite men of figure to undertake them'.[402] As usual, the archbishop's gloom was at odds with the facts. In the city of Derry in the 1750s, a reluctance to serve owing to 'the trouble and difficulty of the office' was reported, but then overcome.[403] In Dublin itself, notables alternated with solid merchants and craftsmen as churchwardens.

In rural communities where Protestants were sparse, adequate officers were harder to find. In the parish of Agher in County Meath, local squires served their turns as churchwardens, but in 1754 the lot fell on two, apparently functionally illiterate.[404] Another hazard lay in the eligibility for parish offices of all householders regardless of confessional alignment. In 1698, it was averred that most churchwardens were Catholics: a situation which may have dissuaded the government from delegating too much to them.[405] Dean Henry Maule, during his incumbencies in the city of Cork, cooperated with a vestry composed of professionals, traders and craftsmen. Visiting his country living in the north of County Cork, at Mourne Abbey, a 'very popish country', he was faced with a throng of Catholics at a vestry meeting. 'There, by a majority of voices, they claimed their right of voting as parishioners against the usual annual rate.' Maule retaliated by tendering the oaths of abjuration and allegiance to those present. With satisfaction, he reported that 'they soon cried *peccavi*, paid their fines and left the affairs of the church and parish to run in the proper channel'. Fearful that not all his clerical colleagues would resist so forcefully, Maule promoted a statute to guarantee that thereafter affairs did follow the 'proper' channels.[406] In 1725, Catholics were statutorily debarred from voting in vestries convened to sanction church repairs.[407]

Elsewhere, Presbyterians troubled incumbents. At Bangor in County Down, they invaded a Church of Ireland vestry to block further taxes intended to embellish the parish church.[408] In Dublin, too, a proposal to add a spire to St Catherine's church provoked dissent. The project, likely to burden the already straitened parishioners, was attributed to a covetous ironmonger, timber merchant and coffin-maker. It also owed something to Presbyterians and Quakers who voted in the vestry: interference, which led to calls that henceforward the dissenters should be excluded.[409] Concern about the ability of the parish to tax and spend provoked a squib of the 1750s that envisaged a figure who had never been in church, 'other than to a vestry to stop salaries or hinder repairs'.[410] Not until the 1770s did a statute debar Protestant nonconformists from voting at vestry meetings.

The debarred found substitutes. Presbyterians through the kirk sessions and Catholics through their parishes regulated (or attempted to regulate) the morals of their congregations, educated the young and aided the poor, infirm and aged. Disappointingly the communal labours, a useful initiation into public service, did not entitle Catholics and Protestant nonconformists to full citizenship. However, the condition of the two biggest groups of the excluded was not identical. Protestant dissenters had a ladder – maybe unsteady – to climb into urban affairs and benevolent voluntaryism. For Catholics, no matter how cultivated or peaceable, there was nothing to occupy them in the public sphere. Frustrations understandably built up and, by the late eighteenth century, would unsettle the country.

Relieving the poor pushed up church rates and annual spending and thickened routine business. Ireland lacked an equivalent of the English statute of 1601 for a concerted assault on poverty.[411] Notwithstanding this gap, the parish was the obvious focus of charity. Irish attitudes and responses matched those in England. Generosity should begin at home. Natives or residents of the parish had first call on its resources. Those most regularly and generously helped were dutiful members of the congregation. Parsimony and confessional discriminations were occasionally conquered by humanity. A Cork preacher reminded his auditors of the 'indispensable obligation [which] lies on every Christian to extend his bounty, as well as his charity, unto every person whom he sees in want'.[412] Surrounded by potential recipients of alms, normally the only practicable solution, adopted also by dissenters and Catholics, was to help those known through membership of the same confessional community. Nevertheless, in emergencies, as in 1720–1, 1729 or 1740–1, the requirements might be waived.[413]

Dublin, harbouring a dense and indigent population, posed intractable problems of poverty. The parishes of St Catherine and St James included parts of the liberties where many textile-workers lived. The operatives were especially prone to trade recession. Despite the possibility of thousands being reduced to poverty, the lists of those allowed parochial relief in the later seventeenth century were short. Fresh crises in the 1720s saw help directed towards the young. In 1728, £120 from a budget of £319 was spent on the foundling or orphan children. The proportion devoted to this work varied from year to year, but always constituted the largest single charge on parish funds. Further assistance was given by employing a schoolmaster, occasionally paying the fees to apprentice youths, and by subsidizing medicines.[414] Many parishes fixed the number of poor regularly to be assisted at between eight and 20.[415] One church in Dublin, St Michan's, specified three categories of beneficiaries: 'reduced' housekeepers (the formerly respectable who through illness or age had fallen on hard times); the poor and sick; and the stated poor. The last group numbered 19 in the 1720s; the other two each fluctuated around 30.[416]

There was a universal reluctance to take responsibility for strangers, unless to return them to their places of origin or – in extreme cases – to bury them at the public charge. Parishes, especially in the larger towns, experimented as how best to help the deserving within their precincts. Schemes were copied from neighbouring districts, other Irish towns, England and continental Europe.[417] Parish worthies gathered and digested information and chose the meritorious. Selection empowered the few. In the mid-eighteenth century, one commentator wrote that 'the common people make as much interest to be put on the list of the parish poor, and be authorized to starve upon charity as their landlords and squires do to get a place or a salary'.[418] The vestry, as it spawned sub-committees and the inner group in the select vestry, differentiated the members of the Protestant interest. The trend towards the few engrossing power was balanced by the semblance of equality which survived among all heads of households within the parish. Each remained eligible for the annual chores.

Church of Ireland congregations seldom reared an alternative hierarchy based on spiritual worth against the one which prevailed in civil society. In practice, the solid and respectable dominated church life. Inside the churches, pews were sold or rented to those who could pay. Seating was also organized according to social rank and income. Generally, the poor either had to stand or stayed away. In 1733, 34,000 of Dublin's estimated 45,000 conformists lacked spaces in which to worship should they wish to do so.[419] Dissenting meeting-houses did not eschew worldly worth as the basis of allocating places. At Dawson Bridge in the Presbytery of the Route (County Antrim), it was stated in 1701 that 'each man in his own proportion have the choice of seats according to his payment'.[420] In other respects, functional equality was stronger among household heads in the nonconformist congregations. Male subscribers in dissenting churches were balloted on whom they would prefer as the next minister.[421] In the kirk session of Connor, elders went from house to house to canvas preferences for empty elderships. Such actions could not be paralleled in Church of Ireland or Catholic parishes.[422] In Catholic chapels, seigneurial insistence on proprietary rights to particular seats close to the altar survived.[423]

There was some scope in the parish for cooperation across denominational boundaries. Evidence of the cool welcome for Catholics and dissenters when they appeared at Church of Ireland vestries suggests that such encounters aggravated rather than alleviated resentments. Those with voracious appetites for public works hastened from manor court to parish meeting, and then on to the Dublin Society, the masonic lodge, the turnpike trust, the boards of hospital or school, before sitting on the grand jury, magistrates' bench or in parliament itself. Parish duties, alone and in combination with the other activities, made manifest the Church of Ireland dominance. One group could not ride to respectability on the back of parish offices. Women as heads of households were rated; they also owned pews.[424] By virtue of their status as householders, they might be entitled, as in eighteenth-century England, to attend the vestry. The one woman known to have done so in Ireland, Lady Orrery at Caledon (County Tyrone) in 1752, came – it seems – on behalf of her absent husband.[425] Otherwise, there was no obvious opening for women in the institutional life of the Church of Ireland. Yet, their prominence as worshippers was noted, and even mocked.[426] Informally, female preferences, in popularizing specific charities, in upholding domestic and conjugal virtues, even in favouring certain styles of preaching, could be powerful. Other than the rare pious exemplar, such as Lady Arbella Denny, the place of women in the recorded life of the established church is hard to detect.[427] The same holds good – again with some notable exceptions like Katherine Conolly, the wife of the Speaker – for their participation in the public life of the secular state.[428] Matters were hardly better in Presbyterian kirk sessions, dissenting congregations and Catholic parishes. In the last, female sodalities may have allowed women a distinctive role, as did the small convents, akin to private houses, which by the 1730s had shadowy existences. Only the Quaker women with separate meetings enjoyed a measure of control over their devotional life.[429]

Trades, crafts, soldiering, the sea and farming offered precarious livelihoods to those below the upper levels of Protestant Ireland. There was little visibly to distinguish the middling and poor of the Church of Ireland from their Catholic and nonconformist counterparts. Incomes were small, possessions few, diet monotonous, housing rudimentary or worse, and the need to find supplements constant. In these conditions, tokens were important in allowing denominations to differentiate themselves one from another. The rituals and society of the several churches offered ways in which to assert and conserve distinctive identities. Geographical and ethnic origins might be cherished and expressed through modes of building, dress, address and furnishing. However, the gradual spread throughout Ireland of fresh commodities and habits was erasing such markers. It is unlikely that by the early eighteenth century, it was possible immediately to identify the Old Irish or Catholics by outward looks. There was an instinct, especially among the hostile from England, to presume that the badly housed and dressed were Irish Catholics. The Protestant bishop of Elphin succumbed to this temptation when he dismissed a visitor as an arrant Irish trull. Soon he was embarrassed to admit that the drab was a penurious English woman.[430] Usually in daily exchanges, religious affiliation had to be inferred. Devotional trinkets, notably rosary beads – wooden, glass or metal – denoted Catholics. In 1760, a young Dublin artist drew papist criminals being carted to execution. Their confession, not itself the reason for their fate, was easily shown by the accessories of crucifixes and rosaries. Priests, monks and nuns, in contrast, wore lay clothing the better to escape detection and arrest.[431] Austere attire might announce Protestant dissenters, particularly the Quakers, who enjoined their members to abstain from worldliness. But, confusingly, it could also signify those indifferent to fashion or the indigent.

Denominational loyalties gave structure to lives outside the circles of the powerful. Protestant Ireland, as much as its Catholic counterpart, was shaped by the dead and departed. Through annual celebrations and informal festivals, the Protestants venerated ancestors who had died, so tradition maintained, at the hands of the Catholics. Trade, education, correspondence, travel, even occasional exile, kept alive contacts with Britain, Protestant and commercial communities throughout Europe, North America and – by the eighteenth century – also in Asia. Thoughtful Protestants conceived of themselves as a component in a community of the chosen. They were taught to regard themselves as members of a world not bounded by terrestrial constraints. Such thoughts may have heartened those otherwise likely to despair at their depressed condition. But it did little to alleviate physical privations or assuage fears.

These cerebrations complemented the material worlds of eighteenth-century Ireland. Opportunities for civic-mindedness and civility expanded. Money and manners commanded entry to modish coffee-houses, clubs, taverns, assemblies and private houses. Cheaper versions of these polite entertainments were soon invented. Alongside, sometimes overlapping with, these voluntary groups were others composed only of communicants of the Church of Ireland. Protestant dissenters were not altogether shut out from the associational life of the parish and the borough; Catholics were. The ambiguities in the situation of the Protestant nonconformists arose from disagreements over how best to treat them, as has been shown above (pp. 69–70). Dissent, no less than Catholicism, defied periodic persecution and thrived. In Dublin itself, among more than 2800 freemen listed in 1749, 14.5 per cent were Protestant dissenters. In the senior guild, that of the merchants, the percentage rose to 22.[432] Some zealots for the Church of Ireland were delighted at the evidence of attrition among the social leaders of dissent. Few squires, even in Ulster, still subscribed to Presbyterianism by George II's reign. This matched the erosion of Catholicism within the landed orders. In 1733, when a fresh bid to repeal the sacramental Test was made, supporters of its retention predicted that within 20 years, there would be no Protestant dissenters worth more than £100 p.a.[433] County surveys aimed to prove such predictions.[434] The returns, while confirming the lack of grandees, showed the alarming strength of the Presbyterians, Quakers and (later) Methodists, and once again disheartened the leaders of the Church of Ireland. The English Presbyterians and Quakers, progeny of the Interregnum, proved tenacious, but remained sparse. The latter may have had 6500 members by 1714. The Baptists, also offspring of the mid-seventeenth century, had dwindled to perhaps 1500 to 2000 by 1725.[435] From the 1740s onwards, the Methodists won many adherents, primarily from the older Protestant denominations.[436]

In the face of such resilience, the rulers of Ireland responded variously: lighten, lift or increase penalties. This mirrored strategies to deal with Catholics: those who viewed dissenters as the greater threat were suspected of generosity towards the Catholics, and vice versa. The Protestants' dramatic increase in their share of Irish land during the seventeenth century was not matched by the increase as a proportion of the total population. They amounted to 20 per cent or (at most) 25 per cent. Many – perhaps half – belonged to the Scottish Presbyterian kirk, not to the established Church of Ireland. In this way, the Protestant interest was splintered. Thanks to the Test of 1704, obstinate dissenters were consigned legally to limbo like the Catholics. Some escaped the sentence through occasional conformity: taking communion according to the Church of Ireland prescript once a year. Others moved easily between worship in the established and dissenting churches, seeing no fundamental differences in their practices and beliefs. Nor were the authorities always rigorous in insisting that the legal obligations should be satisfied. Nevertheless, a large majority of the population was denied full citizenship.

The largest contingent in Ireland consisted of Catholics. Want of property, and so of money and free time, doomed almost all to the frustrations of a life outside official institutions. As intended by English strategists, the longest established and most numerous body of inhabitants in Ireland had been reduced to 'hewers of wood and drawers of water'. Less noticed was the fact that the bulk of the more recently arrived Protestants were in the same condition. What secular tasks attached to the Catholic parish, especially when in Dublin and other towns it took on a fixed and continuing form, have hardly been discerned, so great has been the concentration on bishops, either absent and delinquent or heroic and diligent. The taste for chronicling the clergy, paralleling similar preoccupations among the historians of the Church of Ireland and dissenting churches, reflected both the prevalence among the authors of the clergy and the relative abundance of documentation. It matches the concern until recently with MPs, rather than those who elected them, and with landed patriarchs, not their wives, daughters, tenants, servants and urban suppliers. Even if efforts are made to retrieve the forgotten lives of the Catholic laity, it has mainly to be through the strictures of disapproving clerics or of Protestant officials.[437] Education, charity and even moral regulation may in the course of the eighteenth century have allowed the laity greater scope for useful and communal endeavours comparable to those of the select vestrymen in the Church of Ireland parishes.

From time to time, spies reported to knowing or nervous Protestants what was occurring in Catholic churches. Alarmist stories resulted.[438] Otherwise, what is striking about the routine correspondence of Protestants is the lack of reference to the Catholics who surrounded them. Comment tended towards generalities about the threats of popery, priestcraft, Rome, and the Romans' designs for absolute monarchy. Catholicism in the abstract, whether as political, theological or ecclesiological system, not Catholics as individuals, was discussed. In the 1670s, virulent tracts like Robert Ware's 'Rome's monarchical power blasted' inveighed against a political system of 'popery and papanism' and a doctrine regarded as anti-Christian or 'no religion'. Ware's terrors were excited by a moment when the authorities in Ireland smiled on Catholicism. Throughout this period, the worries lingered.[439] Champions of the Irish Protestant state warned in 1757 of 'Jesuitical subterfuges' to misrepresent and minimize what had happened in the 1640s. Any rewriting of Ireland's history in a mode more creditable to the substantial Catholics belonged to a bid to relax or remove legal penalties. A supporter of moderating the laws appealed to a 'common humanity' which 'would not suffer us to deprive the body of the people of all exercise of their religion'.[440] For the moment, the requests for greater generosity were rebuffed.

In their own households and on their estates, Protestants routinely met Catholics. Squire Edgeworth was evidently gratified when one of his servants, 'Will', converted to Protestantism. Individual conversions were celebrated, but by the eighteenth century only the most optimistic could contend that they augured the conversion of Ireland. Edgeworth, like his contemporaries within the Church of Ireland élite, presided over a household and estate and lived in a neighbourhood where Catholics predominated.[441] A feeling of difference remained palpable, and obliged the ascendant minority to wariness as well as arrogance. Between 1690 and 1760, the minority entrenched itself. Its successes in Dublin and the provinces never altogether disguised its fragility. A small group of privileged Protestants – the likes of Edgeworth – settled into a comfortable existence. A little of their cultivation and prosperity was diffused throughout their localities. However, Ireland was not transformed into the asset that Britain needed. Any state that excluded so large a proportion of its inhabitants from citizenship was storing up trouble for itself. Between 1760 and 1800, Britain, awakening to the Irish Protestants' failures, dismantled what had been so laboriously constructed and started to return Ireland's government to its Catholic majority.

Abbreviations

Barnard, *Ascents and descents*	T. C. Barnard, *Irish Protestant ascents and descents* (Dublin, 2003)
Barnard, *New anatomy*	T. C. Barnard, *A new anatomy of Ireland: the Irish Protestants, 1649–1770* (New Haven and London, 2003)
BL	British Library
Bodleian	Bodleian Library, Oxford
Chatsworth	Chatsworth House, Derbyshire
Christ Church	Christ Church library, Oxford
[C]RO	[County] Record Office
EHR	*English Historical Review*
HJ	*Historical Journal*
HMC	Historical Manuscripts Commission
IAA	Irish Architectural Archive, Dublin
IESH	*Irish Economic and Social History*
IHS	*Irish Historical Studies*
JCHAS	*Journal of the Cork Historical and Archaeological Society*
Johnston-Liik, *HIP*	E. M. Johnston-Liik, *History of the Irish parliament, 1692–1800*, 6 vols (Belfast, 2002)
JRL	John Rylands Library, Manchester
JRSAI	*Journal of the Royal Society of Antiquaries of Ireland*
NA	National Archives, Dublin
NLI	National Library of Ireland, Dublin
NLW	National Library of Wales, Aberystwyth

NUI	National University of Ireland
P & P	*Past and Present*
Petworth	Petworth House, West Sussex
PRIA	*Proceedings of the Royal Irish Academy*
PRO	Public Record Office, Kew
PRONI	Public Record Office of Northern Ireland, Belfast
QUB	The Queen's University, Belfast
RCB	Representative Church Body Library, Dublin
RD	Registry of Deeds, Dublin
RDS	Royal Dublin Society
RIA	Royal Irish Academy, Dublin
RSAI	Royal Society of Antiquaries of Ireland, Dublin
Statutes	*The Statutes at large, passed in the Parliaments held in Ireland*, 21 vols (Dublin, 1796–1804)
TCD	Trinity College, Dublin
TRHS	*Transactions of the Royal Historical Society*
UCNW	Department of Palaeography and Manuscripts, University College of North Wales, Bangor
UL	University Library
V & A	Victoria and Albert Museum, London

Notes

1   *Lands and Peoples*

1. P. O'Flanagan, 'Settlement, development and trading in Ireland', in T. M. Devine and D. Dickson (eds), *Ireland and Scotland, 1600–1850* (Edinburgh, 1983), pp. 146–50.
2. M. Brennan, 'The Smythes of Damma: a Catholic family in the age of the penal laws', *Old Kilkenny Review*, 4 (1989), pp. 614–17; L. M. Cullen, 'Catholic social classes under the Penal laws', in T. Power and K. Whelan (eds), *Endurance and emergence: Catholics in Ireland in the eighteenth century* (Dublin, 1990), pp. 57–83; L. M. Cullen, 'The Black-water Catholics and County Cork society and politics in the eighteenth century', in P. O'Flanagan and N. G. Buttimer (eds), *Cork: history and society* (Dublin, 1993), pp. 535–84; K. Whelan, 'The Catholic community in eighteenth-century Wexford', in Power and Whelan (eds), *Endurance and emergence*, pp. 129–64.
3. D. Dickson, 'Catholics and trade in eighteenth-century Ireland: an old debate revisited', in Power and Whelan (eds), *Endurance and emergence*, pp. 85–100.
4. 'A Briton', *The history of the Dublin election in the year 1749* (London, 1753), p. 9.
5. Ormond to unknown, 7 March 1678[9], Bodleian, Ms. Eng. Hist. C. 266, ff. 15v–16.
6. P. Fagan, *Catholics in a Protestant country: the papist constituency in eighteenth-century Dublin* (Dublin, 1998), pp. 31–7, 43–5; D. Dickson, 'The demographic implications of Dublin's growth', in R. Lawton and R. Lee (eds), *Urban population development in western Europe from the late eighteenth to the early twentieth century* (Liverpool, 1989), pp. 178–87;

D. Dickson, '"Centres of motion": Irish cities and the origins of popular politics', in L. Bergeron and L. M. Cullen (eds), *Culture et pratiques politiques en France et en Irlande XVIe–XVIIIe siècle* (Paris, 1991), pp. 106–7.

7. Hearth money return, Athlone [1724], PRONI, D 4218/L1.

8. Hearth money return, Galway city, 1724, PRONI, D 4218/L1; J. Disney to H. Maxwell, 19 Jan. 1724[5], ibid., D 1556/16/4/5.

9. Summary of hearth tax return, Limerick city, [1724], PRONI, D 4718/L1; S. J. Connolly, *Religion, law and power: the making of Protestant Ireland, 1660–1760* (Oxford, 1992), p. 149.

10. W. Henry, 'Hints towards a natural and typographical [sic] history of the Counties of Sligo, Donegal, Fermanagh and Lough Erne', NA, M. 2533, pp. 404, 433–4; H. Thompson, memoir, Bodleian, Ms. Eng. Hist. d 155; J. A. Oughton, autobiography, National Army Museum, London, Ms. 8808-36-1; N. Peacock, journal, NLI, Ms. 16,091; B. McCormack, *Perceptions of St. Patrick in eighteenth-century Ireland* (Dublin, 2000), pp. 34–54, 69–84; J. Richardson, *The great folly, superstition and idolatry of pilgrimage in Ireland* (Dublin, 1727).

11. J. Kelly, 'The Catholic church in the diocese of Ardagh, 1650–1870', in R. Gillespie and G. Moran (eds), *Longford: essays in county history* (Dublin, 1991), pp. 63–91; J. Kelly, 'The impact of the penal laws', in J. Kelly and D. Keogh (eds), *History of the Catholic diocese of Dublin* (Dublin, 1999), pp. 145–70; F. Ó Fearghail, 'The Catholic church in County Kilkenny, 1600–1800', in W. Nolan and K. Whelan (eds), *Kilkenny: history and society* (Dublin, 1990), pp. 197–248.

12. P. J. Corish, *The Irish Catholic experience: a historical survey* (Dublin, 1985), pp. 96–150; A. Forrestal, *Catholic synods in Ireland, 1600–1690* (Dublin, 1998); R. Gillespie, *Devoted people: belief and religion in early modern Ireland* (Manchester, 1997).

13. W. Gacquin, *Roscommon before the famine. The parishes of Kilcoom and Cam, 1749–1845* (Dublin, 1996), pp. 12–24; B. Gurrin, *A century of struggle in Delgany and Kilcoole: an exploration of the social implications of population change in north-east Wicklow, 1666–1779* (Dublin, 2000); V. Pollock, 'The household economy in early rural America and Ulster: the question of self-sufficiency', in H. T. Blethen and C. W. Wood (eds), *Ulster and North America: transatlantic perspectives on the Scotch-Irish* (Tuscaloosa and London, 1997), pp. 61–75.

14. Roscommon to Cork, 23 Jan. 1665[6], BL, Althorp Ms. B 5; *The economic writings of Sir William Petty*, ed. C. H. Hull, 2 vols (London, 1899), i, pp. 188–91.

15. S. R. Lowry-Corry, earl of Belmore, *The history of the Corry family of Castlecoole* (London and Dublin, 1891), p. 276; S. O'Halloran, *An introduction to the study of the history and antiquities of Ireland* (London, 1772), p. 290; *The secret history and memoirs of the barracks of Ireland*, 2nd edn (London, 1747), p. 32.

16. C. O'Hara, observations, NLI, Ms. 20,397; receipts, 1 July 1760, 21 June 1762, 4 July 1742, 5 Nov. 1762, NLI, Ms. 36,380; D. W. Howell, *The rural poor in eighteenth-century Wales* (Cardiff, 2000), pp. 66–81.

17. Finglas Vestry Book, RCB, P. 307.1.1; Barnard, *New Anatomy*, pp. 285–6; [Anon] *A vindication of the broad cloth weavers* (Dublin, 1749), p. 8; L. M. Cullen, T. C. Smout and A. Gibson, 'Wages and comparative development in Ireland and Scotland, 1565–1780', in R. Mitchison and P. Roebuck (eds), *Economy and society in Scotland and Ireland 1500–1939* (Edinburgh, 1988), pp. 105–16; L. Kennedy and M. Dowling, 'Prices and wages in Ireland, 1700–1850', *IESH*, xxiv (1997), pp. 62–104; F. D'Arcy, 'Wages of labourers in the Dublin building industry, 1667–1918', *Saothar*, xiv (1989), pp. 18–19.

18. D. Dickson, *New Foundations: Ireland, 1660–1800*, 2nd edn (Dublin, 2000), pp. 111–13.

19. 'An act that the king of England, his heirs and successors, be kings of Ireland', 1542, in *Statutes*, i, p. 176; R. Cox, *Hibernia Anglicana*, 2 parts, (London, 1689), i, sig. A3–[A3v].

20. W. Graham (ed.), *The letters of Joseph Addison* (Oxford, 1941), p. 161; *Statutes*, iv, p. 481, summarized in E. Curtis and R. B. McDowell (eds), *Irish historical documents, 1172–1922* (London, 1943), p. 186.

21. C. E. J. Caldicott (ed.), 'P. Darcy, An Argument', *Camden Miscellany*, xxxi (1992), pp. 242–3, 270–1, 306.

22. 'A series of eight anonymous and confidential letters to James II about the state of Ireland', *Notes and Queries*, 6th series, v, no. 122 (1882), pp. 361, 402; no. 131, pp. 2–4.

23. M. Perceval-Maxwell, 'Ireland and the monarchy in the early Stuart monarchy', *HJ*, xxxiv (1991), pp. 279–95.

24. V. Ferguson to H. Sloane, 10 Aug. 1715, BL, Sloane Ms. 4044, f. 84v.

25. The theme is explored by D. W. Hayton, 'Ideas of union in Anglo-Irish political discourse, 1692–1720: meaning and use', in D. G. Boyce, R. Eccleshall and V. Geoghegan (eds), *Political discourse in seventeenth- and eighteenth-century Ireland* (Basingstoke, 2001), pp. 142–68; J. Kelly, 'The origins of the act of Union: an examination of Unionist opinion in Britain and Ireland, 1650–1800', *IHS*, 25 (1987), pp. 236–63; J. Kelly, 'Public and political opinion in Ireland and the

idea of an Anglo-Irish Union, 1650–1800', in Boyce, Eccleshall and Geoghegan (eds), *Political discourse in seventeenth- and eighteenth-century Ireland*, pp. 110–41.

26. R. Lawrence, *The interest of Ireland in its trade and wealth stated*, 2 parts (Dublin, 1682), ii, p. 51; T. C. Barnard, *Cromwellian Ireland*, new edn (Oxford, 2000), p. xxi, n. 37.

27. [W. Henry], *An appeal to the people of Ireland, occasioned by the insinuations and misrepresentations of the author of a weekly paper, entitled 'The Censor'* (Dublin, 1747), p. 10.

28. D. W. Hayton, 'From barbarian to burlesque: English images of the Irish, *c.* 1660–1750', *IESH*, (1988), pp. 5–31; D. W. Hayton, 'Anglo-Irish attitudes: changing perceptions of national identity among the Protestant Ascendancy in Ireland, *ca.* 1690–1760', in *Studies in eighteenth-century culture*, 17 (1987), pp. 145–57.

29. Abp. W. King to Bp. W. Nicolson, 3 Feb. 1717[18], TCD, Ms. 2535/2, p. 77.

30. R. Howard, *A sermon preach'd in Christ-Church, Dublin, before the Incorporated Society for promoting English Protestant schools in Ireland* (Dublin, 1738), p. 21; T. Rundle, *A sermon preach'd in Christ-Church, Dublin, on Thursday, the 23d of October, 1735* (Dublin, 1735), pp. 25–34.

31. Travels of R. Black, 1727, PRONI, T 1073/2.

32. L. A. Clarkson, 'Irish population revisited, 1687–1821', in L. A. Clarkson and J. M. Goldstrom (eds), *Irish population, economy and society* (Oxford, 1981), p. 27; D. Dickson, C. Ó Gráda and S. Daultrey, 'Hearth tax, household size and Irish population change, 1672–1821', *PRIA*, 82, sect. C (1982), pp. 125–55. The earlier figures are more speculative than the later ones.

33. M. Symner, answer to interrogatories, Sheffield UL, Hartlib Mss, lxii (45).

34. D. Dickson, 'Buncrana and Derry in 1744', *Donegal Annual*, 9 (1970), pp. 233–6.

35. R. Smythe to W. Smythe, 10 Oct. 1747, 22 Dec. 1747, Smythe of Barbavilla Mss, private collection, Berkshire; E. B., *Frugal husbandry expressed in short rules and directions for the growth and improvement of hops* (Dublin, 1740); W. Ellis, *The practice of farming and husbandry in all sorts of soils* (Dublin, 1735); *A list of commodities imported into Ireland* (Dublin, 1752); S. Switzer, *A compendious method of the raising of the Italian brocoli, Spanish cardoon, celeriac, finochi, and other foreign kitchen-vegetables* (Dublin, 1729).

36. Dickson, *New Foundations*, p. 114.
37. T. C. Barnard, 'The Protestant interest, 1641–1660', in J. H. Ohlmeyer (ed.), *Ireland from independence to occupation, 1641–1660* (Cambridge, 1995), p. 238; Sir R. Cox, *Antidote*, 4 (1749), p. 13; J. Johnston, *Bishop Berkeley's Querist in historical perspective* (Dundalk, 1970), p. 152 (query 323); *Some thoughts humbly offer'd towards an union between Great-Britain and Ireland* (London, 1708), pp. 2–3.
38. [R. Boyle, earl of Orrery], *The Irish colours displayed* (London, 1662); [R. Boyle, earl of Orrery], *An answer to a scandalous letter lately printed and subscribed by Peter Walsh* (London, 1662); W. Molyneux, *The case of Ireland's being bound by acts of parliament in England, stated* (Dublin, 1696).
39. B. S. Ingram (ed.), *Three sea journals of Stuart times* (London, 1936), p. 196.
40. T. Barnard, 'Protestantism, ethnicity and Irish identities, 1660–1760', in T. Claydon and I. McBride (eds), *Protestantism and National Identity: Britain and Ireland, c. 1650–1850* (Cambridge, 1998), pp. 206–35; Hayton, 'From barbarian to burlesque', pp. 5–31.

2   Rebellions and Reconquests, 1641–1691

41. P. W[alsh], *The Irish colours folded* (London, 1662), p. 3.
42. N. Canny, 'In defense of the constitution? The nature of Irish revolt in the seventeenth century', in Cullen and Bergeron (eds), *Culture et pratiques politiques*, pp. 23–40.
43. J. C. Beckett, 'The confederation of Kilkenny reviewed', reprinted in J. C. Beckett, *Confrontations: studies in Irish history* (London, 1972), p. 53.
44. M. Ó Siochrú, *Confederate Ireland, 1642–1649: a constitutional and political analysis* (Dublin, 1999), pp. 27–54.
45. M. Ní Mhurchadha, 'Contending neighbours: society in Fingal, 1603–60', unpublished Ph.D. thesis, NUI, Maynooth (2002), pp. 368–9.
46. Ó Siochrú, *Confederate Ireland, 1642–1649*, p. 42; T. C. Barnard, '"Parlour entertainment for an evening": histories of the 1640s', in M. Ó Siochrú (ed.), *Kingdoms in crisis: Ireland in the 1640s* (Dublin, 2001), pp. 20–8.
47. P. Lenihan, *Confederate Catholics at war, 1641–1649* (Cork, 2001), pp. 222–3.

48. V. Morley, *Irish opinion and the American revolution, 1760–1783* (Cambridge, 2002), pp. 2–4; Ó Siochrú, *Confederate Ireland, 1642–1649*, p. 11.

49. Lenihan, *Confederate Catholics at war*, pp. 222–3.

50. J. Scott Wheeler, *Cromwell in Ireland* (Dublin, 1999), pp. 23–4.

51. W. C. Abbott (ed.), *The writings and speeches of Oliver Cromwell*, 4 vols (Cambridge, MA, 1937–47), ii, p. 127.

52. T. C. Barnard, '1641: bibliographical essay', in B. MacCuarta (ed.), *Ulster 1641: aspects of the rising* (Belfast, 1993), pp. 173–86; T. C. Barnard, 'The uses of 23 October 1641 and Irish Protestant celebrations', in Barnard, *Irish Protestant ascents and descents*, pp. 111–42.

53. J. W. Blake, 'Transplantation from Ireland to America, 1653–60', *IHS*, iii (1943); P. J. Corish, 'Two seventeenth-century proclamations against the Catholic clergy', *Archivium Hibernicum*, xxxix (1984), pp. 53–7.

54. Privy Council papers prepared for Sir G. Lane, NLI, Ms. 16,974, p. 17.

55. P. Lenihan, 'War and population, 1649–52', *IESH*, 24 (1997), pp. 1–21.

56. Scott Wheeler, *Cromwell in Ireland*, pp. 225–6.

57. S. R. Gardiner, 'The transplantation to Connaught', *EHR*, xiv (1899); T. C. Barnard, 'Crises of identity among Irish Protestants, 1641–1685', *P & P*, 127 (1990), pp. 39–83.

58. R. T. Dunlop, *Ireland under the Commonwealth*, 2 vols (Manchester, 1913), i, pp. cxxxvi–cxxxviii.

59. K. S. Bottigheimer, *English money and Irish land: the 'adventurers' in the Cromwellian settlement of Ireland* (Oxford, 1971), pp. 140, 162–3.

60. A. Clarke, *Prelude to restoration in Ireland: the end of the commonwealth, 1659–1660* (Cambridge, 1999).

61. T. C. Barnard, 'Settling and unsettling Ireland: the Cromwellian and Williamite Revolutions', in Ohlmeyer (ed.), *Ireland from independence to occupation*, pp. 265–91.

62. [J. Boyse], *Some impartial reflections on D[r] Manby's considerations, &c. and Dr. King's answer* (Dublin, 1687); W. King, *An answer to the considerations which obliged Peter Manby, dean of Londonderry … to embrace what he calls the catholique religion* (Dublin, 1687); W. King, *A vindication of an answer to the considerations* (Dublin, 1688); W. King, *A vindication of the Christian religion and reformation against the attempts of a late letter wrote by Peter Manby* (Dublin, 1688); P. Manby, *The considerations which obliged Peter Manby, dean of Derry, to embrace the catholique religion* (Dublin, 1687); P. Manby, *A letter to a friend showing the vanity of the opinion that every man's sense and reason is to guide him in matters of faith* (Dublin, 1688).

63. Abp. J. Vesey to dowager countess of Orrery, 9 July 1687, Petworth, Orrery Mss, general series, 30.

64. HMC, *Ormonde Mss*, new series, vii, pp. 346, 347, 355, 364, 370.

65. Petition, 24 Jan. 1686[7]; licence, 29 Jan. 1686[7], TCD, MUN P/1/ 521; J. Bonnell to J. Strype, 17 April 1686, Cambridge UL, Add. Ms. 1/60; J. Hall to dowager countess of Orrery, 9 Feb. 1687[8], Petworth, Orrery Mss, general series, 30.

66. J. Hall to dowager countess of Orrery, 11, 18 and 22 Jan. 1686[7], ibid.; T. C. Barnard, 'The political, material and mental culture of the Cork settlers, 1649–1700', in Barnard, *Ascents and descents*, pp. 35–83.

67. Reflections on Restoration politics attributed to Lord Mountjoy, Dublin Public Library, Gilbert Mss. 207, 227; P. W[alsh], *The Irish colours folded*, p. 12; Barnard, 'The Protestant interest, 1641–1660', pp. 232–40.

68. W. Harris, *Fiction unmasked* (Dublin, 1752), p. 208.

69. Many reports of these seizures are in the Dopping correspondence, vols 1 and 2 in the Armagh Public Library.

70. List of Catholics sworn as freemen of Limerick, 1672, V & A, Orrery Mss, 1, f. 37; Lord Conway to ?D. Muschamp, 8 March 1672[3], de Vesci Mss, H/15, formerly at Damer House, Roscrea, now in NLI; Barnard, 'Conclusion: settling and unsettling Ireland: the Cromwellian and Williamite revolutions', in Ohlmeyer (ed.), *Ireland from independence to occupation*, p. 274.

71. A. Dopping to abp. of Dublin, 25 March 1686; H. Gwither to A. Dopping, 8 and 10 May 1686; letter of information, 5 June 1686, Armagh, Dopping Mss, 1/51, 53, 54, 56.

72. W. Molyneux to A. Dopping, 19 June 1686, Armagh, Dopping Mss, 1/59.

73. R. Phillips to W. Congreve, 2 July 1691, NLI, Ms. 13,230.

74. Morley, *Irish opinion and the American revolution*, pp. 8–13.

75. *Schemes from Ireland for the benefit of the body natural, ecclesiastical and politick* (Dublin, 1732), p. 9.

76. W. S. Lewis (ed.), *The Yale edition of Horace Walpole's correspondence*, 48 vols (New Haven, 1937–83), ix, p. 401.

77. J. Evelyn, junior, to J. Evelyn, 29 May 1693, formerly in Christ Church, now in BL.

78. Abp. W. King to H. Dodwell, 17 Aug. 1709, 30 Aug. 1710, Bodleian, Ms. Eng. Lett. C. 29, ff. 126, 132.

79. Abp. W. King to S. Molyneux, 10 April 1714, TCD, Ms. 750/4, 260.

3   *Governing Ireland, 1692–1760*

80. Dunlop, *Ireland under the Commonwealth*, i, cxxxvii–cxxxviii; C. I. McGrath, *The making of the eighteenth-century Irish constitution: government, parliament and the revenue, 1692–1714* (Dublin, 2000), p. 53.

81. J. I. McGuire, 'The Irish parliament of 1692', in T. Bartlett and D. W. Hayton (eds), *Penal era and golden age: essays in eighteenth-century Irish history* (Belfast, 1979), pp. 1–32.

82. D. W. Hayton, 'Introduction: the long apprenticeship', in D. W. Hayton (ed.), *The Irish parliament in the eighteenth century* (Edinburgh, 2001), pp. 10–12.

83. The emergence of this system is traced in McGrath, *The making of the eighteenth-century Irish constitution*; and C. I. McGrath, 'Central aspects of the eighteenth-century constitutional framework in Ireland: the government supply bill and the biennial parliamentary sessions, 1715–82', *Eighteenth-Century Ireland*, 16 (2001), pp. 9–34.

84. Receipts, 10 Jan. 1743[4], 21 Jan. 1758, NLI, Ms. 36,380.

85. J. Waller to E. Southwell, 13 Dec. 1698, BL, Add. Ms. 38,150, f. 127; W. Snow to T. Forster, 16 Aug. 1700, Chatsworth, Snow letter book.

86. 'Hibernicus' [Sir R. Cox, the younger], 'Irish politicks or an historical record of proceedings of the house of commons of Ireland in the year, 1737', TCD, Ms. 586, p. 18.

87. T. Carter to Harrington, 19 Jan. 1748[9], PRONI, T 3019/1242; also E. M. Johnston, *Great Britain and Ireland, 1760–1800* (London, 1963), p. 280; Morley, *Irish opinion and the American revolution*, p. 77.

88. Receipt, 17 May 1762, NLI, Ms. 36,380.

89. P. McNally, 'Patronage and politics in Ireland, 1714 to 1727', unpublished Ph.D. thesis, QUB (1993), p. 78; Magennis, *The Irish political system*, p. 47.

90. McGrath, *The making of the eighteenth-century Irish constitution*, pp. 200, 213–14.

91. L. A. Clarkson and E. M. Crawford, *Ways to wealth: the Cust family of eighteenth-century Armagh* (Belfast, 1985), pp. 42–3.

92. Orders of 18 Aug. 1747, 24 April 1758, April 1761, 14 Aug. 1762, 10 Nov. 1763, minute books of Revenue Commissioners, PRO, CUST 1/43, p. 22; 1/61, f. 146; 1/67, f. 155; 1/73, ff. 34v–35; 1/79, ff. 63–3v.

93. Jasper Brett, *The sin of with-holding tribute by running of goods, concealing excise, &c.* (Dublin, 1721), p. 16.

94. Lunnell, memoir, NLI, Ms. 21,521; Brett, *The sin of with-holding tribute by running of goods*, p. 29.

95. W. P. Burke, *The Irish priests in the penal times* (Waterford, 1914), pp. 128, 171–2.
96. Connolly, *Religion, law and power*, p. 276.
97. E. Synge, *The Case of Toleration consider'd with respect both to religion and civil government* (London, 1726).
98. P. Fagan, *The diocese of Meath in the eighteenth century* (Dublin, 2000), pp. 11–12; HMC, *Ormonde Mss*, ii, p. 475.
99. Petition from House of Commons to Ormond, 13 April 1683, NLI, Ms. 4846/9; 'Matters for consideration', *c.* 1678, ibid., Ms. 2492, p. 15–16.
100. Connolly, *Religion, law and power*, pp. 263–313; C. I. McGrath, 'Securing the Protestant interest: the origins and purpose of the penal laws of 1695', *IHS*, xxx (1996), pp. 25–46; J. G. Simms, *War and politics in Ireland, 1649–1730*, ed. D. W. Hayton and G. O'Brien (Dublin, 1986), pp. 225–76.
101. McGrath, *The making of the eighteenth-century Irish constitution*, p. 53.
102. T. Barnard, 'Scotland and Ireland in the later Stewart monarchy', in S. Ellis and S. Barber (eds), *Conquest and union: fashioning a British state, 1485–1725* (Harlow, 1995), pp. 270–3; J. Child, *The army of Charles II* (London, 1976), pp. 203–4; J. Child, *The army, James II and the Glorious Revolution* (Manchester, 1980), pp. 58–76.
103. H. Hatch to Lord Palmerston, 20 Aug. 1733, Southampton UL, BR 142/1/3.
104. List of barrack-masters, 1703, TCD, Ms. 1179; H. Walpole to C. Delafaye, 31 Aug. 1720, Lincolnshire CRO, ASW 1/B/43; lists of barracks, 1725, 1726, BL, Add. Ms. 23,636, ff. 17, 32, 39; J. Jackson to R. Baldwin, 27 May 1731, 9 June 1731, NLW, Powis Castle correspondence, 912, 913; proposals for building barracks on Herberts's lands in Co. Kerry, *c.* 1731, ibid., Powis Castle deeds, 14676–9; R. Lascelles, *Liber munerum publicorum Hiberniae*, 2 vols (London, 1824–30), ii, part vii, pp. 77–9.
105. J. Dennis to E. Southwell, 31 July 1722, NUI, Cork, Boole Library, Kinsale Manorial Papers, U/20; F. Lascelles to M. Ward, 12 Feb. 1727[8], PRONI, D 2092/1/3/235; E. P. McParland, 'The office of surveyor general in Ireland in the eighteenth century', *Architectural History*, 38 (1995), pp. 91–9; *Rules, orders, powers and directions for the good government and preservation of the army in Ireland* (Dublin, 1726); *The secret history and memoirs of the barracks of Ireland*, 2nd edn (London, 1747).

106. J. P. Greene, *Peripheries and center: constitutional development in the extended politics of the British Empire and the United States, 1607–1788* (Athens, GA, 1986), p. 44.

107. Thompson, autobiography, Bodleian, Ms. Eng Hist d 155; J. Wight, journal, Friends' Historical Library, Dublin; T. C. Barnard, 'Athlone, 1685; Limerick, 1710: religious riots or charivarias?', *Studia Hibernica*, 27 (1993), pp. 61–75.

108. Lords justice to W. Blaythwayt, 16 Nov. 1697, 3 Dec. 1698, NA, M 2453; *The case of Sir James Jefferyes, Kt. in answer to the petition of the mayor, sheriffs and citizens of Waterford* (?1697).

109. 'Philopater', *A letter from a member of the corporation of Limerick, to his friend, June 12th 1726* (?Dublin, 1726), p. 2.

110. R. Hickman to H. Ievers, 14 July 1742, NA, M. 5992; *An express from Wexford, by this days post, giving an account of a bloody and desperate engagement* (Dublin, [1754]).

111. Abp. G. Stone to E. Weston, 21 Oct. 1748, PRONI, T 3019/1172.

112. N. Ross and B. Hall, 'The array of the militia in County Louth in 1745', *County Louth Archaeological and Historical Journal*, xxiv (1999), pp. 391–406; N. Ross and B. Hall, 'The array of the militia in County Louth in 1756', ibid., pp. 531–40; Barnard, *New anatomy*, pp. 54–5.

113. H. Ievers to Lord Inchiquin, 7 Nov. 1755; same to E. Brown and others, 10 Dec. 1756, NA, M. 5992.

114. Sir E. O'Brien to H. Boyle, 5 June 1741, PRONI, D 2707/A/1/11, 69.

115. A. Bilbao Acedos, *The Irish community in the Basque country, c. 1700–1800* (Dublin, 2003), pp. 33–4; T. O'Connor and M. A. Lyons (eds), *Irish migrants to Europe after Kinsale, 1602–1820* (Dublin, 2003).

116. *A dialogue between Dean Swift and Tho. Prior, Esq; in the Isles of St. Patrick's Church, Dublin … October 9th, 1753* (Dublin, 1753), pp. 70–3.

117. *A dialogue between Dean Swift and Tho. Prior, Esq,* pp. 101–2; S. Madden, *Reflections and resolutions proper for the gentlemen of Ireland* (Dublin, 1738), p. 77; T. Rundle, *A sermon preach'd in Christ-Church, Dublin, on the 25th day of March 1736* (Dublin, 1736), p. 20.

118. Howard, *Sermon preach'd in Christ-Church, Dublin, before the Incorporated Society for promoting English Protestant schools*, p. 17.

4 Parliament, Improvement and Patriotism, 1692–1760

119. E. McParland, *Public architecture in Ireland, 1680–1760* (New Haven and London, 2001), pp. 177–205.

120. R. Molesworth to Abp. W. King, 28 Sep. 1714, TCD, Mss. 1995–2008/1524.

121. Barnard, *New anatomy*, pp. 21–40; F. G. James, *Lords of the ascendancy. The Irish House of Lords and its members, 1600–1800* (Dublin, 1995).

122. Sir R. Cox to E. Southwell, 26 Nov. 1713, BL, Add. Ms. 38,157, f. 27; McGrath, *The making of the eighteenth-century Irish constitution*, pp. 243, 271; E. Magennis, *The Irish political system, 1740–1765* (Dublin, 2000), p. 82.

123. Hayton, 'Introduction', in Hayton (ed.), *The long apprenticeship*, pp. 12–13.

124. Diary of Winter of Agher, 21 Jan. 1762, 11 Oct. 1763, NLI, Ms. 3855.

125. Johnston-Liik, *HIP*; M. de Bombelles, *Journal de voyage en Grand Bretagne et Irlande 1784*, ed. J. Gury (Oxford, 1989), p. 232.

126. R. Gillespie, 'The Presbyterian revolution in Ulster, 1660–1690', in W. J. Shiels and D. Wood (eds), *The Churches, Ireland and the Irish*, Studies in Church History, 25 (Oxford, 1989), pp. 159–70; R. L. Greaves, *God's other children: nonconformists and the emergence of denominational churches in Ireland, 1660–1700* (Stanford, 1997), pp. 20–1, 161–2; P. Kilroy, *Protestant dissent and controversy in Ireland, 1660–1714* (Cork, 1994), pp. 25–9.

127. R. Ware, *The examinations of Faithful Commin, Dominican Fryar, as Sir James Ware had them from the late Lord Primate Usher* ([London], 1679), p. 2.

128. J. C. Beckett, *Protestant dissent in Ireland, 1687–1780* (London, 1948).

129. Lists of churchmen and dissenters in Ulster, RIA, Ms. 24 K 19; Lambeth Palace Library, London, Ms. 1742, ff. 49–56; D. W. Hayton, 'Exclusion, conformity and parliamentary representation: the impact of the sacramental test on Irish dissenting politics', in K. Herlihy (ed.), *The politics of Irish dissent, 1650–1800* (Dublin, 1997), pp. 52–73.

130. J. Bonnell to J. Strype, 25 Jan. 1698[9], Cambridge UL, Add. Ms. 1, 85; E. Riggs to R. Cox, 26 Dec. 1691, RIA, Ms. 24 G 7; Abp. W. King to Bp. J. Stearne, 25 Sep. 1714, TCD, Ms. 2536, p. 75.

131. P. H. Kelly, 'William Molyneux and the spirit of liberty in eighteenth-century Ireland', *Eighteenth-Century Ireland*, iii (1988), pp. 135–6.

132. D. W. Hayton, 'The crisis in Ireland and the disintegration of Queen Anne's last ministry', *IHS*, xxii (1981), pp. 193–215; J. R. Hill, *From patriots to unionists: Dublin civic politics and Irish Protestant patriotism, 1660–1840* (Oxford, 1997), pp. 70–8.

133. M. Jones to J. Bonnell, [1737], NLI, PC 435; I. Ehrenpreis, *Swift: the man, his works and the age*, 3 vols (London, 1962–83), iii, pp. 858–62.

134. Johnston-Liik, *HIP*, ii, p. 95.

135. PRONI, T 3161/1/4, reproduced in D. W. Hayton (ed.), *Ireland after the Glorious Revolution*, no. 227, with analysis; petition of John Blennerhasset to parliament, ?1661, TCD, Ms. 3821/285; *The case of James Lennox, esq; in relation to an election of a knight of the shire in the county of Londonderry* (?Dublin, 1697).

136. PRONI, T. 1522; Genealogical Office, Dublin, Ms. 443; NLI, Ms. 16,093.

137. R. Nutley to Sir T. Vesey, [Sep. 1727], de Vesci Mss, J/1, formerly at Damer House, now in NLI; J. Echlin to R. Smythe, 9 Dec. 1760, NLI, PC 448; F. Trench to S. Bagshawe, 22 Nov. 1760, JRL, B 2/3/809; R. Smythe to W. Smythe, 31 May 1748, Smythe of Barbavilla Mss, private collection, Berkshire; E. Magennis, 'Politics and administration of Ireland during the Seven Years' War, 1750–63', unpublished Ph.D. thesis, QUB (1996), p. 151.

138. Tripartite agreement of Sir M. Crosbie, A. Denny and J. Blenner-hasset, 6 July 1727, TCD, Ms. 3821/175; agreement of W. Flower and E. Deane, 15 Sep. 1727, NLI, D 20,237.

139. Lady Ranelagh to Bp A. Dopping, 15 April 1682, Armagh Public Library, Dopping Mss, 1/21.

140. T. C. Barnard, 'Reforming Irish manners: the religious societies in Dublin during the 1690s', in Barnard, *Ascents and descents*, pp. 143–78.

141. T. C. Barnard, 'Protestants and the Irish language, *c.* 1675–1725', in Barnard, *Ascents and descents*, pp. 179–207.

142. D. W. Hayton, 'Did Protestantism fail in early eighteenth-century Ireland? Charity schools and the enterprise of religious and social reformation in Ireland, *c.* 1690–1730', in A. Ford, J. I. McGuire and K. Milne (eds), *As by law established: the Church of Ireland since the Reformation* (Dublin, 1995), pp. 166–86.

143. D. W. Hayton, 'Patriots and legislators: Irishmen and their parliaments, *c.* 1689–*c.*1740', in J. Hoppit (ed.), *Parliaments, nations and identities in Britain and Ireland, 1660–1850* (Manchester, 2003), pp. 116–17.

144. *The secret history and memoirs of the barracks of Ireland*, 2nd edn (London, 1747), p. 23.

145. *A dialogue between Dean Swift and Tho. Prior, Esq*, pp. 15–16.

146. E. Magennis, 'Coal, corn and canals: the dispersal of public moneys, 1695–1772', in Hayton (ed.), *The long apprenticeship*, pp. 71–86;

D. Broderick, *The first toll-roads: Ireland's turnpike roads, 1729–1858* (Cork, 2002), pp. 34–83.

147. J. Kelly, 'Harvests and hardships: famine and scarcity in Ireland in the late 1720s', *Studia Hibernica*, xxvi (1992), pp. 65–106.

148. *The Dublin Society's weekly observations* (Dublin, 1739), pp. 6–7.

149. *A dialogue between Dean Swift and Tho. Prior, Esq*, p. 44.

150. McGrath, *The making of the eighteenth-century Irish constitution*, p. 77.

151. W. H. Crawford, *The handloom weavers and the Ulster linen industry*, 2nd edn (Belfast, 1994); L. M. Cullen, *Anglo-Irish trade, 1660–1800* (Manchester, 1968), pp. 58–66; Dickson, *New foundations*, pp. 138–41.

152. List of Linen Board Trustees, *c.* 1727, NA, M. 2537, pp. 272–5.

153. NA, M. 2537, pp. 272–5; [James Corry], *Precedents and abstracts*, p. 1; H. D. Gribbon, 'The Irish linen board, 1711–1828', in L. M. Cullen and T. C. Smout (eds), *Comparative aspects of Scottish and Irish economic and social history, 1600–1900* (Edinburgh, 1977), pp. 77–87.

154. [Corry], *Precedents and abstracts* , pp. 66, 115, 129–30.

155. W. Crosbie to Sir M. Crosbie 26 April 1753, NLI, Talbot-Crosbie Mss, folder 53.

156. R. Smythe to W. Smythe, 13 March 1730[1], Smythe Mss, private collection, Berkshire.

157. *The Great Importance of the Shannon Navigation to the Whole Kingdom of Ireland* (Dublin, 1746), p. 12; *Particulars relating to the life and character of the late Brockhill Newburgh, esq.* (n.p, 1761), p.23; *Remarks on the Present State of the Linnen-Manufacture of this kingdom* (Dublin, 1755), p. 16.

158. A. Dobbs, *An Essay on the Trade and Improvement of Ireland* (Dublin, 1729), p. 47.

159. Bp. E. Synge to Lord Limerick, 25 and 29 May 1753, 8 and 15 Dec. 1753, PRONI, Roden Mss, MIC 147/9; [W. Bruce], *Some facts and observations relative to the fate of the late Linen Bill* (Dublin, 1753), pp. 9, 14, 28.

160. RDS, Minutes, 6 and 13 Jan. 1731[2], 15 March 1738[9], 29 Jan. 1740[1], 12 and 26 Feb. 1740[1], 25 June 1741, 28 Jan. 1741[2], 30 May 1745; M. Dunlevy, 'Samuel Madden and the scheme for the encouragement of useful manufactures', in A. Bernelle (ed.), *Decantations: a tribute in honour of Maurice Craig* (Dublin, 1992), pp. 16–20; L. Slator, *Instructions for the cultivating and raising of flax and hemp* (Dublin, 1724).

161. T. Carter to Sir M. Crosbie, 1 June 1750, NLI, Talbot-Crosbie Mss., folder 32; same to same, 27 Aug. 1750, 17 Sep. 1750, ibid., folder 33; draft petitions of William Smythe to Linen Board, c. 1740, NLI, PC 449; [Corry], *Abstracts and precedents*, pp. 129–30.

162. RDS, minute book, 1758–1761, s.d. 4, 6 and 9 May 1758; *A letter from Sir Richard Cox, Bart. to Thomas Prior, Esq* (Dublin, 1749); H. Brooke, *The interests of Ireland considered, stated and recommended* (Dublin, 1759), p. 94.

163. [Corry], *Precedents and abstracts*, pp. 11, 45, 50, 52, 73, 74, 77, 94, 96, 101, 102, 109, 117.

164. J. Kelly (ed.), *The letters of Lord Chief Baron Edward Willes to the earl of Warwick, 1757–1762* (Aberystwyth, 1990), p. 95.

165. Hume, report on Wentworth estate, c. 1732, NLI, Ms. 6054; *An essay on the antient and modern state of Ireland* (Dublin, 1759); R. J. S. Hoffman (ed.), *Edmund Burke, New York agent, with his letters to the New York Assembly and intimate correspondence with Charles O'Hara*, Memoirs of the American Philosophical Society, 41 (Philadelphia, 1956), pp. 281–4.

166. P. Delany to M. Ward, 1 June 1746, PRONI, D 2092/1/7/33; 13 Geo. II, c. viii; *Statutes*, vi, pp. 506–14.

167. PRONI, D 695/51; D 695/M; C. Casey, 'Books and builders: a bibliographical approach to Irish eighteenth-century architecture', unpublished Ph.D. thesis, 2 vols (Dublin, 1991), i, pp. 202–4; *Hydrographia Hibernica*, (Dublin, 1710); Hayton (ed.), *Ireland after the Glorious Revolution*, no. 229; W. A. McCutcheon, *The industrial archaeology of Northern Ireland* (Antrim, 1980), pp. 52–3.

168. Casey, 'Books and builders', i, pp. 205–7; R. Delany, *A celebration of 250 years of Ireland's inland waterways* (Belfast, 1986), p. 11.

169. T. Carter to Sir M. Crosbie, 27 Aug. 1750, NLI, Talbot-Crosbie Mss, folder 33; T. Smythe to ?R. Smythe, 11 Nov. 1755, NLI, PC 448; J. Ponsonby to Sir T. Taylor, before 6 Sep. 1760, NLI, Headfort Mss, F/5/49.

170. S. Bagshawe to Hartington, 23 Jan. 1752, JRL, B 15/1/25; T. Smythe to R. Smythe, 11 Nov. 1755, 15 Dec. 1755, NLI, PC 448/38; McCutcheon, *The industrial archaeology of Northern Ireland*, pp. 49–52.

171. 'Publicola', *The Irish collieries and canal defended* (Dublin, 1752), p. 21; *Reasons why the canal for the inland navigation from the Shannon to Dublin, should be cut thro' the Bog of Allen* (Dublin, 1756), pp. 9–11.

172. *A Letter to a Member of the Irish Parliament relative to the Present State of Ireland* (London, [1755]), p. 10.

173. G. Westgate to O. St George, 11 April 1730, PRO, C 110/46, 807; W. Colles to R. Griffiths, 12 Dec. 1751; same to J. Perry, 15 Nov. 1753, NA, Prim Mss, 87.

174. Lease of 25 Oct. 1706; sale by R. Whaley to T. Pierson, 5 Feb. 1719[20], IAA, Castletown deposit, box 47; papers relating to Drumglass colliery, including receipt of 26 March 1754; and Abp. J. Ryder to A. Hill, 29 March 1758, Denbighshire RO, DD/BK/I/321; Johnston-Liik, *HIP*, vi, pp. 36–7; [Anon] *A letter to a commissioner of the inland navigation concerning the Tyrone collieries* (Dublin, 1752); McCutcheon, *An industrial archaeology of Northern Ireland*, p. 49, 58–65; Francis Seymour, *Remarks on the scheme for supplying Dublin with coals* (Belfast, 1729).

175. *A list of commodities imported into Ireland* (Dublin, 1752).

176. B. Boydell, *A Dublin musical calendar, 1700–1760* (Dublin, 1988), pp. 81–3; D. Hunter, 'The audience for Handel's *Messiah*', forthcoming. (I am grateful to David Hunter for allowing me to read his article in advance of its publication.)

177. H. Boyle to Sir M. Crosbie, 23 March 1748[9], NLI, Talbot-Crosbie Mss, folder 46; *An account of the life, character, and parliamentary conduct of the Right Honourable Henry Boyle, esq.* (Dublin, ?1754); *The pr-te vindicated and the affairs of I-d set in a true light in a letter from the honourable Hellen O'Roon* (Dublin and London, 1754), pp. 16, 23.

178. Minutes of the Barber-Surgeons' Company, s.d. 23 July 1750, TCD, Ms. 1447/8/1, f. 113v; T. C. Barnard, *The abduction of a Limerick heiress: political and social relations in mid-eighteenth-century Ireland* (Dublin, 1998), pp. 37–9; C. Massy, *A collection of resolutions, queries, &c. wrote on the occasion of the present dispute in the city of Limerick* (Limerick, 1769); E. O'Flaherty, 'Urban politics and municipal reform in Limerick, 1723–62', *Eighteenth-Century Ireland*, 6 (1991), pp. 112–19.

179. Rev. C. Massy to F. Burton, 29 Feb. 1739[40], 7 March 1739[40], Chatsworth, Devonshire letters, 1740–3, 273.0, 273.2; J. Potter to E. Weston, 27 May 1740, PRO, SP 36/50/443; Barnard, *New Anatomy*, pp. 91–2.

180. *An address from the independent electors of the antient, loyal and ever memorable town of Inniskillen* (Belfast, 1754), pp. 14–16; *Address from the independent electors of the County of Westmeath, to Anthony Malone, esq; late prime serjeant at law* (London, 1754), pp. 14–16.

181. Mss verses, 'When Liffey's silver tide shall backward run', Smythe Mss, private collection, Berkshire. For division lists circulating in England, see: *A list of the members of the Hon. House of Commons of Ireland, who voted on the question previous to the expulsion of Arthur Jones Nevill, Esq.* (London, 1753); *Insula sacra et libera* (London, 1753).

182. James Walton (ed.), *'The king's business': letters on the administration of Ireland, 1740–1761 from the papers of Sir Robert Wilmot* (New York, 1996), p. 62.

183. Hayton, 'Ideas of union', pp. 142–68; Magennis, *Irish political system*, pp. 67, 88.

184. M. Moore to J. Moore, 11 Dec. 1759, Brabazon Mss, private collection, London; S. Murphy, 'The Dublin anti-union riot of 3 December 1759', in G. O'Brien (ed.), *Parliament, politics and people: essays in eighteenth-century Irish history* (Dublin, 1988), pp. 49–68.

185. Michael Dalton, *The countrey justice* went through at least nineteen editions between 1619 and 1742.

186. Edgeworth accounts, s.d. 20 Feb. 1733[4], NLI, Ms. 1510, p. 97.

187. Edgeworth accounts, s.d. 8 March 1733[4], NLI, Ms.1510, p. 102; J. Corry to D. Muschamp, 10 April 1685, de Vesci Mss, H/8, now in NLI; Barnard, *New anatomy*, p. 217.

188. Edgeworth accounts, s.d. 29 and 31 March 1734, 1, 23 and 24 April 1734, NLI, Ms. 1510, pp. 104, 105, 106.

189. Edgeworth accounts, 2 April 1734, ibid., p. 105.

190. Edgeworth, accounts, 17 Dec. 1735, NLI, Ms. 1511, p. 73, account book of J. Pickard, Dorset CRO, D/BLX, B1, f. 40.

191. M. Smythe to W. Smythe, 2 and 5 Jan. 1733[4], NLI, PC 448; *Statutes*, vi, p. 220.

192. Account book of J. Pickard, Dorset CRO, D/BLX, B1, ff. 39, 40.

193. Edgeworth accounts, 23 Feb. 1735[6], 4 March 1735[6], NLI, Ms. 1511, pp. 81, 82–3; *Statutes*, vi, pp. 220, 311.

194. Edgeworth accounts, 1 and 25 June 1736, 22 July 1736, 13 Aug. 1736, 3 Sep. 1736, 13 Jan. 1736[7], 12 April 1737, NLI, Ms. 1511, pp. 114, 115, 119, 123, 127, 142, 157.

195. Crown entry book, County Dublin, 1 Dec. 1746, 14 Feb. 1747, NA; Edgeworth accounts, s.d. 23 Nov. 1746, NLI, Ms. 1517, p. 57.

196. Edgeworth accounts, s.d. 6, 7 and 10 May 1737, 16 and 24 Aug. 1737, 24 Sep. 1737, 18 and 19 Oct. 1737, NLI, Ms. 1512, pp. 21, 22, 39, 42, 48–52.

197. Accounts of D. Foulke, after 15 Nov. 1756, PRONI, D 1556/12/1/48.

198. Edgeworth accounts, s.d. 30 Nov. 1755, 26 Feb. 1756, 5 April 1756, 31 Jan. 1758, NLI, Mss. 1522, pp. 67, 110, 120; 1524, p. 58.

199. Edgeworth accounts, s.d. 18 Dec. 1749, 14 Feb. 1752, NLI, Mss. 1518, p. 190; 1519, p. 208.

200. Hartington's dinner guests, NLI, Ms. 1466; Edgeworth, accounts, s.d. 31 Jan. 1756, NLI, Ms. 1522, p. 106.

201. Robert, Viscount Molesworth, *Some considerations for the promoting of agriculture, and employing the poor* (Dublin, 1723), pp. 28–9.

202. Dublin City Library, Gilbert Mss. 207, pp. 11–18; 227, pp. 43–6; W[alsh], *The Irish colours folded*, p. 12.

203. M. Coghill to E. Southwell, 5 April 1733, 20 Oct. 1733, BL, Add. Ms. 21,123, ff. 33, 62.

204. H. Boyle to Sir M. Crosbie, 23 March 1748[9], NLI, Talbot-Crosbie Mss, folder 46.

5   *Rulers and Ruled*

205. D. W. Hayton, 'The beginnings of the "Undertaker System"', in Hayton and Bartlett (eds), *Penal era and golden age*, pp. 32–54.

206. RDS, Minutes, s.d. 10 Nov. 1737, 22 Nov. 1759.

207. Ormond to Rochester, 7 Jan. 1684[5], BL, Add. Ms. 15,892, 178, 182–2v; list of Irish privy council, 9 Jan. 1724[5], PRO, SP 63/385, 11–12; D. W. Hayton, 'Ireland and the English ministers, 1707–1716', unpublished D. Phil. thesis, University of Oxford (1975), pp. 43–5; *Hiberniae notitia* (Dublin, 1723), pp. 50–1.

208. Abp. H. Boulter to ?Devonshire, 16 May 1737, Chatsworth letters, box 1737–1739, 242.0.

209. W. Coughlan to W. Crotty, 16 July 1726, NLI, Ms. 13,246; A. Crotty to J. Coughlan, 25 July 1726; same to Captain Supple, 11 Aug. 1726; same to W. Coughlan, 11 Aug. 1726, Chatsworth, Crotty letter-book; E. Southwell to Sir T. Taylor, 29 July 1731, Headfort Mss, NLI, F/2/13; *Letters written by his excellency Hugh Boulter ... lord primate of all Ireland*, 2 vols (Dublin, 1770), i, p. 81.

210. Magennis, 'Politics and administration', pp. 183–4.

211. K. Whelan, 'An underground gentry? Catholic middlemen in eighteenth-century Ireland', *Eighteenth-Century Ireland*, 10 (1995), pp. 9–66, reprinted in K. Whelan, *The tree of liberty: radicalism, Catholicism and the construction of Irish identity, 1760–1830* (Cork, 1996), pp. 3–58.

212. H. R. French, '"Ingenious and learned gentlemen"- social percep-
tions and self-fashioning among parish élites in Essex, 1680–1740',
Social History, 25 (2000), pp. 44–66; M. Goldie, 'The unacknow-
ledged republic: office-holding in early modern England', in
T. Harris (ed.), *The politics of the excluded, c. 1500–1850* (Basingstoke
and New York, 2001), pp. 153–94; S. Hindle, 'A sense of place?
Becoming and belonging in the rural parish, 1550–1650', in
A. Shepard and P. Withington (eds), *Communities in early-modern
England* (Manchester, 2000), pp. 96–114.

213. M. Braddick, *State formation in early modern England, c. 1550–1700*
(Cambridge, 2000), pp. 136–75; D. Eastwood, *Government and
community in the English provinces, 1700–1870* (Basingstoke, 1997);
C. Herrup, *The common peace: participation and the criminal law in
seventeenth-century England* (Cambridge, 1987); J. Kent, 'The rural
"middling sort" in early modern England, *circa* 1640–1740: some
economic, political and socio-cultural characteristics', *Rural History*,
10 (1999), pp. 19–54; K. Wrightson and D. Levine, *Poverty and piety
in an English village: Terling, 1525–1700* (New York and London,
1979), pp. 73–185.

214. F. Bernard to E. Southwell, 24 Dec. 1725, BL, Add. Ms. 9713, f. 84;
J. Smythe to W. Smythe, 10 Oct. 1741, NLI, PC 449.

215. *Statutes*, iv, p. 27.

216. D. Mac Íomhair, 'Clergy and churchwardens of Termonfeckin
parish', *County Louth Archaeological and Historical Journal*, xvii (1970),
p. 84; Sheila Roe, 'The Roe family of Arthurstown, Charlestown,
Glack and Tallanstown, County Louth: their lives and times', ibid.,
xxiv (2000), p. 547; Lusk vestry book, RCB, p. 453.

217. Hoffman (ed.), *Edmund Burke, New York agent*, pp. 281–2.

218. W. H. Crawford and R. H. Foy (eds), *Townlands in Ulster: local history
studies* (Belfast, 1998); Johnston-Liik, *HIP*, iii, pp. 18–19; B. Ó
Dálaigh, D. A. Cronin and P. Connell (eds), *Irish townlands: studies
in local history* (Dublin, 1998); *Economic writings of Petty*, ed. Hull, i,
p. 215.

219. J. H. Andrews, 'Plantation Ireland: a review of settlement history',
in Barry (ed.), *Settlement in Ireland*, p. 149; A. J. Otway-Ruthven,
'The character of Norman settlement in Ireland', *Historical Studies*,
5 (1965), pp. 75–84.

220. Charles II's letter incorporating Charleville, NA, M 2449, pp. 74–6;
Ormonde to Abp. J. Vesey, 15 Sep. 1713, De Vesci Mss, G/10a,
formerly at Damer House, Roscrea, now in NLI.

221. W. H. Crawford, 'The significance of landed estates in Ulster, 1600–1820', *IESH*, xvii (1990), pp. 48–9, 58; R. Gillespie (ed.), *Settlement and survival on an Ulster estate* (Belfast, 1988), pp. lvi–lviii.

222. J. B. Hamilton, *Records of the Court Leet, manor of Dunluce, County Antrim, held in Ballymoney, 1798–1847* (Ballymoney, 1934).

223. Barnard, *Cromwellian Ireland*, pp. 249–54.

224. R. Gillespie, 'Finavarra and its manor court in the 1670s', *The Other Clare*, 25 (2000), pp. 45–8.

225. Misset to Blundell, PRONI, D 607/A/12, 16 Nov. 1723, 1725.

226. Second Lord Burlington to Bagge, Foulke, Power, 19 Nov. 1700, NLI, Ms. 13,255.

227. R. Smythe to W. Smythe, 24 April 1731, 26 June 1731, Smythe Mss, private collection, Berkshire; E. Curtis, 'The court book of the manor of Esker and Crumlin, 1592–1600', *JRSAI*, 59 (1929), pp. 45–64, 128–48; 60 (1930), pp. 38–51, 137–49; R. Gillespie, 'A manor court in seventeenth-century Ireland', *IESH*, xxv (1998), pp. 81–7; B. Ó Dálaigh (ed.), *Corporation book of Ennis* (Dublin, 1990), pp. 349–66.

228. H. Owen, papers concerning Castleisland, NLI, Ms. 7861, ff. 156, 164v–5; report on Ballynakill, 8 Oct. 1696, de Vesci Mss, H/18, formerly at Abbey Leix, now in NLI; W. J. Smith (ed.), *Herbert correspondence* (Cardiff and Dublin, 1963), pp. 236, 244, 248.

229. T. Samson to ?Ormonde [?1703], private collection, Co. Waterford; T. Doolittle to W. Smythe, 22 Feb. 1724[5], NLI, PC 448.

230. Lord Cork and Burlington to W. Congreve, 4 Sep. 1694, Chatsworth, Londesborough Mss. 1 (v) 15, Irish letter book, 1694; J. Taaffe to W. Smythe, 6 Dec. 1713, NLI, PC 436.

231. Bp. F. Hutchinson, account book, 1721–1729, PRONI, DIO 1/22/1.

232. Bp. F. Hutchinson, account book from 1729, PRONI, DIO 1/22/2.

233. Rowan account book, PRONI, D 1614/3, 21 Feb. 1672 [3], 4 May 1674, 14 Oct. 1674, 24 July 1676, 1 Oct. 1676, 25 July 1677, 4 June 1678, 17 Sep. 1679, 9 Jan. 1679[80].

234. R. Purcell to Lord Perceval, 27 July 1746, BL, Add. Ms. 47,002A, f. 56.

235. R. Fitzsimons to W. Smythe, 4 Sep. 1721, NLI, PC 445; E. French to same, 29 April 1721, NLI, PC 449.

236. C. Crofts to Sir R. Southwell, 19 June 1686, NUI, Cork, Boole Library, Kinsale manorial papers, Ms. U/55; J. Waller to ?E. Southwell, 20 Feb. 1701[2], National Maritime Museum, Greenwich, Southwell Ms. 19.

237. Lord Palmerston to L. Roberts, 22 Oct. 1723; same to B. Birne, 22 Oct. 1723, 11 March 1724[5]; same to Corkran, 31 Dec. 1724, 11 March 1724[5], Southampton UL, BR 2/4, copy book of H. Temple, 1st Viscount Palmerston's letters, 1720–1727.

238. R. Purcell to Lord Perceval, 26 Aug. 1746, BL, Add. Ms. 47,002A, f. 62v.

239. R. Lloyd to A. H. Herbert, 24 April 1718, NLW, Powis Castle correspondence, 847; R. Meredith to R. Davies, 30 May 1719, ibid., 853.

240. H. Hatch to Lord Blundell, 14 May 1747, 1 June 1747, PRONI, D 607/A/12.

241. J. Usher to Sir W. Abdy, 13 July 1743, NLI, Ms. 7180; Chatsworth, Lismore Ms. 36/136.

242. W. Conner to Sir A. Abdy, 22 Dec. 1753, Chatsworth, W. Conner letter book, 1749–58.

243. J. Usher to Sir W. Abdy, 13 July 1743, NLI, Ms. 7180.

244. Lord Perceval to W. Taylor, 6 Feb. 1730[1], BL, Add. Ms. 46,982, f. 12.

245. Chatsworth, J. Waite letter book, 29 Oct. 1706, 22 and 25 Nov. 1707; A. Spurrett letters, 23 March 1703[4], 1 Aug. 1704.

246. Sheffield City Archives, WWM A 759, pp. 398, 404, 419; Barnard, *Ascents and descents*, pp. 35–83.

247. Address from Co. Mayo, 1 Aug. 1724, PRO, SP 63/384, 171–8; address from Co. Cavan, 6 Oct. 1724, PRO, SP 63/384, 191; loyal addresses from Counties Clare, Tyrone, Louth, Londonderry, Cavan, Down, Westmeath, Limerick, Donegal, Fermanagh, Armagh, Leitrim, Longford, Waterford, 24 Sep.–14 Nov. 1745, ibid., SP 63/408/114, 124, 153, 179, 181, 183, 185, 187, 193, 202, 211, 213.

248. A. Smith to unknown, 20 May 1696; E. Hoare to same, 18 May 1696, PRO, C 104/12, box 1, pp. 2v, 3; Sheffield City Archives, A 759, pp. 398, 404, 419.

249. J. Ingram to W. Smythe, 27 Feb. 1736[7], NLI, PC 445; N. Evans to A. Brodrick, 29 March 1720, 8 July 1723, Brodrick Mss, Surrey History Centre, Woking, G145/box 98/1.

250. Sir R. Cox to W. Harris, 17 Feb. 1740[1], Physico-Historical Society papers, Armagh Public Library; *The great importance of the Shannon navigation*, p. 20; W. Harris, *The antient and present state of the County of Down* (Dublin, 1764), preface; [F. Hutchinson], *A Letter to a Member of Parliament, concerning the Imploying and Providing for the Poor* (Dublin, 1723), p. 9; E. Nicholson, *A method of charity Schools*, p. 34.

251. E. Spencer to F. Price, 14 Feb. 1743[4], 26 March 1744, NLW, Puleston
      Ms. 3580E; R. O'Flaherty to S. Molyneux, n.d. [1709], Southampton
      Corporation Archives, Molyneux Mss, D/M, 1/2, p. 130.

252. J. Hamilton to J. Bonnell, 20 Aug. 1739, NLI, PC 435/35.

253. H. Oxburgh to Sir L. Parsons, 10 Oct. 1687, Birr Castle Archives,
      Co. Offaly, A/1/149; 2nd Lord Burlington to unknown, *c.* 1700,
      NLI, Ms. 13,255; accounts of J. Crawford with R. Maxwell, s.d. 14
      Sep. 1749, PRONI, D 1556/16/14/17; R. Brown, accounts with R.
      Maxwell, 1762, PRONI, D 1556/16/11/15; T. Medlycott to ?H.
      Maxwell, *c.* 1725, PRONI, D 1556/16/4/20.

254. Indenture, 23 March 1686[7], PRONI, D 929/HA/F1/3/1; indenture,
      25 Feb. 1713, NLI, PC 346, box 2; C. Casey, 'Court houses, market
      houses and town halls of Leinster', unpublished MA thesis, University
      College, Dublin (1982); T. King, *Carlow, the manor and town, 1674–
      1721* (Dublin, 1997), p. 39.

255. A. Lock to Lady Ardglass, 15 Sep. 1688, and undated, PRONI, D
      970/1, pp. 18, 19; W. Conner to H. Boyle, 16 June 1741, PRONI, D
      2707/A/1/11, 75; J. Cooley to W. Smythe, 3 Feb. 1750[1], 31 March
      1751; same to R. Smythe, 10 Sep. 1758, NLI, PC 446; T. C. Barnard,
      'The cultures of eighteenth-century Irish towns', in P. Borsay and
      L. Proudfoot (eds), *Provincial towns in early modern England and Ireland;
      change, convergence and divergence*, Proceedings of the British Academy,
      108 (2002), pp. 195–222; McParland, *Public architecture*, p. 31 and
      plate 26; E. Parkinson, 'The vestry book of the parish of Down',
      Ulster Journal of Archaeology, xiv (1908), p. 149.

256. Journal of B. Fletcher, s.d. 23 Oct. 1684, private collection,
      Berkshire; E. Herbert to W. Hickman, [c. 1716], NLW, Powis Castle
      correspondence, no. 903; R. Smythe to W. Smythe, 22 Oct. 1751,
      NLI, PC 436; HMC, *Ormonde Mss*, iii, p. 454; King, *Carlow*, p. 32.

257. C. L. Falkiner, 'The counties of Ireland: an historical sketch of
      their origin, constitution and gradual delimitation', *PRIA*, xxiv
      (1902–4), pp. 170–93.

258. Sir M. Fenton to Cork, 12 April 1659, NLI, Ms. 13,228; Orrery to
      Cork, 6 May 1663, Chatsworth, Lismore Ms. 33/16.

259. R. Cox to ?J. Barry, 26 Aug. 1703, NLI, Ms. 13,247.

260. Anne Crosbie to W. Crosbie, 31 March 1733, TCD, Ms. 3821/194.

261. List of 1679, Bodleian, Carte Ms. 53, f. 162; lists after 1 Aug. 1714,
      PRO, SP 63/371, 17–18, 65–6; H. S. Upton, 'A list of the governors
      and deputy governors of counties in Ireland in 1699', *JRSAI*, lv
      (1925), pp. 36–53.

262. Lord Perceval to B. Taylor, 18 Aug. 1715, 17 and 20 Sep. 1715, 6 and 18 Oct. 1715, 12 Nov. 1715, BL, Add. Ms. 46,966, ff. 91, 97, 105, 106, 111v–12, 118, 123v; account book of O. Wynne of Hazelwood, 1737–1751, NLI, Ms. 5780, pp. 353–85; Barnard, *New anatomy*, p. 206.

263. Cf. J. M. Rosenheim, 'Party organization at the local level: the Norfolk sheriff's subscription of 1676', *HJ*, 29 (1986), p. 718.

264. R. Power to G. Roche, 29 Jan. 1683[4], Chatsworth, Lismore Ms. 33/126.

265. Account of H. Crofton, late high sheriff of Leitrim, 1682–3, NA, M. 2203; account of W. Flower as sheriff, Feb. 1733[4], NLI, D 20,234; W. Taylor to Sir J. Perceval, 23 May 1702, BL, Add. Ms. 46,964A, f. 14; S. Waring to M. Ward, 30 Nov. 1723, PRONI, D 2092/1/3, 66.

266. J. Bysse to R. Southwell, [1665], Boole Library, NUI, Cork, Southwell shrievalty papers; R. Edgeworth, Edgeworth accounts, 1741–2, NLI, Ms. 1515, p. 262.

267. Southwell shrievalty papers, NUI, Cork, Boole Library, Ms. U/55.

268. Memorandum on clause in the sheriffs' bill, *c*. 1729, PRONI, D 4718/L1; 10 July 1764, PRO, CUST 1/82, ff. 127–7v.

269. T. C. Barnard, 'Integration or Separation? Hospitality and display in Protestant Ireland, *c*. 1660–1800', in L. Brockliss and D. Eastwood (eds), *A union of multiple identities: the British Isles, c. 1750–1850* (Manchester, 1997), pp. 127–46; T. C. Barnard, 'Public and private uses of wealth in Ireland, *c*. 1660–1760', in J. R. Hill and C. Lennon (eds), *Luxury and austerity: Historical Studies, XXI* (Dublin, 1999), pp. 66–83.

270. N. Ogle to W. Smythe, 9 Feb. 1740[1], NLI, PC 436; Matthew Dutton, *The Office and Authority of Sheriffs, Under-Sheriffs, Deputies, County Clerks and Coroners* (Dublin, 1721), p. 586.

271. Southwell shrievalty papers, NUI, Cork, Boole Library, Ms. U/55.

272. Dutton, *The Office and Authority of Sheriffs*, pp. 257–60.

273. Hillsborough to Hartington, 4 Oct. 1755, Chatsworth, Devonshire letters, 414.4; Dutton, *The Office and Authority of Sheriffs*, p. 257.

274. Complaint against fees, Bodleian, Carte Ms. 36, f. 454; Sir W. Petty to T. Crookshank, 26 Sep. 1676, McGill UL, Osler Ms. 7612; J. Rutter to Sir W. Petty, 28 Dec. 1672, Petty Papers, 14, now BL, Add. Ms. 72,861; J. Waller to C. Petty, 9 March 1696[7], Petty Papers, 18, now BL, Add. Ms. 72,864.

275. J. Jones to W. Legge, 15 May 1664, 16 Sep. 1665; N. Jones to same, 23 Feb. 1668[9], 20 March 1668[9], 30 March 1669, Staffordshire CRO, DW 1778/I/i/134, 161, 266, 269, 270.

276. Sir W. Petty to T. Crookshank, McGill UL, Osler Ms. 7612.

277. J. Petty to J. Phillips, 6 June 1671; same to J. Rutter, 25 July 1671, Petty Papers, vol. 12, now in BL, Add. Ms.

278. Sir W. Petty to J. Rutter, 14 and 28 Jan. 1667[8], McGill UL, Osler Ms. 7612.

279. T. Waller to Sir W. Petty, 27 March 1675, Petty Papers, 16, now BL, Add. Ms.72,860; petition of Robert Marshall, ibid., D 7; J. Rutter to Sir W. Petty, 7 Oct. 1672, Petty Papers, 14, now BL, Add. Ms. 72,861.

280. Sir W. Petty to J. Mahony, 9 Feb. 1685[6]; same to Lord Longford, 26 June 1686, Petty papers, 17, pp. 26, 92, now BL, Add. Ms. 72,863; W. M. Brady (ed.), *The McGillicuddy papers* (London, 1867), p. xxviii.

281. J. Bonnell to J. Strype, 7 Dec. 1687, Cambridge UL, Add Mss. 1/59; 'Account of last assizes at Down', *c.* 1686, Bodleian, Clarendon Ms. 89, f. 102.

282. Petition of R. Moore to Arran, *c.* 1676, TCD, Ms. 10,721, ff. 114–15v.

283. Affidavit of Sir Edward Tyrrell, after 1690, Marsh's Library, Dublin, Ms. Z3.2.6/11.

284. Tyrconnell to J. Bellew, 20 Aug. 1687, NLI, Ms. 27,249.

285. W. M. Brady, *Clerical and parochial records of Cork, Cloyne and Ross*, 3 vols (London, 1864), i, p. li.

286. C. Crofts to H. Owen, 29 Dec. 1694, NLW, Powis Castle correspondence, 671; indenture between Sir R. Adair and P. McCormick, 29 Dec. 1725, PRONI, D 929/HA/F1/2/12; deposition of M. Purdon, *c.* 1743, NLI, PC 438; account of R. Maxwell and A. Browne, 21 May 1744, PRONI, D 1556/16/11/3; N. Garnham, *The courts, crime and the criminal law, 1692–1760* (Dublin, 1996), pp. 95–7.

287. Bp. S. Digby to 'cousin', 6 June 1691, RCB, C 6/1/26 (6), no. 23; another copy in Dopping correspondence, 2/188, Armagh Public Library.

288. A. C. Elias, jr. (ed.), *Memoirs of Laetitia Pilkington*, 2 vols (Athens and London, 1997), i, pp. 77–9.

289. N. Peacock, journal, s.d. 8 and 9 Feb. 1743[4], 4 March 1743[4], 9 April 1744, NLI, Ms. 16,091.

290. J. Thompson to W. Smythe, 1 April 1733, NLI, PC 445/12.

291. Cork and Burlington to D. Foulke, 14 Sep. 1695; same to Kingston, 12 Oct. 1696, Chatsworth, letter books of Cork and Burlington, 1695 and 1696; PRONI, D 638/18/45; J. Smythe to W. Smythe, 'Tuesday night', *c.* 1750, NLI, PC 449; 16 Jan. 1743, NLI, PC 436.

292. R. Molesworth to Abp. W. King, 7 Oct. 1713, TCD, Mss. 1995–2008/ 1470; T. Knox to W. Conolly, 28 July 1710, IAA, Castletown deposit, box 57.

293. F. Burton to Devonshire, 19 Nov. 1740, Chatsworth, Devonshire letters, 1740–3, 283.0.

294. J. Bayly to M. Ward, 4 Jan. ?1725[6]; F. Cuffe to same, 29 July 1727, PRONI, D 2092/1/3/138,196.

295. C. Colclough to A. Vesey, 1 July 1722, 26 Aug. 1722, NA, Sarsfield-Vesey Mss, nos 174, 179.

296. C. Colclough to A. Vesey, 26 Aug. 1722, ibid.; Johnston-Liik, *HIP*, iii, pp. 447–9.

297. T. Colley to Lord Digby, 26 May 1761, Dorset CRO, D/SHC, 3C/81.

298. M. Travers, *A justice of the peace of Ireland* (Dublin, 1750), pp. 87–8; N. Garnham, 'Local élite creation in early Hanoverian Ireland: the case of the county grand jury', *HJ*, 42 (1999), pp. 623–42.

299. N. Garnham, 'The courts, crime and the criminal law in Ireland, 1692–1760', unpublished Ph.D. thesis, University of Ulster (1995), p. 122.

300. Lord Grandison to ?Newport, 2 Jan. 1733 [4], 8 May 1734, Dromana, Co. Waterford, Villiers-Stuart Mss, T 3131/D5/1, 2.

301. C. Robinson, *The charge given to the grand juries of the city of Dublin and county of Dublin* (1749) p. 7. Cf. deposition about the Danish silver robbery, 1731, NLI, Talbot-Crosbie Mss, folder 150.

302. I am grateful to Dr Neal Garnham for these calculations.

303. Barnard, *New anatomy*, pp. 53–5.

304. J. C. Lyons, *The grand juries of the county of Westmeath from the year 1727 to the year 1853* (Ledenstown, 1853), unpaginated.

305. Grand jury presentments, Co. Tyrone, 12 Jan. 1673[4], BL, Stowe Ms. 204, f. 77; presentments at Waterford, 13 April 1708, Chatsworth, Lismore Ms. 35/46; J. Waite to T. Baker, 1 May 1708; same to C. Musgrave and T. Baker, 29 May 1708, ibid., Waite letter book, 1708–1710; Blair, 'An analysis of the Donegal Grand Jury Presentments', pp. 61–71; Brady, *Clerical records*, i, pp. xlviii–lv; R. Cox. *A charge delivered to the grand-jury, at a general quarter sessions of the peace held for the County of Cork at Bandon-Bridge, on the 13th of January 1740[1]* (Dublin, 1741); R. Cox, *A charge delivered to the Grand Jury at the Quarter Sessions for the County of Cork, held at Bandon-Bridge, on Jan. 14 1755* (Dublin, 1755); [F. Hutchinson], *A letter to a member of parliament concerning the imploying and providing for the poor* (Dublin, 1723), p. 9.

306. *The Case of the Grand Jury of the County of Down with relation to a petition exhibited against them … by Hugh Savage, esq. And David Echlin, gent … 26 October 1719* ([Dublin, 1719]).
307. Complaint against Abp. M. Boyle, 1673, NLI, Ms. 17,845.
308. HMC, *Ormonde Mss*, n.s, vii, p. 361.
309. Sir P. Rycaut to E. Cooke, 27 June 1686, BL, Lansdowne Ms. 1135/A/2, f. 42v.
310. S. W. Singer (ed.), *The correspondence of Henry Hyde, earl of Clarendon*, 2 vols (London, 1828), ii, p. 6.
311. Z. Sedgwick to J. Evelyn, 16 March 1693[4], BL, Evelyn Mss.
312. *Statutes*, vi, pp. 20–1; 7 Geo II, c. vi.
313. Lord Conway, Bp. J. Taylor and E. Rawdon to Ormond, 1 Aug 1663, Bodleian, Carte Ms. 32, ff. 740, 742.
314. Sir R. Cox to E. Southwell, 23 Dec. 1714, BL, Add. Ms. 38,157, f. 145 R. Smythe to W. Smythe, 23 Dec. 1714, Smythe of Barbavilla Mss, private collection, Berkshire.
315. Sir R. Cox to E. Southwell, 9 Oct. 1714, BL, Add. Ms. 38,157, f. 133; petition of the high sheriff, knights of the shire and some JPs of Co. Clare to Lord Chancellor Midleton, [1717], NA, M. 5992/33.
316. HMC, *Ormonde Mss*, n.s, vii, pp. 68–9.
317. J. Smythe to W. Smythe, 20 May 1732, 19 April 1733, 14 March 1733 [4], NLI, PC 449.
318. R.Fitzgerald to M. Crosbie, 13 Nov. 1750, NLI, Talbot-Crosbie Mss, folder 47.
319. HMC, *Various collections*, viii, pp. 274–5.
320. L. K. J. Glassey, *Politics and the appointment of justices of the peace, 1675–1720* (Oxford, 1979), pp. 15–17.
321. G. Rawdon to Lord Conway, 14 March 1656[7], PRO, SP 63/287, 39v.
322. R. Whitelaw to Bp. W. Smythe [1695], NLI, PC 436/24.
323. W. Peard to F. Price, 11 Jan. 1740[1], NLW, Puleston 3579E.
324. R. Cox to Lord Nottingham, 10 July 1707, Leicestershire CRO, Finch Mss. Box 4950.
325. *Journals of the House of Commons of the Kingdom of Ireland*, 20 vols (Dublin, 1796–1804), iv, s.d. 4 Dec. 1733, 1, 4 and 9 Jan. 1733[4].
326. *Statutes*, v, p. 416.
327. M. A. Hickson, *Selections from old Kerry records, historical and genealogical, 2nd series* (London, 1874), pp. 182–3; B. MacMahon, 'New light on "The Golden Lion" and the Danish silver robbery at Ballyheighe, 1731', *Kerry Archaeological and Historical Society Journal*, 24 (1991), p. 129.

328. J. Smythe to W. Smythe, 6 Jan. 1733[4], NLI, PC 449.

329. Bp. R. Howard to H. Howard, 2 Feb. 1735[6], NLI, PC 227.

330. 'Case of Mr. Nugent and Mr. Maguire', 1737, Chatsworth, Devonshire Letters, box 1737–1739; lords justice to Devonshire, 7 June 1737; Abp. H. Boulter to same, 7 June 1737, ibid.

331. R. Bolton, *A justice of peace for Ireland*, 2 parts, 2nd edn (Dublin, 1683), i, pp. 13–15; M. Dutton, *The office and authority of a justice of peace for Ireland*, 2nd edn (Dublin, 1727).

332. Sir C. Porter to T. Coningsby, 19 Nov. 1694, PRONI, D 638/18/29; Barnard, 'Reforming Irish manners'; F. Hutchinson, *A sermon preached in Christ-Church, Dublin, on Friday, November 5. 1731*, 3rd edn (Dublin, 1731), p. 27; J. Story, *A sermon preach'd before the Honourable House of Commons ... on the Fifth of November, 1737* (Dublin, 1737), p. 24.

333. PRO, SP 63/367/243.

334. Dumas to Shelburne, 4 May 1729, BL, Add. Ms. 72,903/90.

335. Journal of Fletcher, 1684, Smythe of Barbavilla Mss, private collection, Berkshire; R. Christmas to D. Muschamp, 2 May 1685, de Vesci Mss, H/8, formerly at Abbey Leix, now in NLI; R. Hedges to J. Dawson, 22 Oct. 1704, Bodleian, Ms. Top. Ireland, c. 2, p. 29; Hickson, *Selection from old Kerry records*, 2nd series, p. 147.

336. H. Hatch to Lord Blundell, 20 May 1758, PRONI, D 607/A/12; J. Wight, journal, Friends' Historical Library; T. C. Barnard, 'Sir William Petty as Kerry ironmaster', *PRIA*, lxxxii, sect C (1982), pp. 1–32; T. C. Barnard, 'An Anglo-Irish industrial enterprise: iron-making at Enniscorthy, 1657–1692', ibid., lxxxv, sect C (1985), pp. 101–44; [Corry], *Precedents and abstracts*, pp. 73–4.

337. H. Hamilton to S. Waring, 14 April 1711, private collection, Co. Down; T. Pakenham to W. Smythe, 'Friday', NLI, PC 449.

338. Barnard, *Abduction of a Limerick heiress*, pp. 36–7.

339. E. Spencer to F. Price, 1 March 1747[8], NLW, Puleston Mss. 3580E.

340. J. Cooley to W. Smythe, fragment, n.d. [early 1750s?], NLI, PC 446.

341. N. Garnham, 'The criminal law 1692–1760: England and Ireland compared', in S. J. Connolly (ed.), *Kingdoms united? Essays in the history of England, Scotland, Ireland and Wales* (Dublin, 1999), pp. 215–24; Garnham, 'How violent was eighteenth-century Ireland?', *IHS*, xxx (1996–7), pp. 377–92.

342. Hayton, 'Introduction', in Hayton (ed.), *The long apprenticeship*, p. 12; N. Garnham, 'Criminal legislation in the Irish parliament, 1692–1760', ibid., pp. 55–70.

343. Essex to Arlington, 16 May 1674, Bodleian, Add. Ms. C. 34, f. 118v; E. Magennis, 'The politics and administration of Ireland, 1750–63', p. 195.

344. Chatsworth, diary of the second earl of Cork, s.d. 18 Jan. 1657[8], Chatsworth; J. W. Blake, 'Transportation from Ireland to America, 1653–1660', *IHS*, iii (1942–3), pp. 267–81; P. Fitzgerald, 'A sentence to sail: the transportation of Irish convicts and vagrants to colonial America in the eighteenth century', in P. Fitzgerald and S. Ickringill (eds), *Atlantic crossroads: historical connections between Scotland, Ulster and North America* (Newtownards, 2001), pp. 114–32.

345. R. Gillespie, 'The transformation of the borderlands, 1600–1700', in R. Gillespie and H. O'Sullivan (eds), *The Borderlands: essays on the history of the Ulster–Leinster border* (Belfast, 1989), pp. 84–6; T. Morris (ed.), *A collection of the state letters of … Roger Boyle, the first earl of Orrery* (London, 1742), p. 88; M. Mulcahy (ed.), *Calendar of Kinsale documents*, 7 (Kinsale, 1998), pp. 39, 101–2, 104–7; *Statutes*, iii, pp. 321–5, 396–402, 7 William III, c. xxi; 9 William III, c. ix; R. R. Steele, *Tudor and Stuart proclamations*, 2 vols (Oxford, 1910), ii, no. 443a, 460a, 553, 902, 1292, 1482 (Ireland).

346. M. Ward, 'Observations on the new barrack scheme of Ireland', between 1745 and 1759, PRONI, D 2092/1/4, 38.

347. M. Mulcahy (ed.), *Calendar of Kinsale documents*, 5 (Kinsale, 1996), p. 10.

348. Hayton, 'Exclusion, conformity and parliamentary representation', pp. 52–73; M. Wall, *Catholic Ireland in the eighteenth century* (Dublin, 1989).

349. R. Day (ed.), 'Cooke's memoirs of Youghal, 1749', in *JCHAS*, ix (1903), p. 63; B. Kirby, 'Civic politics and parliamentary representation in Waterford city, 1730–1807', unpublished Ph. D. thesis, NUI, Maynooth (2002), pp. 78–89.

350. Dickson, 'Catholics and trade in eighteenth-century Ireland', pp. 85–100.

351. G. H, *A genuine letter from a freeman of Bandon, to George Faulkner* (Dublin, 1755), pp. 11–12; H. G, *A just and true answer to a scandalous pamphlet call'd a genuine letter from a freeman of Bandon to George Faulkner* (Dublin, 1755), pp. 6, 15.

352. *A letter from Patrick Taylor, of Bally-James-Duff to his cousin Jemmy in Dublin, upon a late paper war in the metropolis* (Dublin, 1749). See also: *A letter from a burgess of Monaghan to the parish-clerk of Ardbraccan* (Dublin, 1754); *A narrative of the dispute in the corporation of Kinsale, in*

a letter from a buff to his friend in Dublin (Dublin, 1756); *The adventures and metamorphose of Queen Elizabeth's pocket pistol, late of Charles-Fort, near Kinsale* (Dublin, 1756).

353. Barnard, 'Considering the inconsiderable', pp. 107–27.

6 Catholic Masses and Protestant Élites

354. Barnard, *New anatomy*, pp. 128–39; Fagan, *Catholics in a Protestant country*, pp. 77–100.

355. W. Dalton to T. Dillon, 5 Feb. 1727[8], NA, 1096/9/2.

356. R. Lloyd to A. H. Herbert, 15 March 1717[18], NLW, Powis Castle correspondence, no. 846.

357. 'Report on the state of popery, Ireland 1731', *Archivium Hibernicum*, i (1912), p. 11.

358. P. O'Connell, 'The early modern Irish college network in Iberia, 1590–1800', in T. O'Connor (ed.), *The Irish in Europe, 1580–1815* (Dublin, 2001), pp. 49–64.

359. P. Levinge to W. Smythe, 15 Aug. 1746, NLI, PC 449; Fr. White, Annals of Limerick, NLI, Ms. 2714, p. 120.

360. T. Daly to H. Owen, 19 April 1694, 23 Dec. 1694, 23 June 1698; C. Daly to same, 24 June 1698, NLW, Powis Castle correspondence, nos. 192, 212, 239, 251.

361. H. Fenning, *The undoing of the friars of Ireland. A study of the novitiate question in the eighteenth century* (Louvain, 1972).

362. W. J. Smyth, 'Ireland as a colony: settlement implications of the revolution in military-administrative, urban and ecclesiastical structures, *c.* 1550–*c.* 1730', in Barry (ed.), *A history of settlement in Ireland*, pp. 172–4.

363. J. Brady, *Catholics and catholicism in the eighteenth-century press* (Maynooth, 1965), pp. 5–73; P. J. Larkin, '"Popish riot" in south County Derry, 1725', *Seanchas Ard Mhacha*, viii (1975–6), pp. 97–110.

364. Fr. White, Annals of Limerick, NLI, Ms. 2714, p. 120.

365. Abp. H. Boulter to Newcastle, 11 June 1726, PRO, SP 63/387 209; T. Orpen to A. Herbert, 9 Feb. 1760; T. Hutchins to T. Orpen, 7 and 8 April 1762, NA, M. 1857; C. Massy to F. Burton, 29 Feb. 1739[40], 7 March 1739 [40], Chatsworth, Devonshire letters, box 1740–43, 273.0, 273.2; R. Purcell to Lord Perceval, 14 and 24 Feb. 1743[4], 2 March 1743[4], BL, Add. Ms. 47001B, ff. 45, 47, 49;

journal of N. Peacock, NLI, Ms. 16,091, s.d. 6 and 8 March 1743[4], 24 Nov. 1745; Fr. White, annals of Limerick, NLI, Ms. 2714, p. 114; *Seasonable advice to Protestants, containing some means of reviving and strengthening the Protestant interest*, 2nd edn (Cork, 1745).

366.   W. Macartney to M. Ward, 28 Oct. 1745, PRONI, D 2092/1/7, 43; J. H. Gebbie, *An introduction to the Abercorn letters (relating to Ireland, 1736–1816)* (Omagh, 1972), pp. 11–15.

367.   Crown entry books, city of Dublin, 24 Oct. 1745, 12 Dec. 1745, 12 Dec. 1748, NA.

368.   Thomas Rundle, *A sermon preach'd ... the.23d of October, 1731* (Dublin, 1735), p. 23; Edward Synge, *A sermon preach'd ... the.23d of October, 1731* (London, 1731), p. 29. The view recurs in, for example, Nicholas Forster, *A sermon preach'd ... November, 5th. 1721* (Dublin, 1721), pp. 11–12; H. Jenney, *A sermon preach'd ... the 5th of November, 1731* (Dublin, 1731), pp. 15, 18–20; J. Leland, *A sermon preach'd ... on November the 5th, 1728* (Dublin, 1728), p. 26; Edward Maurice, *A sermon preached ... the 23d of October, 1755* (Dublin, 1755), pp. 15–16; George Story, *A sermon preach'd ... October the 23d, 1714* (London, 1714), pp. 16–17; Joseph Story, *A sermon preach'd ... on the Fifth of November, 1737* (Dublin, 1737), p. 6; Charles Whittingham, *A sermon preach'd ... November the 4th, 1733* (Dublin, 1733), p. 23.

369.   J. Byrne, *War and peace: the survival of the Talbots of Malahide, 1641–71* (Dublin, 1997); R. Gillespie, 'A question of survival: the O'Farrells and Longford in the seventeenth century', in R. Gillespie and G. Moran (eds), *Longford: essays in country history* (Dublin, 1991), pp. 13–30; E. MacLysaght, *Short study of a transplanted family in the seventeenth century* (Dublin, 1935); K. Whelan, 'An underground gentry?', pp. 3–58.

370.   Rundle, *A sermon preach'd ... the 23d of October, 1731*, p. 23; Story, *A sermon preached ... on the Twenty Third of October, 1735*, p. 19.

371.   Fagan, *Diocese of Meath*, pp. 11–17; K. Harvey, *The Bellews of Mount Bellew: a Catholic gentry family in eighteenth-century Ireland* (Dublin, 1998); H. O'Sullivan, *John Bellew: a seventeenth-century man of many parts, 1605–1679* (Dublin, 2000).

372.   Bp. J. Evans to Abp. W. Wake, 21 May [1718], Christ Church, Wake Ms. 12, f. 267; T. Caulfield to K. O'Hara, 15 June 1703, NLI, Ms. 20,388; NA, Chancery Bill Books, 1682–7, 1692–6, 1710–12, 1713–16; Brady, *Catholics and Catholicism*, p. 35; T. Butler, 'Sir Toby Butler', *Journal of the Butler Society*, 5 (1973–4), pp. 361–76;

6 (1975–6), pp. 455–64; *An elegy on the very much lamented death of Sir Toby Buttler, Knight, Barrister at Law, [11 March 1720/1], aet. 78* ([Dublin, 1721]).

373. Sir H. Tuite to Bp. H. Maule, 12 April 1745; Bp. H. Maule to W. Smythe, 15 April 1745; NLI, PC 449; Johnston-Liik, *HIP*, v, pp. 183–7; Magennis, *The Irish political system*, pp. 34–5.

374. Abjuration of J. Radcliffe, 5 June 1703, vestry book, St Peter's, Dublin, 1686–1736, pp. 127–8, RCB, P 45/6.1; N. Carolan, 'Motives of conversion to the Catholic faith as it is professed in the reformed church of Ireland', NLI, PC 519; Barnard, *Ascents and descents*, pp. 179–207; J. Clayton, *A sermon preach'd at St Michan's Church in Dublin … upon receiving into the communion of the Church of England, the Honble. Sir Terence Mac-Mahon, Knt. and Barnet. And Christopher Dunn, converts from the Church of Rome* (Dublin, [1701]) R. Fanning, *A lost sheep returned home* (Dublin, 1705); *The recantation of Cornelius O Donnel, prior of Trim* (London, 1664); *The whole reasons and abjuration of the Roman religion by Father J. L. on Monday, the 9th of this instant Decemb. 1728* ([Dublin, 1728]).

375. *The recantation sermon of R[edmon]d A[rchbol]d, Esq; a professed Jesuit, put into metre* (Dublin, 1755), pp. 13, 16.

376. T. C. Barnard, 'The worlds of a Galway squire: Robert French of Monivae, 1716–1779', in G. Moran and R. Gillespie (eds), *Galway: history and society* (Dublin, 1996), pp. 271–96; D. A. Cronin, *A Galway gentleman in the age of improvement: Robert French of Monivea, 1716–1779* (Dublin, 1995); Johnston-Liik, *HIP*, iv, pp. 249–51.

377. D. H. Akenson, *If the Irish ran the world: Montserrrat, 1630–1730* (Liverpool, 1997).

378. N. Genet-Rouffiac, 'The Irish Jacobite exile in France, 1692–1715', in Barnard and Fenlon (eds), *The dukes of Ormonde*, pp. 195–210; R. Moulinas, 'James Butler, second duke of Ormonde in Avignon', in ibid., pp. 255–62; G. Rowlands, *An army in exile: Louis XIV and the Irish forces of James II in France, 1691–1698*, The Royal Stuart Society, paper lx (2001).

379. A. Bilbao Acedos, *The Irish community in the Basque country, c. 1700–1800* (Dublin, 2003).

380. L. M. Cullen, 'The Irish diaspora of the seventeenth and eighteenth centuries', in N. P. Canny, (ed.), *Europeans on the move* (Oxford, 1994), pp. 190–6; G. Henry, *The Irish military community in Spanish Flanders, 1586–1621* (Dublin, 1992); E. Ó hAnnracháin, 'Corkmen in the Hôtel des Invalides', *JCHAS*, 105 (2000), pp. 129–54; E. Ó

hAnnracháin, 'Irish veterans in the Invalides: the Tipperary contingent', *Tipperary Historical Journal* (1998), pp. 158–89; E. Ó hAnnracháin, 'Sidy Macnamara and sixty-two others: Claremen in the Hôtel Royal des Invalides', *North Munster Antiquarian Journal*, 41 (2001), pp. 1–22; E. Ó hAnnracháin, 'Some wild geese of the west', *Journal of the Galway Archaeological and Historical Society*, 54 (2002), pp. 1–24; R. A. Stradling, *The Spanish monarchy and Irish mercenaries: the wild geese in Spain, 1618–68* (Dublin, 1994).

381. H. Ievers to Lords Justice, 23 July 1726, PRO, SP 63/387/33; R. White to W. Lingen, 6 Sep. 1726, PRO, SP 63/387/65; C. Massy to F. Burton, 29 Feb. 1739[40], 7 March 1739 [40], Chatsworth, Devonshire letters, box 1740–43, 273.0, 273.2.

382. Dumas to Shelburne, 4 May 1729, BL, Add. Ms. 72,903/90; Ó Ciardha, *Ireland and the Jacobite cause*, pp. 186–90, 236–7.

383. K. W. Nicholls, 'Rectory, vicarage and parish in the western Irish dioceses', *JRSAI*, ci (1971), pp. 53–6.

384. Report on diocese of Killaloe, 1693, PRONI, DIO/4/4; C. C. Ellison, 'Bishop Dopping's visitation book, 1682–1685', *Riocht na Midhe*, vi/1 (1976), p. 13; P. Loupès, 'Bishop Dopping's visitation of the diocese of Meath', *Studia Hibernica*, 24 (1984–8), p. 134; T. A. Lunham, 'Bishop Dive Downes' visitation of his diocese, 1699', *JCHAS*, xiv (1908), pp. 1–14.

385. D. W. Hayton, 'The development and limitations of Protestant ascendancy: the Church of Ireland laity in public life, *c*. 1660–1740', in R. Gillespie and W. G. Neely (eds), *The laity and the Church of Ireland, 1000–2000: all sorts and conditions* (Dublin, 2002), pp. 104–32.

386. *The autobiography and correspondence of Mary Granville, Mrs. Delany*, 6 vols (London, 1861–2), 1st series, ii (1861), pp. 347–53.

387. J. Taaffe to W. Smythe, 1 Jan. 1713[14], NLI, PC 436; R. Edgeworth accounts, s.d. 22 Dec. 1741, NLI, Ms. 1516, p. 83; Barnard, 'Protestantism, ethnicity and Irish identities, 1660–1760', pp. 206–7; Mulcahy, *Kinsale documents*, 7, p. 42.

388. Broderick, *The first toll-roads*, pp. 34–83; W. H. Crawford, *The management of a major Ulster estate in the late eighteenth century* (Dublin, 2001), pp. 40–5; Johnston-Liik, *HIP*, i, pp. 222–8.

389. F. Hutchinson, *The State of the Case of Loughneagh and the Bann* (Dublin, 1738), p. 20.

390. *Statutes*, iii, pp. 505–7; iv, pp. 87, 258; E. McCracken and D. McCracken, *A register of trees for County Londonderry, 1768–1911* (Belfast, 1984).

391. Vestry book, St Catherine's Dublin, 1693–1730, p. 105, RCB, P. 117/5.2; vestry book, St Paul's, Dublin, 1698–1750, RCB, P. 273/6.1, p. 3.

392. R. Dudley, 'Dublin's parishes, 1660–1729: the Church of Ireland parishes and their role in the civic administration of the city', unpublished Ph.D. thesis, TCD, 2 vols (1995); R. Dudley, 'The Dublin parishes and the poor, 1660–1740', *Archivium Hibernicum*, liii (1999), pp. 80–94.

393. T. C. Barnard, 'Parishes, pews and parsons: lay people and the Church of Ireland, 1647–1780', Gillespie and Neely (eds), *The laity and the Church of Ireland, 1000–2000*, pp. 70–103.

394. Vestry minute book, St Michan's, 1724–1760, RCB, P 276/4.1; J. Johnston, 'Clogher parish – some early sidesmen, 1662–1734', *Clogher Record*, xiv (1991), pp. 89–91.

395. Petition of J. Bell to lords justice, 1718, Marsh's Library, Ms. Z3.1.1; Barnard, 'Parishes, pews and parsons', pp. 82–4; *Records of the general synod of Ulster from 1691–1820*, 3 vols (Belfast, 1890–8), i, p. 33; *Statutes*, iv, p. 511.

396. *Statutes*, iv, pp. 508–14.

397. R. Gillespie (ed.), *The vestry records of the parish of St John the Evangelist, Dublin, 1595–1658* (Dublin, 2002), pp. 10–18.

398. Vestry book, St Bride's, Dublin, 1662–1742, RCB, P 327/3.1, pp. 17, 18, 19, 28, 56, 133, 134; vestry book, St John's, Dublin, 1711–1762, s.d. 2 April 1719, 20 Jan. 1725, RCB, P. 328/5.3.

399. R. Caulfield, 'Annals of St Mary, Shandon', p. 11, St Finbarre's Cathedral, Cork; F. X. McCorry, *Lurgan: an Irish provincial town, 1610–1970* (Lurgan, 1993), pp. 18, 20.

400. St Michan's, churchwardens' accounts, 1723–1761, RCB, P. 276/8.2, p. 159; Dudley, 'Dublin's parishes', i, pp. 76–8, 173–4, 154.

401. F. Hutchinson, *A Sermon Preach'd by … Francis [Hutchinson], Lord Bishop of Down and Connor, at his Primary Visitation, held at Lisburn, May 3. 1721* (Dublin, 1721), pp. 14–15.

402. W. King, *The Mischief of Delaying Sentence against an Evil Work* (Dublin, 1707), p. 34.

403. Rev. F. Houston to Lord Strangford, 23 March 1755, PRONI, D 668/E/38.

404. Agher vestry book, from 1745, NLI, Ms. 5246.

405. J. Waller to E. Southwell, 12 June 1698[9], BL, Add. Ms. 38,151, ff. 3v–4; *Statutes*, iv, p. 27.

406. H. Maule to Abp. W. Wake, 22 Aug. 1724, Christ Church, Wake Mss, 14/213.

407. 12 Geo 1, *c.* 9. Its operations are indicated in J. Smythe to W. Smythe, 'Easter Day', [1745], NLI, PC 449; J. Thompson to same, 8 April 1745, ibid., PC 445.

408. J. Clelow to M. Ward, 19 Feb. 1738[9], 20 Nov. 1740, 2 March 1740[1], 10 Oct. 1741, PRONI, D 2092/1/5, 33, 72, 88, 98; petition of Seapatrick to Dean John Leslie, *c.* 1695–1700, Denbighshire Record Office, DD/BK/I, 391.

409. J. Devereux, *Mr. Devereux's letter to the inhabitants of St Catherine's parish* ([Dublin], 1740).

410. *To all Prime Ministers, Chief-Governors, Deputies, Justices and Secretaries* (Dublin, [1755]), p. 7.

411. D. Dickson, 'In search of the old Irish poor law', in R. Mitchison and P. Roebuck (eds), *Economy and society in Scotland and Ireland, 1500–1939* (Edinburgh, 1988), pp. 149–59; Dudley, 'Dublin parishes and the poor', pp. 80–94.

412. R. Davies, *The right use of riches* (Dublin, 1717), p. 12.

413. Ballymodan vestry book, RCB, P. 140/7.

414. Vestry book, St Catherine's, 1693 to 1730, RCB, P. 117.5.2, ff. 339–40, 351, 356, 365, 371v, 375v, 380, 385, 390.

415. Vestry book, St Catherine's, 1657–1692, RCB, P. 117.5.1, at end, unpaginated.

416. Poor book, St Michan's, Dublin, 1723–1734, RCB, P. 276/8.1, pp. 8, 10, 117, 189, 262, 271, 313.

417. Vestry book of St Catherine's. 1657–92, RCB, P. 117.5.1, p. 233; ibid., 1693–1730, f. 365; St Michan's, Dublin, vestry minutes, 1724–60, RCB, P.276/4/1, p. 117; Barnard, *New anatomy*, pp. 316–27.

418. *A dialogue between Dean Swift and Tho. Prior, Esq.*, p. 95.

419. Monck Mason Collections, iii, part 1, pp. 151–6; iii, part 2, pp. 237, 247, 277, 341; Dublin Public Library, Gilbert Mss. 68 and 69.

420. Minute book of Duncomb Marsh Presbyterian congregation Cork, s.d. 28 April 1726, Cork Archives Institute, U/87(1); minutes of the Route Presbytery, 1701–1706, s.d. 30 Dec. 1701, Presbyterian Historical Society, Belfast; minutes of sub-synod of Derry, 1706–1736, pp. 2, 8, ibid.

421. Minute book of Duncomb Marsh Presbyterian congregation Cork, s.d. 19 and 26 June 1757, Cork Archives Institute, U/87(1); *Records of the general synod of Ulster*, ii, pp. 444–5, 501, 509, 562.

422. Minutes, Connor kirk session, 1693–1735, s.d. 12 Dec. 1705, Presbyterian Historical Society.

423. White, Annals of Limerick, NLI, Ms. 2714, p. 121.

424. Sales of pews, St Michan's parish, Dublin, 1725–1761, RCB, P 276/12.2; cess applotment, St Michan's parish, Dublin, 1711, ibid., P 276/10.1; pew-holders, St Werburgh's parish, Dublin, 1725, ibid., P 326/13.1.

425. Lady Orrery to Sir A. Acheson, 16 March 1752, PRONI, D 1606/1/3A; J. J. Marshall, *Vestry records of the church of St John parish of Aghadow Caledon, Co. Tyrone* (Dungannon, 1935), p. 30.

426. H. Alcock to J. Mason, 14 June 1718, Villiers-Stuart Mss, Dromana, T 3131/B/1/9.

427. Barnard, *New anatomy*, pp. 73, 322.

428. T. C. Barnard, 'A tale of three sisters: Katherine Conolly of Castletown', in Barnard, *Ascents and descents*, pp. 266–89.

429. P. J. Corish, 'Women and religious practice', in M. MacCurtain and M. O'Dowd (eds), *Women in early-modern Ireland* (Edinburgh, 1991), pp. 212–20; D. Hempton and M. Hill, 'Women and Protestant minorities in eighteenth-century Ireland', ibid., pp. 197–211; P. Kilroy, 'Women and the reformation in seventeenth-century Ireland', ibid., pp. 179–96.

430. M. Legg (ed.), *The Synge letters. Bishop Edward Synge to his daughter Alicia, Roscommon to Dublin 1746–1752* (Dublin, 1996), pp. 300, 301.

431. J. Brady and P. J. Corish, 'The Church under the penal code', in P. J. Corish (ed.), *A history of Irish Catholicism*, iv/2 (Dublin, 1971), pp. 51–3; W. Laffan (ed.), *The cries of Dublin, drawn from the life by Hugh Douglas Hamilton, 1760* (Dublin, 2003), pp. 70–1.

432. *An alphabetical list of the freemen and freeholders of the city of Dublin who polled at the election for members of parliament ... 1749* (Dublin, 1750); J. R. Hill, 'Dublin corporation, Protestant dissent, and politics, 1660–1800', in Herlihy (ed.), *Politics of Irish dissent*, pp. 34–7.

433. M. Coghill to E. Southwell, 18 Oct. 1733, BL, Add. Ms. 21,123, f. 59.

434. Sir R. Cox to E. Southwell, 2 May 1704, BL, Add. Ms. 38,153, f. 50v; lists of churchmen and dissenters in Ulster, RIA, Ms. 24 K 19; Lambeth Palace Library, London, Ms. 1742, ff. 49–56.

435. O. M. Goodbody, 'Anthony Sharp: a Quaker merchant of the liberties', *Dublin Historical Record*, 14 (1955), pp. 12–19; R. Greaves, *Dublin's Merchant-Quaker: Anthony Sharp and the community of Friends, 1643–1707* (Stanford, 1998); D. Hempton, 'Methodism in Irish

society', *TRHS*, 5th series, 36 (1986), pp. 117–42; D. Hempton and M. Hill, *Evangelical Protestantism in Irish society, 1740–1890* (London, 1992); K. Herlihy, 'The early eighteenth-century Irish Baptists: two letters', in *IESH*, xix (1992), pp. 71–2; Kilroy, *Protestant dissent and controversy in Ireland*, pp. 25–6, 42, 90.

436. Greaves, *God's other children*, p. 270; K. Herlihy, 'The Irish Baptists, 1650–1780', unpublished Ph.D. thesis, TCD (1992).

437. Brady, *Catholics and Catholicism*; W. H. Grattan Flood, 'The diocesan manuscripts of Ferns during the rule of Bishop Sweetman', *Archivium Hibernicum*, 2 (1913), pp. 100–5; 3 (1914), pp. 113–23; C. O'Dwyer, 'Archbishop Butler's visitation book', ibid., 33 (1975), pp. 1–90; 34 (1976–7), pp. 1–49.

438. Depositions, 1668, Petworth, Orrery Mss, general series, 12; Abp. M. Boyle to Lord Orrery, 31 Aug. 1678, 23 Nov. 1678, ibid., general series, 29; Orrery to Sir R. Southwell, 29 Oct. 1678, 1, 12 and 26 Nov. 1678, V & A, Orrery Mss, vol. 2; diary of Bp. S. Digby, 1688, Lambeth Palace Library, Ms. 3152, ff. 7v, 19; C. Massy to F. Burton, 29 Feb. 1739[40], 4, 7 and 11 March 1739[40], Chatsworth, Devonshire letters, 273.0–2; Larkin, '"Popish riot" in south Co. Derry, 1725', pp. 98–101.

439. R. Ware, 'Looking glass for the reformed church and state of Ireland', JRL, Eng. Ms. 1028; R. Ware, 'Rome's monarchical power blasted', *c.* 1683, QUB, Ms. 1/149; *The ax laid the root, or reasons humbly offered for putting the popish clergy of Ireland under some better regulations*, 3rd edn (Dublin, 1749); minutes of the Medico-Politico-Physico-Classico-Ethico-Puffical Society, s.d. 7 April 1757, RIA, Ms. 24 K 31, pp. 84–5; T. Barnard, '1641: a bibliographical essay', in MacCuarta (ed.), *Ulster 1641*, pp. 181–3; W. D. Love, 'Charles O'Conor of Belanagare and Thomas Leland's "philosophical" history of Ireland', *IHS*, xiii (1962), pp. 1–25.

440. Draft letter of Lord Clanbrassil, Dec. 1757, PRONI, Mic 147/9.

441. R. Edgeworth, accounts, s.d. 22 March 1735[6], NLI, Ms. 1511, p. 86.

Further Reading

Two excellent accounts cover much of this period: S. J. Connolly, *Religion, law and power: the making of protestant Ireland* (Oxford, 1992); D. Dickson, *New foundations: Ireland, 1660–1800*, new edn. (Dublin, 2000). J. C. Beckett, *The making of modern Ireland, 1603–1923* (London, 1966), although some of its concerns belong to an earlier time, has the merit of clarity. Many chapters – especially those on social, economic and cultural themes – in *A new history of Ireland*, iii, ed. T. W. Moody, F. X. Byrne and F. X. Martin (Oxford, 1975), and iv. *Eighteenth-century Ireland, 1691–1800*, ed. T. W. Moody and W. E. Vaughan (Oxford, 1986) help. On society and economy there is much to ponder in L. M. Cullen, *The emergence of modern Ireland, 1600–1900* (London, 1981) and his *Life in Ireland* (London, 1969, paperback edn, 1979).

In the last 20 years, a sluggish stream of writings on the period has turned into a torrent. The quality varies, but the benefit – cumulatively if not always individually – is great. Currently out of fashion but often in advance of it are E. MacLysaght, *Irish life in the seventeenth century*, 3rd edn (Shannon, 1969); and C. Maxwell, *Country and town in Ireland under the Georges*, 2nd edn (Dundalk, 1949). An effort to convey more of the complexity of Protestant Ireland, and incidentally to throw fresh light on the Catholic majority, is made in T. C. Barnard, *A new anatomy of Ireland: the Irish protestants, 1649–1760* (New Haven and London, 2003).

The sixteenth-century scene is set expertly by S. G. Ellis, *Ireland in the age of the Tudors, 1447–1603* (Harlow, 1998); and C. Lennon, *Sixteenth-century Ireland: the incomplete conquest* (Dublin, 1994). The renewed interest in the sixteenth and seventeenth centuries among a younger generation of scholars, including Ellis and Lennon, led to an important collaborative volume: C. Brady and R. Gillespie (eds), *Natives and newcomers: essays on the making of Irish colonial society, 1534–1641* (Dublin, 1986), which heralds much of the work of the next decades. Plantations are fully delineated in R. Gillespie, *Colonial Ulster: the settlement of east Ulster, 1600–1641* (Cork, 1985); M. MacCarthy-Morrogh, *The Munster plantation: English migration to southern Ireland, 1583–1641* (Oxford, 1986); and P. Robinson, *The plantation of Ulster* (Belfast, 1984). Their and others' work is summarized and supplemented in inimitable fashion by N. Canny, *Making Ireland British, 1580–1650* (Oxford, 2001). As guides to the indigenous societies, K. Nicholls, *Gaelic and Gaelicised Ireland in the middle ages* (Dublin, 1972, reprinted, 2003); D. B. Quinn, *The Elizabethans and the Irish* (Ithaca, 1966); and a recent collection edited by P. J. Duffy, D. Edwards and E. Fitzpatrick, *Gaelic Ireland: land, lordship and settlement, c. 1250–c. 1650* (Dublin, 2001) can be recommended.

On politics immediately before 1641, H. Kearney, *Strafford and Ireland, 1633–1641* (Manchester, 1959; reprinted Cambridge, 1989); and Aidan Clarke, *The Old English in Ireland, 1625–42* (London, 1966, paperback, 2000), although amplified by later works, have neither been superseded nor bettered. The uprising itself has attracted a wide-ranging collection edited by B. MacCuarta, *Ulster 1641: aspects of the rising* (Belfast, 1993); a full narrative and minute analysis by M. Perceval-Maxwell, *The outbreak of the Irish rebellion of 1641* (Dublin, 1994); and enlightening coverage in Canny, *Making Ireland British*. Thereafter, order is imposed on confusion by M. Ó Siochrú, *Confederate Ireland 1642–1649: a constitutional and political analysis* (Dublin, 1999); and by the collections edited respectively by J. H. Ohlmeyer, *Ireland from Independence to Occupation, 1640–1660* (Cambridge, 1995); and by M. Ó Siochrú, *Kingdoms in crisis: Ireland in the 1640s* (Dublin, 2001). On the Confederate Catholics, military matters are explored in J. I. Casway, *Owen Roe O'Neill and the struggle for Catholic Ireland* (Philadelphia, 1984) and P. Lenihan, *Confederate Catholics at war, 1641–1649* (Cork, 2001); diplomatic and ecclesiastical by Tadgh Ó hAnnracháin, *Catholic reformation in Ireland: the mission of Rinuccini, 1645–1649* (Oxford, 2002) and in J. H. Ohlmeyer, *Civil war and restoration in three Stuart kingdoms: the career of Randal MacDonnell, marquis of Antrim, 1609–1683* (Cambridge, 1993). The convoluted responses of the Protestants are untangled by R. Armstrong, 'Ormond, the confederate peace talks and protestant royalism', in Ó Siochrú, *Kingdoms in crisis*; and K. S. Bottigheimer, *English money and Irish land* (Oxford, 1971), pp. 30–98; P. Little, 'The marquess of Ormond and the English parliament, 1645–1647', in T. Barnard and J. Fenlon (eds), *The dukes of Ormonde,*

1610–1745 (Woodbridge, 2000); J. A. Murphy, 'The politics of the Munster Protestants, 1641–49', *JCHAS*, lxxvi (1971). John Adamson, 'Strafford's ghost: the British context of Viscount Lisle's lieutenancy', in Ohlmeyer (ed.), *Ireland from independence to occupation*, pp. 128–59; K. Bottigheimer, *English money and Irish land*, pp. 99–114; and P. Little, 'The English parliament and the Irish constitution, 1641–1649', in Ó Siochrú (ed.), *Kingdoms in crisis* follow the dealings of the Westminster parliament with Ireland. Relations with Scotland are charted in D. Stevenson, *Scottish covenanters and Irish confederates: Scottish-Irish relations in the mid-seventeenth century* (Belfast, 1981); D. Stevenson, *Alasdair MacColla and the highland problem in the seventeenth century* (Edinburgh, 1980), reprinted as *Highland warrior: Alasdair Maccolla and the civil wars* (2003); and Ohlmeyer, *Antrim*.

The eventual reconquest of 1649 to 1653 is the subject of J. Scott Wheeler, *Cromwell in Ireland* (Dublin, 1999); and Tom Reilly, *Cromwell: an honourable enemy* (Dingle, 1999), a work spoilt by exaggeration and repetition. The 1650s is the subject of T. C. Barnard, *Cromwellian Ireland* (Oxford, 1975, paperback edn, 2000). R. T. Dunlop (ed.), *Ireland under the Commonwealth*, 2 vols (Manchester, 1913) prints documents most of which were destroyed in 1922, and therefore remains useful. Fresh light is thrown on the dark decade by P. Little, 'The first unionists? Irish Protestant attitudes to Union with England, 1653–9', *IHS*, pp. 44–58. Its end is detailed in A. Clarke, *Prelude to restoration in Ireland: the end of the commonwealth, 1659–1660* (Cambridge, 1999). To his meticulous account can be added J. I. McGuire, 'The Dublin Convention, the protestant community and the emergence of an ecclesiastical settlement in 1660', in A. Cosgrove and J. I. McGuire (eds), *Parliament and community: Historical Studies*, xiv (Belfast, 1983).

For the reigns of Charles II and James II, it is best to turn to the chapters by J. G. Simms, in *A new history of Ireland*, iii; although R. Hutton, *Charles the Second, king of England, Scotland and Ireland* (Oxford, 1989) incorporates Irish affairs. Continuities with earlier problems are suggested by T. C. Barnard, 'Settling and unsettling Ireland: the Cromwellian and Williamite revolutions', in Ohlmeyer (ed.), *Ireland from Independence to Occupation*; and Barnard and Fenlon (eds), *The dukes of Ormonde, 1610–1745*. For the Catholic camp A. Clarke, 'Colonial identity in early-seventeenth-century Ireland', in T. W. Moody (ed.), *Historical studies, xi: nationality and the pursuit of national independence* (Belfast, 1978); and M. A. Creighton, 'The Catholic interest in Irish politics in the reign of Charles II', unpublished Ph.D. thesis, QUB (2000) are suggestive. On James VII and II's policies, R. Gillespie, 'The Irish protestants and

James II, 1688–1690', *IHS*, 28 (1992), pp. 124–33; J. Miller, 'The earl of Tyrconnell and James II's Irish policy, 1685–1688', *HJ*, 20 (1977) offer contrasting views; but the fullest account remains J. G. Simms, *Jacobite Ireland, 1685–91* (London, 1969, reprinted Dublin, 2000). For the fighting, see R. Doherty, *The Williamite war in Ireland, 1688–1691* (Dublin, 1998); and P. Wauchope, *Patrick Sarsfield and the Williamite war* (Dublin, 1992). In the absence of a modern biography of Tyrconnell, the interested can unearth P. W. Sergeant, *Little Jennings and fighting Dick Talbot. A life of the duke and duchess of Tyrconnel*, 2 vols (London, 1913). W. A. Maguire (ed.), *Kings in conflict: the revolutionary war in Ireland and its aftermath, 1689–1750* (Belfast, 1990) contains brief accounts, which prefigure continuing reinterpretations. It is supplemented by the beguiling catalogue of an exhibition in the Ulster Museum: E. Black (ed.), *Kings in conflict: Ireland in the 1690s* (Belfast, 1990). Different insights are afforded by three essays arising from the celebration of the Glorious Revolution: K. Bottigheimer, 'The glorious revolution and Ireland', in L. G. Schwoerer (ed.), *The revolution of 1688–1689* (Cambridge, 1992); D. W. Hayton, 'The Williamite revolution in Ireland, 1688–1691', in J. I. Israel (ed.), *The Anglo-Dutch moment: essays on the glorious revolution and its world impact* (Cambridge, 1991); and P. H. Kelly, 'Ireland and the Glorious Revolution: from kingdom to colony', in R. Beddard (ed.), *The revolutions of 1688* (Oxford, 1991). On William himself, there is W. Troost, *William III and the Treaty of Limerick (1691–1697)* (Leiden, 1983).

Parliamentary politics after 1692 can now be followed with relative ease. Much of the groundwork was done by D. W. Hayton in 'Ireland and the English ministers, 1707–16', unpublished D.Phil. thesis, University of Oxford (1975), and is reported in his (presently) scattered articles, which include 'The beginnings of the "undertaker system"', in T. Bartlett and D. W. Hayton (eds), *Penal era and golden age: essays in eighteenth-century Irish history* (Belfast, 1979), pp. 32–54; 'British Whig ministers and the Irish question, 1714–25', in S. Taylor, C. Jones and R. Connors (eds), *Hanoverian Britain and empire* (Woodbridge, 1998); 'Patriots and legislators: Irishmen and their parliaments, c. 1689–c. 1740, in J. Hoppit (ed.), *Parliaments, nations and identities in Britain and Ireland, 1660–1850* (Manchester, 2003); and 'Walpole and Ireland', in J. Black (ed.), *Britain in the age of Walpole* (London, 1984), pp. 95–119. Versions of these and other penetrating investigations are now available in D. W. Hayton, *Ruling Ireland, 1685–1742: politics, politicians and parties* (Woodbridge, 2004). Another pioneering investigation is J. I. McGuire, 'The Irish parliament of 1692', in Bartlett and Hayton (eds), *Penal era and golden age*, pp. 1–32.

Fuller analyses – C. I. McGrath, *The making of the eighteenth-century Irish constitution: government, parliament and the revenue, 1692–1714* (Dublin, 2000); P. McNally, *Parties, patriots and undertakers: parliamentary politics in early Hanoverian Ireland* (Dublin, 1997); and E. Magennis, *The Irish political system, 1740–1765* (Dublin, 2000) – recover more of the detail and dynamics. In advance of these monographs, S. J. Connolly, *Religion, law and power* provided a provocative interpretation. A helpful summary of the present state of knowledge and argument is offered by David Hayton in his introduction to D. W. Hayton (ed.), *The long apprenticeship: the Irish parliament in the eighteenth century* (Edinburgh, 2001); and in his 'The development and limitations of Protestant ascendancy: the Church of Ireland laity in public life, *c.* 1660–1740', in R. Gillespie and W. G. Neely (eds), *The laity and the Church of Ireland, 1000–2000: all sorts and conditions* (Dublin, 2002). Older but intermittently valuable accounts are to be found in R. E. Burns, *Irish parliamentary politics in the eighteenth century*, 2 vols (Washington, DC, 1989); and F. G. James, *Lords of the ascendancy. The Irish House of Lords and its members, 1600–1800* (Dublin, 1995). The introductory sections of E. M. Johnson-Liik, *History of the Irish parliament, 1690–1800*, 6 vols (Belfast, 2002), belong to the same tradition. The *History* includes lists of statutes, analysis of county and borough constituencies, and an invaluable biographical register of more than 2000 members of the Irish Commons, few of whom appear in other reference works. A *Dictionary of Irish Biography* under the general editorship of James McGuire is being compiled. Holders of Irish peerages can be retrieved from G. E. C., *The Complete Peerage of England, Scotland, Ireland, Great Britain and the United Kingdom*, ed. V. Gibbs and H. A. Doubleday, 13 vols (London, 1910–40).

Political ideas have of late received extensive, even disproportionate coverage. Collections, all curate's eggs, include H. Morgan (ed.), *Political ideology in Ireland, 1541–1641* (Dublin, 1999); J. Ohlmeyer (ed.), *Political thought in seventeenth-century Ireland* (Cambridge, 2000); S. J. Connolly (ed.), *Political ideas in eighteenth-century Ireland* (Dublin, 2000); D. G. Boyce, R. Eccleshall and V. Geoghegan (eds) *Political discourse in seventeenth- and eighteenth-century Ireland* (Basingstoke and New York, 2001). Elsewhere excellent studies of individual writers have appeared: M. Brown, *Francis Hutcheson in Dublin* (Dublin, 2002); B. Cunningham, *The world of Geoffrey Keating: history, myth and religion in seventeenth-century Ireland* (Dublin, 2000); J. Hill, 'Ireland without Union: Molyneux and his legacy', in J. Robertson (ed.), *A Union for empire: political thought and the British Union of 1707* (Cambridge, 1995); P. H. Kelly, 'William Molyneux and the spirit of liberty in eighteenth-century Ireland', *Eighteenth-Century Ireland*, iii (1988); I. McBride, 'The school of virtue: Francis Hutcheson, Irish Presbyterians and the Scottish enlightenment', in D. G. Boyce, R. Eccleshall and V. Geoghegan (eds), *Political thought in Ireland since the seventeenth century* (London, 1993), pp. 73–99; and J. G. Simms, *William Molyneux of Dublin* (Dublin, 1982). These studies contrast strikingly with the absence of biographies of most leading politicians. Not just Tyrconnell, but Conolly and Henry Boyle are among the victims. The curious can consult Barnard and Fenlon (eds), *The dukes of Ormonde*; L. Boylan, 'The Conollys of Castletown, a family history', *Bulletin of the Irish Georgian Society*, 11/4 (1968); K. Lynch, *Roger Boyle, first earl of Orrery* (Knoxville, 1965); and R. W. Ramsey, *Henry Cromwell* (London, 1933). Tentative looks at a vital institution are T. Barnard 'The viceregal court in the later-seventeenth-century Ireland', in E. Cruickshanks (ed.), *The Stuart Courts* (Stroud, 2000), pp. 256–65; and Barnard, *Making the grand figure*, ch. 1. Patrick Little's illuminating doctoral thesis on Orrery (London University, 2000) is in course of publication. An unfamiliar perspective is offered in T. C. Barnard, 'A tale of three sisters: Katherine Conolly of Castletown', in Barnard, *Irish Protestant ascents and descents* (Dublin, 2003). The volume includes other investigations of the behaviour and attitudes of the Protestant minority.

The history of Ireland gains from being set in other contexts. Approaches via the British and north Atlantic worlds include D. J. Baker and W. Maley (eds), *British identities and English renaissance literature* (Cambridge, 2002); B. Bradshaw and J. Morrill (eds), *The British problem, c. 1534–1707: state formation in the Atlantic archipelago* (Basingstoke, 1996); B. Bradshaw and P. Roberts (eds), *British consciousness and identity: the making of Britain, 1533–1707* (Cambridge, 1998); S. G. Ellis and S. Barber (eds), *Conquest and union: fashioning a British state, 1485–1725* (London, 1995). Equally, if not more, rewarding are the collaborations between historians of Ireland and France, and Ireland and Scotland. The products of the former include L. Bergeron and L. M. Cullen (eds), *Culture et pratiques politiques en France et en Irlande XVIe–XVIIIe siècle* (Paris, 1991); P. Butel and L. M. Cullen (eds), *Cities and merchants: French and Irish perspectives on urban development, 1500–1900* (Dublin, 1986); L. M. Cullen and F. Furet (eds), *Irlande et France XVIIe–XXe siècles: pour une histoire rurale comparée* (Paris, 1980); and L. M. Cullen and P. Butel (eds), *Négoce et industrie en France et en Irlande aux xviiie et xix siècles* (Paris, 1980). The latter have yielded L. M. Cullen and T. C. Smout (eds), *Comparative aspects of Scottish and Irish economic and social history, 1600–1900* (Edinburgh,

1977); T. M. Devine and D. Dickson (eds), *Ireland and Scotland, 1600–1850* (Edinburgh, 1983); R. Mitchison and P. Roebuck (eds), *Economy and society in Scotland and Ireland, 1500–1939* (Edinburgh, 1988); S. J. Connolly, R. A. Houston and R. J. Morris (eds), *Conflict, identity and economic development: Ireland and Scotland, 1600–1939* (Preston, 1995); and S. J. Connolly (ed.), *Kingdoms united? Great Britain and Ireland since 1500* (Dublin, 1999). Sustained comparisons are offered by D. W. Hayton, 'Constitutional experiments and political expediency, 1689–1725', in Ellis and Barber (eds), *Conquest and union*; and Jim Smyth, *The making of the United Kingdom, 1660–1800* (Harlow, 2001).

Generally, it has proved easier and more rewarding, especially in terms of career, to write about ideas rather than physical realities. Among the most persuasive enquiries into attitudes are D. W. Hayton, 'From barbarian to burlesque: English images of the Irish, *c.* 1660–1750', *IESH*, (1988), pp. 5–31; D. W. Hayton, 'Anglo-Irish attitudes: changing perceptions of national identity among the Protestant Ascendancy in Ireland, *ca.* 1690–1760', in *Studies in eighteenth-century culture*, 17 (1987), pp. 145–57; and J. T. Leerssen, 'Anglo-Irish patriotism and its European context' in *Eighteenth-Century Ireland*, iii (1988).

Studies of localities are starting to indicate the complexities of Ireland. Notable in this genre are investigations of Dublin led by J. Hill, *From patriots to unionists: Dublin civic politics and Irish protestant patriotism, 1660–1840* (Oxford, 1997); P. Clark and R. Gillespie (eds), *Two capitals: London and Dublin, 1500–1840*, Proceedings of the British Academy, 107 (2001); R. V. Dudley, 'Dublin's parishes, 1660–1729: the Church of Ireland parishes and their role in the civic administration of the city', unpublished Ph.D. thesis, TCD, 2 vols (1995). The provinces are well served with the outstanding doctoral thesis of David Dickson, 'An economic history of the Cork region in the eighteenth century', unpublished Ph. D. thesis, TCD, 2 vols (1977), soon to be published; and T. P. Power, *Land, politics and society in eighteenth-century Tipperary* (Oxford, 1993); Jean Agnew, *Belfast merchant families in the seventeenth century* (Dublin, 1996); D. M. Beaumont, 'The gentry of the king's and queen's counties: Protestant landed society, 1690–1760', unpublished Ph.D. thesis, TCD, 2 vols, (1999); and R. Richey, 'Landed society in mid-eighteenth-century County Down', unpublished Ph.D. thesis, QUB (2000). Other rewarding investigations include L. A. Clarkson and E. M. Crawford, *Ways to wealth: the Cust family of eighteenth-century Armagh* (Belfast, 1985); D. A. Cronin, *A Galway gentleman in the age of improvement: Robert French of Monivea, 1716–1779* (Dublin, 1995); B. Gurrin, *A century of struggle in Delgany and*

Kilcoole: an exploration of the social implications of population change in north-east Wicklow, 1666–1779 (Dublin, 2000); T. King, *Carlow, the manor and town* (Dublin, 1997); H. Murtagh, *Athlone: history and settlement to 1800* (Athlone, 2000); M. Ní Mhurchadha, *The customs and excise service in Fingal, 1684–1765* (Dublin, 1999); B. Ó Dálaigh, *Ennis in the eighteenth century* (Dublin, 1995); and M. O'Dowd, *Power, politics and land: early modern Sligo, 1568–1688* (Belfast, 1991).

Matters are further advanced by P. Borsay and L. Proudfoot (eds), *Provincial towns in early modern England and Ireland; change, convergence and divergence*, Proceedings of the British Academy, 108 (2002). Vignettes are offered in H. B. Clarke (ed.), *Irish cities* (Cork, 1995); A. Simms and J. H. Andrews (eds), *Irish towns* (Cork, 1994); A Simms and J. H. Andrews (eds), *More Irish country towns* (Cork, 1995); and T. C. Barnard, *The abduction of a Limerick heiress: social and political relationships in eighteenth-century Ireland* (Dublin, 1998). The operations of government outside Dublin are most convincingly uncovered in N. Garnham, *The courts, crime and the criminal law in Ireland, 1692–1760* (Dublin, 1996); and his articles 'How violent was eighteenth-century Ireland?', *IHS*, xxx (1997), pp. 377–92, and 'Local élite creation in early Hanoverian Ireland: the case of the county grand jury', *HJ*, 42 (1999), pp. 623–42. These works can be supplemented by D. M. Beaumont, 'Local office-holding and the gentry of Queen's County, *c.* 1660–1760', in P. G. Lane and W. Nolan (eds) *Laois: history and society* (Dublin, 1999), pp. 435–58. An innovative anthology is James Kelly, *Gallows speeches from eighteenth-century Ireland* (Dublin, 2001). Some insights into military matters can be gleaned from Barnard, *A new anatomy*, ch. 7; T. Bartlett and K. Jeffery (eds), *A military history of Ireland* (Cambridge, 1996); and H. McAnally, 'The militia array of 1758 in Ireland', *The Irish Sword*, i (1950), pp. 94–104

Religious practice, as yet, has been treated less fully than the lives – and complaints – of bishops and clergy. The essentials, and much more besides, are provided in P. J. Corish, *The Irish Catholic experience: a historical survey* (Dublin, 1985), pp. 96–150. A. Forrestal, *Catholic synods in Ireland, 1600–1690* (Dublin, 1998); H. Fenning, *The undoing of the friars of Ireland* (Louvain, 1972); H. Fenning, *The Irish Dominican province, 1698–1797* (Dublin, 1990); and P. Ferté and L. W. Brockliss, 'Irish clerics in France in the seventeenth and eighteenth centuries: a statistical study', *PRIA*, lxxxvii, sect. C (1987). Raw material is set out in J. Brady, *Catholics and Catholicism in the eighteenth-century press* (Maynooth, 1965); and W. P. Burke, *Irish priests of the penal times, 1660–1760* (Waterford, 1914).

The latter exploits material most of which has since been burnt. Useful biographies are P. Fagan, *Dublin's turbulent priest. Cornelius Nary, 1658–1738* (Dublin, 1991); P. Fagan, *An Irish bishop in penal times: the chequered career of Sylvester Lloyd, OFM, 1680–1747* (Dublin, 1993); T. O'Connor, *An Irish theologian in enlightenment France: Luke Joseph Hooke 1714–96* (Dublin, 1995); and P. Power, *A bishop of the penal times, being letters and reports of John Brenan* (Cork, 1932) (a different subject from Fagan's). Recent diocesan histories vary from the traditional – P. Fagan, *The diocese of Meath in the eighteenth century* (Dublin, 2001); I. Murphy, *The diocese of Killaloe in the eighteenth century* (Dublin, 1991); and L. Swords, *A hidden church: the diocese of Achonry 1689–1818* (Dublin, 1997) – to the more innovative. To sample the latter, consult: J. Kelly, 'The Catholic Church in the diocese of Ardagh, 1650–1870', in R. Gillespie and G. Moran (eds), *Longford: essays in county history* (Dublin, 1991), pp. 63–91; J. Kelly, 'The impact of the penal laws', in J. Kelly and D. Keogh (eds), *History of the Catholic diocese of Dublin* (Dublin, 1999), pp. 145–70; the early pages of D. Keogh, *'The French disease': the Catholic Church and radicalism in Ireland, 1790–1800* (Dublin, 1993); F. Ó Fearghail, 'The Catholic Church in County Kilkenny 1600–1800', in W. Nolan and K. Whelan (eds), *Kilkenny: history and society* (Dublin, 1990), pp. 197–248; and B. McCormack, *Perceptions of St Patrick in eighteenth-century Ireland* (Dublin, 2000). An excellent collection is T. P. Power and K. Whelan (eds), *Endurance and emergence: Catholics in Ireland in the eighteenth century* (Dublin, 1990). P. Fagan, *Catholics in a Protestant country: the papist constituency in eighteenth-century Dublin* (Dublin, 1998), is similarly innovative and important. However, it is still necessary to turn back to the invaluable investigations collected in M. Wall, *Catholic Ireland in the eighteenth century*, ed. G. O'Brien (Dublin, 1989).

Sources are made accessible in C. O'Dwyer, 'Archbishop Butler's visitation book', *Archivium Hibernicum*, 33 (1975), pp. 1–90; 34 (1976–7), pp. 1–49; H. Fenning (ed.), *The Fottrell papers* (Belfast, 1980); W. H. Grattan Flood, 'The diocesan manuscripts of Ferns during the rule of Bishop Sweetman', *Archivium Hibernicum*, 2 (1913), pp. 100–5, and 3 (1914), pp. 113–23; B de Breffni, 'Letters from Connaught to a wild goose', *The Irish ancestor*, x/2 (1978); and J. Hanly (ed.), *Letters of Saint Oliver Plunkett, 1625–1681* (Dublin, 1979). Writings in the Irish language are exploited by B. Ó Buachalla in *Aisling Ghéar: Na Stíobhartaigh agus an tAos Léinn, 1603–1788* (Dublin, 1996); V. Morley, *Irish opinion and the American revolution, 1760–1783* (Cambridge, 2002); and É. Ó Ciardha, *Ireland and the Jacobite cause, 1685–1766* (Dublin, 2001). Introductions to the views of the first are in 'James our true king: the ideology of Irish royalism in the seventeenth century', in Boyce, Eccleshall and Geoghegan (eds), *Political thought in Ireland since the seventeenth century*. These interpretations can be compared with those in J. Leerssen, *Mere Irish and Fíor-Ghael* (Amsterdam, 1986; 2nd edn Cork, 1996).

On the established church, two collections serve as good introductions: A. Ford, K. Milne and J. I. McGuire (eds), *As by law established: the Church of Ireland since the Reformation* (Dublin, 1995); and R. Gillespie and W. G. Neely (eds), *The laity and the Church of Ireland, 1000–2000: all sorts and conditions* (Dublin, 2002). One of the commanding presences is the subject of a careful biography in P. O'Regan, *Archbishop William King of Dublin (1650–1729) and the constitution of church and state* (Dublin, 2000). For King's own utterances, there is C. S. King, *A great archbishop of Dublin. William King, D.D. , 1650–1729* (London, 1906). Ecclesiastical initiatives are traced in Barnard, *Irish Protestant ascents and descents*; D. W. Hayton, 'Did Protestantism fail in early eighteenth-century Ireland? Charity schools and the enterprise of religious and social reformation, *c*. 1690–1730', in Ford et al., *As by law established*; and K. Milne, *The Irish charter schools, 1730–1830* (Dublin, 1997). Although focused on a later period, the brilliance from A. P. W. Malcomson, *Archbishop Charles Agar: churchmanship and politics in Ireland, 1760–1810* (Dublin, 2002), irradiates the preceding era.

Protestant dissent has attracted considerable interest as is attested in the four compilations edited by K. Herlihy, *The Irish dissenting tradition, 1650–1750* (Dublin, 1995); *The religion of Irish dissent* (Dublin, 1996); *The politics of Irish dissent* (Dublin, 1997); and *Propagating the word of Irish dissent* (Dublin, 1998). In addition, P. Brooke, *Ulster Presbyterianism: the historical perspective*, 2nd edn (Belfast, 1994); C. E. J. Caldicott, H. Gough and J. P. Pittion (eds), *The Huguenots and Ireland: the anatomy of an emigration* (Dun Laoghaire, 1987); R. L. Greaves, *God's other children: Protestant nonconformists and the mergence of denominational churches of Ireland, 1660–1700* (Stanford, 1997); R. L. Greaves, *Dublin's merchant Quaker: Anthony Sharp and the community of Friends, 1643–1707* (Stanford, 1998); P. Griffin, *The people with no name: Ireland's Ulster Scots, America's Scots Irish, and the creation of a British Atlantic world, 1689–1764* (Princeton, 2001); and P. Kilroy, *Protestant dissent and controversy in Ireland, 1660–1714* (Cork, 1994), explore a variety of groups. The origins of many are uncovered in St. J. D. Seymour, *The Puritans in Ireland, 1647–1661* (Oxford, 1921, reprinted 1969); and J. C. Beckett, *Protestant dissent in Ireland, 1687–1780* (London, 1948). Two ambitious studies, informed by contrasting methodologies, cover the troubled confessional life of the period: A. Ford, *The Protestant reformation in Ireland, 1590–1641* (Frankfurt-am-Main, 1985; paperback edn, Dublin, 1997); and R. Gillespie, *Devoted people: belief and religion in early modern Ireland* (Manchester, 1997).

The bulk of the inhabitants, singularly resistant to resuscitation, come into focus chiefly thanks to historical demographers and geographers. Their insights can be sampled in J. H. Andrews, *Shapes of Ireland: maps and their makers, 1564–1839* (Dublin, 1997); T. Barry (ed.), *A history of settlement in Ireland* (London, 2000); W. H. Crawford, 'The political economy of linen: Ulster in the eighteenth century', in C. Brady, M. O'Dowd and B. Walker (eds), *Ulster: an illustrated history* (London, 1989), pp. 134–57; D. Dickson, *Arctic Ireland. The extraordinary story of the great frost and forgotten famine of 1740–41* (Dundonald, 1997); and B. J. Graham and L. J. Proudfoot (eds), *Urban improvement in provincial Ireland, 1700–1840* (Athlone, 1994). A succinct guide is R. Gillespie, *The transformation of the Irish economy, 1550–1700*, 2nd edn (Dublin, 1998). Another neglected subject is probed by M. MacCurtain and M. O'Dowd (eds), *Women in early modern Ireland* (Edinburgh, 1991).

Shifts in landownership are expertly measured by K. S. Bottigheimer, *English money and Irish land: the 'adventurers' in the Cromwellian settlement of Ireland* (Oxford, 1971), and in his 'The restoration land settlement in Ireland: a structural view', in *IHS*, xviii (1972); and also by J. G. Simms, *The Williamite confiscation in Ireland, 1690–1703* (London, 1956). Helpful case studies are offered in K. McKenny, 'The seventeenth-century land settlement in Ireland: towards a statistical interpretation', in Ohlmeyer (ed.), *Ireland from independence to occupation*, pp. 181–200; and in L. J. Arnold, *The restoration land settlement in County Dublin, 1660–1688* (Dublin, 1993). Important, too, is L. M. Cullen, *Anglo-Irish trade, 1660–1800* (Manchester, 1968).

Intellectual life is explored in T. Barnard, 'The Hartlib circle and the cult and culture of improvement in Ireland', in M. Greengrass, M. Leslie and T. Raylor (eds), *Samuel Hartlib and universal reformation* (Cambridge, 1994), pp. 381–97; T. C. Barnard, 'Sir William Petty, Irish landowner', in H. Lloyd-Jones, V. Pearl and A. B. Worden (eds), *History and imagination: essays in honour of H. R. Trevor-Roper* (London, 1981), pp. 201–17; D. Clarke, *Thomas Prior 1681–1751, founder of the Royal Dublin Society* (Dublin, 1951); I. Ehrenpreis, *Swift: the man, his work and the age*, 3 vols (London, 1962–83); A Harrison, *The dean's friend: Anthony Raymond 1675–1726, Jonathan Swift and the Irish language* (Dublin, 1999); K. T. Hoppen, *The common scientist in the seventeenth century: a study of the Dublin*

Philosophical Society, 1683–1708 (London, 1970); and P. H. Kelly, "'A light to the blind": the voice of the dispossessed elite in the generation after the defeat at Limerick', *IHS*, xxiv (1985). Collective schemes of improvement can be studied through H. F. Berry, *A history of the Royal Dublin Society* (London, 1915); and J. Meenan and D. Clarke (eds), *The Royal Dublin Society* (Dublin, 1981). B. Cunningham and M. Kennedy (eds), *The Experience of reading: Irish historical perspectives* (Dublin, 1999); and G. Long (ed.), *Books beyond the Pale: aspects of the provincial book trade before 1850* (Dublin, 1996) can be recommended. A wonderful treasure trove of information about printers and printing (and incidentally of life and work in Dublin) is contained in M. Pollard, *Dictionary of members of the Dublin book trade, 1550–1800* (London, 2000); to which must be added her indispensable account of *Dublin's trade in books, 1550–1800* (Oxford, 1989). The worlds of print are further explored in R. Munter, *The history of the Irish newspaper, 1685–1760* (Cambridge, 1967).

Theatre has attracted H. Burke, *Riotous performances* (Chapel Hill, 2003); W. S. Clark, *The Irish stage in the country towns, 1720–1800* (Oxford, 1965); W. S. Clark, *The early Irish stage: the beginnings to 1720* (Oxford, 1955); J. C. Greene, *Theatre in Belfast, 1736–1800* (Lehigh, 2000); J. C. Greene and G. Clark, *The Dublin stage, 1720–1745* (Lehigh, 1993); E. K. Sheldon, *Thomas Sheridan of Smock-Alley* (Princeton, 1957); and La Tourette Stockwell, *Dublin theatres and theatre customs, 1637–1820* (Kingsport, 1938). On music there are B. Boydell, *A Dublin musical calendar, 1700–1760* (Dublin, 1988); D. O'Sullivan, *Carolan: the life, times and music of an Irish harper*, 2 vols (Dublin, 1958); and H. White, *The keeper's recital: music and cultural history in Ireland, 1770–1970* (Cork, 1998). Other aspects of material life dazzle in A. Crookshank and D. Fitzgerald, *Ireland's painters, 1600–1940* (New Haven and London, 2002); E. McParland, *Public architecture in Ireland, 1680–1760* (New Haven and London, 2001); and P. Francis, *Irish delftware* (London, 2000). Humbler experiences are sketched by T. C. Barnard in 'The world of goods and County Offaly in the early eighteenth century', in T. O'Neill (ed.), *Offaly: history and society* (Dublin, 1998), pp. 371–92. A pioneering study yet to be superseded is R. Loeber, 'Irish country houses of the late Caroline period: an unremembered past recaptured', in *Bulletin of the Irish Georgian Society*, xvi (1973). T. Barnard, *Making the grand figure: lives and possessions in Ireland, 1641–1770* (New Haven and London, 2004) builds on these specialist works.

IESH publishes an annual list of publications on Irish history. It remains the most reliable and comprehensive, and may well be accessible electronically by the time this appears. In the interim, the bibliography compiled by the Royal Historical Society (www.rhs.ac.uk/bibwel.html) includes much Irish material. Finally, for sampling of what was written at the time – the best way to re-enter the era – there are two excellent anthologies: S. Ó Tuama (ed.), *An Duanaire 1600–1900: poems of the dispossessed* (Mountrath, 1981); and A. Carpenter (ed.), *Verse in English from eighteenth-century Ireland* (Cork, 1998), soon to be joined by a seventeenth-century volume from the same anthologist. Two minor poets, Thomas Sheridan and Thomas Parnell, have had their work collected and edited, respectively by R. G. Hogan (Delaware, 1994) and by C. Rawson and F. P. Lock (Delaware, 1989). *The correspondence of Jonathan Swift*, ed. H. A. Williams, 5 vols (Oxford, 1963–5), which is being supplemented by a new edition edited by David Woolley, Frankfurt-am-Main (1999, continuing); and H. A. Williams (ed.), *The poems of Jonathan Swift*, 3 vols, 2nd edn (Oxford, 1958) afford endless entertainment and instruction. Finally, three exemplary editions tell of the times: J. Swift and T. Sheridan, *The Intelligencer*, ed. J. Woolley (Oxford, 1992); *Memoirs of Laetitia Pilkington*, ed. A. C. Elias, Jr., 2 vols (Athens, GA, and London, 1997); and M. L. Legg (ed.), *The Synge letters. Bishop Edward Synge to his daughter Alicia, Roscommon to Dublin 1746–1752* (Dublin, 1996).

Index

Catholicism and Catholics
(*Continued*)
  penalized, 20–1, 43, 69–70, 73,
    91, 97–8, 119, 125
  pilgrimage, 6
  women, 139
  worship, 6, 21, 37, 127–8, 134
  see also clergy, Catholic; land;
    office; statutes
Chapelizod, Co. Dublin, 120
charity, 89, 101, 134–5, 137–9, 142
Charles I, king of England,
  Ireland and Scotland, 15–17,
  20, 24, 27, 31, 36, 37, 39, 45,
  55, 69, 71, 102, 122
Charles II, king of England,
  Ireland and Scotland, 27, 31,
  34, 36, 44, 48, 55, 64, 74, 101,
  106, 112, 122
Charles Edward Stuart, Prince, the
  young pretender, 59, 60, 129
Chester, 40, 92
Chesterfield, Philip Dormer
  Stanhope, earl of, 89
church buildings, 21–2, 34, 37, 80,
  89, 94, 95, 130, 133–5, 137–8
Church of Ireland (Protestant),
  3–4, 49, 79–80, 99, 104,
  132–9; threatened, 34, 37
Clanricarde, Ulick Bourke,
  marquess of, 18, 111
Clare, county, 29, 57, 58, 76, 90,
  91, 107, 113, 117
clergy
  Catholic, 2, 5, 6, 15–16, 19, 21,
    26, 28, 47, 51–3, 59, 61–2,
    65, 69–70, 116, 125–8, 131,
    132, 140, 142
  Church of Ireland, 19, 34, 40,
    61, 67, 79–80, 91, 93, 100,
    115, 117, 125, 142
  curates, 124, 131
  dissenting, 142
Clonmel, 108
cloth and clothing, 7–8, 18, 51,
  60, 139–40
  shoes, 12
  silk, 48

stockings, 12
  velvet, 48
  see also linen
coal, 88–9
Coalisland, Co. Tyrone, 88
coinage, 68, 75
Colclough, Caesar, 114
Coleraine, Co. Londonderry, 123
Connacht, province, 4, 21, 22,
  25, 28, 29, 85, 120, 130
Connor, kirk session, 138
Conolly, Katherine, 92, 139
Conolly, William, Speaker of the
  Irish House of Commons, 50,
  66, 73, 88, 92, 93, 98, 100,
  103, 113, 139
constable, 104, 105, 115, 120, 135
Coote, Sir Charles, 1st earl of
  Mountrath, 25
Coote, Thomas, 85
Cootehill, Co. Cavan, 85
Cork, city, 1, 30, 40, 50, 60, 108,
  111, 123, 128, 135–7
Cork, county, 86, 106–7, 109, 113
Cork, Richard Boyle, 1st earl of,
  18, 25, 35, 110, 113, 119
cottiers, 7, 13
county, government of, 2, 21,
  23, 30, 33, 76, 86, 104,
  106–10, 113, 118
Court of Claims, 35, 110
Cox, Sir Richard, lord chancellor,
  109
Cox, Sir Richard, MP, 86
craftsmen, 3, 7, 59, 68, 71, 84,
  90, 123–5, 129, 135–6, 139
Cromwell, Oliver, 4, 26–8, 31,
  36, 38–40, 43–4, 51, 63–4
Crosbie, William, 85
Cruoverghan, Co. Clare, 106
Curragh, Co. Kildare, 101
Cust, Henry, 50

Dalton, Michael, 94
Darcy, Patrick, 21
Dawson Bridge, Co. Antrim, 138
Denmark, 10
Denny, Lady Arbella, 139